Murder along the Cape Fear

A North Carolina Town
in the Twentieth Century

The Market House, Fayetteville's most famous landmark, was built in 1832 on the site of the old State House which was destroyed by fire in 1831. The building and the landscaping has been refurbished numerous times. Sometimes called the "old slave market" because it was rumored that slaves had once been bought and sold there, it was primarily a place where area farmers sold their produce. Four major Fayettville streets—Hay, Green, Gillespie, and Person—converge at this famous structure. (Photo courtesy of Biz Tools One, Inc., Fayetteville NC.)

Murder along the Cape Fear

A North Carolina Town
in the Twentieth Century

ALABASTER

by
David T. Morgan

For Albert L. Scott Library, with gratitude to its fine staff and with best wishes.

David T. Morgan

1-21-06

Mercer University Press
Macon, Georgia USA

ISBN 0-86554-966-4   MUP/H692

Murder along the Cape Fear.
A North Carolina Town in the Twentieth Century.
Copyright ©2005
Mercer University Press
All rights reserved
Printed in the United States of America
First edition, September 2005

Library of Congress Cataloging-in-Publication Data

Morgan, David T.
    Murder along the Cape Fear : a North Carolina town
in the twentieth century / by David T. Morgan. — 1st ed.
    p. cm.
Includes bibliographical references.
ISBN-13: 978-086554-966-1 (hardcover : alk. paper)
ISBN-10: 0-86554-966-4 (hardcover : alk. paper)
    1. Murder—North Carolina—Fayetteville—History—20th century.
2. Fayetteville (N.C.)—History—20th century. I. Title.
    HV6534.F38M67 2005
    364.1'523'09756373—dc22
                                            2005020710

Table of Contents

List of Murders Discussed or Mentioned

1. Sam Melvin (aka Murchison) shoots and kills
   Police Chief James Herbert Benson (1908)
2. Henry Spivey shoots and kills his father-in-law and hangs for it (1910)
3. George Hobbs (presumably) shoots and kills
   sheriff's deputies Herman Butler and W. G. Moore (1920)
4. David Marshall ("Carbine") Williams shoots and kills Deputy Al Pate (1921)
5. A man named Waddell guns down another man named Covington (1921)
6. Frank McLaurin dies of a gunshot wound. Kenneth O. Boone
   and Mae Belle Phillips are tried for the murder and are acquitted (1927)
7. Lenward Hair shoots and kills police officer Willis Genes (1939)
8. Marvin Strickland pleads guilty to involuntary manslaughter
   in the death of Julius Lee (1939)
9. Wall Ewing beats his wife, Douglas Southerland Ewing, to death (1946)
10. Lenward Hair stabs and kills Pfc. Lawrence Simmons (1947)
11. Raymond Hair shoots and kills Roy Coble (1949)
12. Robert Williams shoots and kills Ricky Monsour (1954)
13. Haywood Honeycutt shoots and kills Wilbert Signal (1969)
14. Jeffrey MacDonald stabs and beats to death his wife Colette
    and his two daughters, Kimberly and Kristen (1970)
15. Norris Carlton Taylor shoots and kills Mildred Murchison and others (1978)
16. Velma Barfield poisons Stuart Taylor and others (1978 and earlier)
17. Kathryn Eastburn and two of her daughters are murdered.
    Sgt. Timothy Hennis is charged, but he is ultimately acquitted (1983)
18. Jeffrey Meyer and Mark Thompson, the "ninja killers,"
    stab Paul Kutz, Sr. and Janie Lee Meares Kutz to death (1986)
19. Ronald Gray murders Linda Jean Coats, 22, and Tammy Wilson, 18 (1987)
20. William Edgar Weller murders Margaret Best Jensen (1988)
21. Sgt. Kenneth Junior French shoots and kills
    four people at Luigi's Restaurant (1993)
22. Jim Burmeister, aided and abetted by Malcolm Wright,
    shoots and kills a black couple on Hall Street (1995)
23. Sgt. William Kreutzer shoots and kills Major Stephen Badger
    and wounds 18 other paratroopers (1995)
24. Tilmon and Kevin Golphin shoot and kill
    police officers Ed Lowry and David Hathcock (1997)
25. Paco Tirado, Eric "E" Queen, and Christina "Queen" Walters
    murder two women as part of a gang initiation (1998)
26. Captain Marty Theer is shot and killed in December
    just before the century ends (2000). Sgt. John Diamond is tried
    and convicted. Michelle Theer, the captain's wife, is charged in 2002.

Dedicated to
 Judy, Cindi, Brian, Matt, Willene,
 all my other kinfolks
 (both mentioned and unmentioned in these pages),
 and to the Fayetteville High School class of 1955
 for enriching my life.

Acknowledgments

No one writes a book and gets it published without being indebted to a goodly number of people. In doing the research for this book I received a tremendous amount of help from Daisy Maxwell, the librarian at the *Fayetteville Observer* Library, and from Sharon Masters, a staff member at the library. Both of them helped me find newspaper articles, books, and photographs that proved indispensable. I will always be grateful for their help.

Although I did not get to know them personally, a number of staff members at the Cumberland County Library in Fayetteville assisted me many times, and I appreciate what they did to help. I used a vast amount of material, particularly newspaper articles and city directories, at both libraries. I could not have finished my research without access to the complete run of the *Fayetteville Observer* located on microfilm at the county library. It was a location where I felt right at home, for it is just across the street from where my old grammar school—Central—once stood. I was a little nostalgic every time I walked out of this impressive library building and looked over into what is now a parking lot but was once a schoolyard where my classmates and I played softball.

Several of my relatives and a number of friends in Fayetteville provided helpful information. My mother, Bessie Herring Morgan, told me about her experiences with some of the people whose names appear in the book, and her youngest brother, Gilbert Herring, related interesting personal encounters with two of the murderers highlighted in this story. Charles Cox, my first cousin, who was married to Velma Barfield's sister-in-law, shared his observations of Velma with me, and he himself is prominently mentioned in the book because of a bizarre stunt he pulled while a student at Fayetteville High School. Clara Koonce, a fellow member of the Class of '55, put me in touch with Mickey Thompson, the daughter of Willis Genes, a Fayetteville policeman who was murdered in 1939. Mrs. Thompson offered some personal insights into her father's murder and the man who killed him. Clara also steered me to other people who were kind enough to provide information. Some of them asked that I not reveal their names, and I am obliged to honor their request. Even so, I do want to thank these anonymous sources whose contributions were important.

Last, but certainly not least, I am deeply indebted to my cherished friends of many years, Judy and Joe Hardison, on two counts. First, they lent me their copy of Weeks Parker's *Fayetteville, North Carolina: A Pictorial History*—and, Judy, I promise that I will return it! Second, during my research trips to Fayetteville, they took me in on numerous occasions as their houseguest and sometimes turned their house over to me when they were out of town. I have no better friends in this world than the Hardisons, and I can't thank them enough.

I would also like to acknowledge the writers of some very fine books— books upon which I relied, sometimes heavily. I will give titles and comment further on their work when I list sources at the end of this book. For now I just want to note that I found valuable information in books by John A. Oates, Weeks Parker, Jerry Bledsoe, Joe McGinniss, and Fred Bost and Jerry Potter. They all have made valuable contributions to understanding Fayetteville and/or to helping me write about *Murder along the Cape Fear: A North Carolina Town in the Twentieth Century*.

Preface

The end of the twentieth century was just days away. It was Sunday night, 17 December 2000—the time approximately 11:00. Air Force Captain Marty Theer, stationed at Pope Air Force Base near Fayetteville, North Carolina, would not be around to see the twenty-first century arrive. On the night of the seventeenth he and his wife Michelle, a psychologist, were returning home from a Christmas party. Michelle wanted to stop by her office at 2500 Raeford Road in Fayetteville to pick up some paperwork. She claimed later that she went into the building alone. Not long after she left the car, Captain Theer apparently decided to follow her inside. As he climbed an outside staircase of the building, shots rang out, shots that riddled his body with five bullets. One bullet struck him in the head. The captain died that dark night on that staircase, allegedly the victim of pre-meditated murder and conspiracy to commit murder.

Thus Fayetteville, North Carolina saw the outgoing twentieth century end in violence. A hundred years earlier, when Fayetteville had been tiny and more tranquil, the twentieth century had arrived without violence. It was not that Fayetteville was free of crime or even devoid of murder in 1900; it was just that the town was only a small place surrounded by cotton farms, and times were more peaceful. The coming of Fort Bragg in the first quarter of the new century would result in a tremendous increase in population in the whole area, especially after World War II. As the little town grew and embraced modernity, its character changed. People wanted to let the good times roll. While hell-raising was nothing new in this town that sat on the west bank of the Cape Fear River, there was a whole lot more of it as more and more soldiers were assigned to Fort Bragg. Murder cases, too, seemed to increase as a mounting number of soldiers took up their post ten miles west of town. The man convicted of killing Captain Theer was a Fort Bragg soldier, Staff Sergeant John Diamond.

Because both the victim and the accused were in the military, the Army chose to prosecute the case. At the trial, the story behind the shooting unfolded. On 20 August 2001 Diamond pled guilty to committing adultery with Michelle Theer and to transporting a privately owned gun to Fort

Bragg, but he denied shooting Captain Theer or anybody else. His defense attorney, Coy Brewer, argued before a military court that Michelle Theer, not Diamond, had pulled the trigger and pumped five shots into her husband. Brewer called Mrs. Theer "cold, hard, and ruthless" and claimed that she had set Sergeant Diamond up to take the fall. Michelle Theer maintained, however, that she was inside her office building when her husband was shot.

When all the evidence was heard, the military jury deliberated three hours and fifteen minutes before returning a verdict of guilty on the counts of premeditated murder and conspiracy to commit murder. The sergeant was given life without parole, a sentence to be served at Fort Leavenworth in Kansas. Diamond broke down after the jury rendered its verdict. Sobbing, he told the jurors, "I did not kill anyone, and I did not conspire to kill anyone. My whole life, honor, integrity, and discipline have meant more to me than anything else." According to Deborah Dvorak, Sgt. Diamond's sister, Diamond later admitted to helping Michelle cover up the murder, after she shot her husband.

As for Michelle Theer, the Army had no jurisdiction over her. Fayetteville District Attorney Ed Grannis gathered evidence against Mrs. Theer, all the while refusing to comment on "a pending case." Eventually, when he felt he had the evidence to convict, Grannis brought murder charges against the captain's widow. Indicted by a Cumberland County grand jury on 21 May 2002, she fled the state and went to Lauderdale-by-the-Sea, Florida and rented an apartment under the assumed name of Lisa Pendragon. She told the landlady, Cindy Geesey, that she was fleeing from an abusive husband and asked her to say nothing if anybody came looking for her. Theer eluded capture until early August when U.S. marshals arrested her outside her apartment. A few weeks earlier she had had a laser peel on her face, apparently in an attempt to alter her appearance. Arrested on a federal warrant for unlawful flight to avoid prosecution, Michelle Theer was returned to Fayetteville where, near the end of 2002, she awaited trial.

Almost certainly the murder of Captain Theer grew out of marital infidelity. That was nothing new in Fayetteville. Love triangles and arguments over women provided the motives for a number of murders in Fayetteville during the twentieth century, but there were other murders that grew out of alcohol abuse, human anger, and downright meanness. Sex and alcohol were the catalysts in a number of cases, but there were other cases when people were simply disturbed and lost it, as Sergeant Kenneth Junior

French did in 1993 when he opened fire in Luigi's Restaurant and killed four people and caused injury to eight others. He was upset because of President Bill Clinton's policy on gays in the military. Two other soldiers, Mark Edward Thompson and Jeffrey Meyer, allegedly robbed and killed a couple as they acted out a game called "Dungeons and Dragons" in 1989. Their foul deed came to be known as the "ninja murders." Decades earlier, in 1921, Marshall Williams of Godwin, a small community north of Fayetteville, shot and killed a deputy sheriff simply because his whiskey still was being confiscated. By the year 2000, murder along the Cape Fear had become a common occurrence. During the century there was a long list of murder cases, some committed by locals, some by transients, and more than a few by soldiers stationed at Fort Bragg. The following pages tell the story of numerous gruesome tales of murder, but they also tell a bigger story—the story of a little town lying along the west bank of the Cape Fear River.

The reader should know that this book is meant to tell the story of Fayetteville, North Carolina during the twentieth century. Not the *history* of the town, but the *story* of the town. The word *history* stirs up connotations of tedious documentation and rigorous analysis, all written in a deadly serious tone. I hope to be far less formal here by telling the story of a fascinating place based on stories told to me by people who lived through many of the events and by using newspaper accounts drawn mainly from the city's own newspaper, the *Fayetteville Observer*, the oldest North Carolina newspaper still in existence. Finally, I draw on my own personal experiences as a Fayetteville native, experiences that, in some cases, were part of the story. I want very much for the focus to be on the town, but I realize that the focus will sometimes shift to me, because I am telling the story as a native son who became fascinated with his hometown while still a young boy. Still, I hope the reader will continuously bear in mind that it is the town I want him or her to see. For the first eleven years of my life (1937–1948) it was the only world I knew firsthand. As a boy I became a junky on stories about Fayetteville and Fort Bragg, the army post ten miles to the west. As a teenager I went to the Cumberland County Courthouse and listened to cases being tried by lawyers who spoke eloquently and who offered highly creative explanations for why their clients could not have committed the crimes of which they had been accused. I saw what Fayetteville was then, and I heard what it had once been. I was intrigued with the town then, and more than a half-century later, I still am.

It was during the twentieth century that the small town of Fayetteville became a much bigger town, one that gained a national reputation. Unfortunately its reputation included tales of bootleg whiskey, pool sharks, hookers, and violence in abundance. Symbolizing the old Fayetteville was the Market House, an odd-looking structure that stood, and still stands, in the center of downtown. It was built in 1832, presumably to replace the old State House that burned down in 1831 during what local historians call "the great fire of 1831." This very destructive fire engulfed and destroyed a large part of the town's commercial district. The loss of the State House was of great historical significance, for it was in that building that North Carolina had ratified the Constitution of the United States in 1789. The Market House, which replaced the State House, came to be used for many functions upstairs in the enclosed part, but down below in the open part, with its arched entryways, farmers from the area came to sell their meat and produce. (Rumor had it that one or more slaves were sold there at one time or another.) Throughout the nineteenth century Fayetteville was a market town dependent economically upon agriculture, and the most important staple of the area was cotton. So, fittingly, the Market House symbolized the town.

With the coming of Fort Bragg to the area early in the twentieth century, that changed. The new symbols for Fayetteville eventually became Army artillery and the insignia of the 82nd Airborne Division, along with countless stories of murder. Fayetteville became nationally and internationally known because of Fort Bragg and Jeffrey MacDonald and, to a lesser extent, Velma Barfield. MacDonald's case is known all over the world, while Barfield's was long in the national spotlight. Booming guns, the proud 82nd, war (Fayetteville even came to be called Fayettenam during the years of the Vietnam War!), and murder-most-foul came to define Fayetteville in the twentieth century.

While all of this is true, there is another side to the story. Fayetteville was and is a town where good people live, work, go to church, raise their families, and enjoy life. To be sure there was murder along the Cape Fear, but there was also civilization and glory. My purpose here is to tell the whole story so that the reader will know that murder along the Cape Fear defines my hometown only in part. I am part of the story, but the real story is the intriguing town that I will always proudly call my hometown.

A Fayetteville Photo Album

This 1982 photo shows the Market House, Fayetteville's most-famous landmark, 150 years after it was erected. (Photo courtesy of Weeks Parker, Fayetteville. For a more recent view of the Market House, see the frontispiece, page ii above.)

A view of downtown Fayetteville in the late 1960s, before most downtown businesses moved to the suburban malls. This view looks down Hay Street from the west towards the Market House. Three landmarks are in plain view—the Kress store, the First Citizens Bank Building, and the Market House. (Photo courtesy of Weeks Parker, Fayetteville.)

Two Fayetteville landmarks for many years—the Prince Charles Hotel and the Sears, Roebuck & Company store—during the 1950s and 1960s. Both buildings stood on the north side of Hay Street. The Sears store was torn down in recent years. (Photo courtesy of Weeks Parker, Fayetteville.)

The Confederate Monument. In this early 20th-century picture the monument stood in a square upon which four streets converged—Green, Grove, Rowan, and Ramsey. Eventually the monument was moved over to the side (corners of Grove and Ramsey) to make way for a major traffic intersection. (Photo courtesy of Weeks Parker, Fayetteville.)

(See chapter 1.) *Sheriff Neill Hector McGeachy about 1920. McGeachy was elected to office in 1910 and remained sheriff of Cumblerland County until December 1950. No other Fayetteville politician has held a public office for forty years. McGeachy was involved in the arrest and/or trial of several of the murders discussed in this book.* (Public domain photo.)

(See chapter 1.) *First automobile in Fayetteville, November 1902. The owner of the automobile, Wade T. Saunders, Sr., is in the driver's seat. This car sold for $1,200, a considerable sum in 1902.* (Photo courtesy of Weeks Parker, Fayetteville.)

(See chapter 2.) *"Camp Bragg" (later Fort Bragg) during its earliest beginnings. From the inconspicuous start it became one of the largest and most important military bases in the world.* (Public domain photos.)

(See chapter 3.) *David Marshall "Carbine" Williams (with the hat on) looks on at Governor Terry Sanford (holding the gun) with Gordon Williams, the youngest brother of the great firearms inventor. Convicted of murdering a Cumberland County sheriff's deputy in 1921, Williams invented the M-1 carbine while a prisoner. He received a pardon from the governor of North Carolina in 1929.* (Photo courtesy of the *Fayetteville Observer*.)

(See chapter 5.) *Soldiers drinking at the Town Pump, Fayetteville's most notorious nightspot during World War II. At one time its owner boasted of having the longest bar in the world. There was a riot there in 1942. Many stories of that event were blown out of proportion.* (Photo courtesy of Weeks Parker, Fayetteville.)

(See chapter 7.) *Dr. Jeffrey MacDonald, the most famous murderer ever convicted in North Carolina, goes to court with his two attorneys, Bernard Segal on his left and Wade Smith on his right. The Green Beret captain was convicted of murdering his pregnant wife and two young daughters and sentenced to three life terms in federal prison. Twenty-five years after his conviction he remains incarcerated.* (Photo courtesy of the *Fayetteville Observer.*)

(See chapter 7.) *Helena Stoeckley who was the mystery woman in the Jeffrey MacDonald murder case. MacDonald and his attorneys claimed that she was in the MacDonald house the night of the murders and was part of a drug-crazed hippy group that committed the murders. Stoeckley, simultaneously an addict and a police informant, told conflicting stories, saying to some that she thought she was there and to others that she was so wasted on drugs the night in question that she could not remember where she was or what she did. (Photo courtesy of the Fayetteville Observer.)*

(See chapter 8.) *Velma Barfield in a pose taken weeks before her execution by lethal injection in 1984. Convicted of the poisoning death of Stuart Taylor, her boyfriend, she poisoned at least three others, including her mother.* (Photo courtesy of the *Fayetteville Observer.*)

(See chapter 8.) *Norris Carlton Taylor, flanked by two police officers. Taylor was charged with murder, rape, and various other serious crimes. His crime spree of 1978 along the Cape Fear reached unprecedented proportions. Sentenced to death for his numerous murders and other crimes, Taylor remains on Death Row more than a quarter century after his conviction and death sentence.* (Photo courtesy of the *Fayetteville Observer.*)

(See chapter 9.) *Sgt. Timothy B. Hennis who was charged in the deaths of Kathryn Eastburn and two of her daughters, all three of whom had their throats slashed. Found guilty at his first trial and sentenced to death, Hennis appealed, was granted a second trial, and was acquitted.* (Photo courtesy of the *Fayetteville Observer*.)

(See chapter 9.) *Jeffrey Meyer, one of the "ninja killers" who stabbed a couple to death in 1986. Meyer apparently was influenced by the game called "Dungeons and Dragons." Sentenced to death, he was still on Death Row in 2004.* (Photo courtesy of the *Fayetteville Observer*.)

(See chapter 9.) *Mark Edward Thompson, one of the "ninja killers." Unlike his accomplice Jeffrey Meyer, who was given the death penalty, Thompson was sentenced to life in prison.* (Photo courtesy of the *Fayetteville Observer.*)

(See chapter 9.) *An aerial photo of Fayetteville in 1984. Most of the merchants had abandoned downtown for the suburban malls by this time.* (Photo by Sam Edge and made available courtesy of Weeks Parker, Fayetteville.)

(See chapter 10.) *Kenneth Junior French who went on a shooting spree at Luigi's Restaurant in Fayetteville in 1993, killing four people and wounding others. Presumably the catalyst that pushed French over the edge and drove him to act was President Clinton's policy on gays in the military.* (Photo courtesy of the *Fayetteville Observer.*)

(See chapter 10.) *Jim Burmeister (forward) and Malcolm wright (behind) who are escorted by a black police officer. In December 1995, these two Skinheads went in search of a black person to kill. Egged on by Wright, Burmeister gunned down a black couple on Hall Street in Fayetteville. Both men received two life sentences.* (Photo courtesy of the *Fayetteville Observer*.)

(See chapter 10.) *Tilmon Golphin, age 19. Along with his brother, Kevin, in 1997, he shot and killed police officers Ed Lowry and David Hatchcock. In 1998, he was sentenced to death, as was his brother, and, at last word, remains on Death Row.* (Photo courtesy of the *Fayetteville Observer*.)

(See chapter 10.) *Kevin Golphin, age 17. In 1997, Kevin and his brother Tilmon shot and killed two police officers on Interstate 95 outside Fayetteville. Sentenced to death the next year, along with his brother, he is still on Death Row.* (Photo courtesy of the *Fayetteville Observer*.)

(See chapter 10.) *Sgt. John Diamond who was convicted of killing Captain Marty Theer in December 2000. Diamond admitted to having an affair with Theer's wife but vigorously denied murdering anyone. An Army tribunal sentenced him to life without parole, to be served at Fort Leavenworth in Kansas.* (Photo courtesy of the *Fayetteville Observer*.)

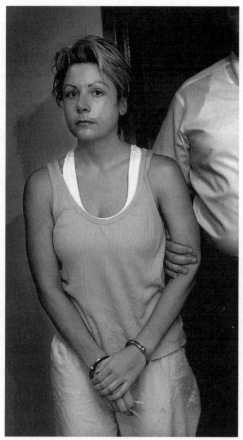

(See chapter 10.) *Michelle Theer, wife of Captain Marty Theer and implicated in his murder, who fled to Florida after Sgt. John Diamond was convicted of the crime. Although she tried to alter her appearance and hide from the law, she was found and returned to Fayetteville. Accused of doing the shooting by Diamond's attorney, she was awaiting trial for murder at the time of this writing.* (Photo courtesy of the *Fayetteville Observer*.)

Growing Up along the Cape Fear

There is a river, no Nile or Amazon to be sure, but a river that has figured prominently in the history and economic development of eastern North Carolina—Cape Fear River. Formed by the confluence of Deep River and Haw River in Chatham County, not too many miles from Greensboro, the Cape Fear meanders diagonally through North Carolina from its center down to its southeastern corner at Southport, where it empties into the Atlantic Ocean. Along the way, it spills over the fall line at a little place called Linden, and then, just a few miles south, it flows by the town of Fayetteville and then, ninety or so miles farther south, through the port city of Wilmington, about thirty miles north of Southport. In colonial times there was another port on the river between Wilmington and Southport. That was Brunswick Town, now a tourist attraction after a successful effort by archaeologists to uncover its remains.

Fayetteville, one of the most important river towns of early North Carolina, is the focus of this story. It was up the Cape Fear that Highland Scots came in the eighteenth century to found the town of Campbellton on the river, as well as the community of Cross Creek about a mile to the west. After the Revolutionary War, the town, then making up the two communities, finally was named Fayetteville in honor of LaFayette, the famous Frenchman who fought alongside George Washington for American independence and who would, in 1825, visit the first American town named for him. Fayetteville, although never a large city, was, and is, important. Many a well-known person has lived there or passed through. Flora MacDonald, supporter of Bonnie Prince Charlie and his pretensions to the British throne in the eighteenth century, was once a resident for a brief period. Lord Cornwallis, the British commander of the southern theater during the last years of the Revolutionary War, marched through with his army of Redcoats. And, since 1918 when Fort Bragg was established ten miles west of town, soldiers and politicians of renown have paraded down Hay Street (the city's main drag) at various times—for instance, Franklin D. Roosevelt and Dwight D. Eisenhower. General George C. Marshall retired to Pinehurst, North Carolina, which is almost in the western shadows of Fort Bragg. The famous general's search for entertainment sometimes took him to the old Colony Theater in Fayetteville where, as a teenager, I was employed as an usher. On several occasions I greeted this great American general and statesman and took his ticket. A dignified gentleman, General Marshall always greeted me with a smile and a "How are you, son?" Fayetteville produced some of its own celebrities, too. Only a decade and a half after World War II ended, Terry Sanford, a Fayetteville attorney, was elected governor of North Carolina in 1960. Having had a rich history, Fayetteville is a place that one is pleased to call his hometown. Not everyone can say, as I can, that his state ratified the Constitution of the United States in the town of his birth.

Yes, I was born in Fayetteville, less than a mile from the banks of the Cape Fear. While growing up in that river town I fished in the Cape Fear's waters and hunted squirrels along its banks. As a small boy I saw the famous river overflow its banks and spread up Person Street westward, almost to the center of downtown. The waters reached to within a block of what is known to natives as the "old Market House," a unique structure that stands where four of the city's main streets—Hay, Green, Gillespie, and Person—meet. Local lore says that the Market House was once a slave market, but it was primarily a farmers' market where cotton and produce were bought and sold, and there is little evidence that it was ever a real marketplace for slaves. Standing on the eastern side of this landmark and looking eastward down Person Street, one looks directly toward the Cape Fear.

I know this town, which was symbolized for so long by its unique landmark. I attended Fayetteville's schools, worked in some of its business establishments, learned its stories, and perhaps even gloried a bit in being a "Fedvillian." (We natives never took time to enunciate all the syllables. We shortened Fayetteville to "Fed-vul," and to this day, many years later, I find myself still doing so unless I stop and think about what I am saying.)

There is so much about Fayetteville that is interesting to tell, but nothing so much as those high-profile murder cases that are a dramatic part of the town's story in the twentieth century. For that reason, a considerable portion of this book will tell the story of those murders. Some of the murders made national and even international headlines. The two most sensational cases were those involving Jeffrey MacDonald and Velma Barfield. Dr. MacDonald, a Green Beret captain at Ft. Bragg at the time his family was killed, remains in prison today, convicted of murdering his wife and two daughters.

Velma Barfield, whom I knew as a friend when she was Velma Burke, was found guilty of poisoning her fiancé, and it became known that she poisoned three others, including her mother. Given the death penalty at her trial, she finally became the first woman in North Carolina to be executed by lethal injection. The stories surrounding the gruesome deeds of MacDonald and Barfield will be told below, along with those of others who are less widely known—for instance, Wall Ewing who beat his wife to death and Marshall "Carbine" Williams who went to prison for shooting sheriff's deputy Al Pate while the latter was participating in a raid on Williams's whiskey still.

The MacDonald and Barfield murders occurred after I had left my hometown to find my place in the world. Williams, who would prove to be a genius as an inventor and a firearms expert, was convicted sixteen years before I was born, while Wall Ewing was found guilty and went to prison when I was a young boy. Ewing was a very prominent citizen in town, and his evil deed shocked those who knew him. The details of the Williams and Ewing stories will follow in due course. I will be able to speak more personally about Ricky Monsour, a tavern owner who was murdered by a taxi driver. I knew Monsour, whom I always thought had the mannerisms and looks of Groucho Marx. I saw him regularly on the streets of Fayetteville and in the pool hall called Brunswick Billiards, a place where the law said I was too young to be, but where I could often be found—much to my mother's horror!

The story of the murders mentioned above, along with a number of others, will be woven into the story of Fayetteville, which I will tell from the perspective of a native son. Regarding this native son, I was born on 5 January 1937 at home in an apartment on the corner of Person and Cool Spring Streets. The apartment was part of a large house, which was torn down late in the twentieth century. While I was still a toddler we moved a short distance from the house where I was born to Cool Spring Lane. Just up the lane was Mr. Watson's grocery store, a place where I first revealed, at least publicly, my fiery temper. One day my mother took me to Mr. Watson's store. I was three. I saw a bushel basket full of beautiful red apples and told my mother I wanted one. When she said no, I became angry and pushed the basket over, causing the apples to roll all over the floor. Some of them even rolled out the door and down the street. Instinctively, my mother snatched me up and began whipping me with her hand while at the same time apologizing profusely to Mr. Watson, who observed that I would certainly be in a reformatory school before I reached the age of fifteen! Mother, highly embarrassed, picked up the apples, dragged me out of the store, and down the lane, spanking me all the way home. She continued the spanking until our maid intervened and begged her not to spank me anymore. The maid, Annie Mae Holmes, was my mother's age. The two had become friends when they were in their teens. Annie Mae, as a young girl, ironed clothes for my maternal grandmother, and that is how she and my mother met. I would know and love Annie Mae until she died, long after I had married and was the father of grown children.

A year or two after the apple incident at Mr. Watson's store, we moved to Dick Street. It was while living there that I first heard about World War II, as the adults who were part of my life had discussions about how long it would take to conquer Germany and Japan. One of those adults was Esdale Edens, whom I called Dale. My earliest recollections include her and her husband Hubert, whom my mother and father called "Squirty." I never knew the story behind that nickname, but the Edenses were dear to me in my early years. I was about seven or eight when Esdale died of cancer. Even though I was so young, I felt a sense of deep despair and emptiness when my mother told me that Dale was gone. Hubert married again and opened a florist shop—Edens' Florist—virtually next door to where my paternal grandparents lived in Red Springs, twenty-six miles from Fayetteville. When I married in 1958, Hubert was in charge of the flowers for our wedding. He was a funny man, a hoot to be around. I loved him dearly, and I will never forget him. When he died, I felt a sense of loss akin to losing a family member.

Before World War II ended we moved again, this time to a new house on Robeson Street, literally within a stone's throw of Fayetteville High School. Behind FHS were Alexander Graham Junior High School and the high school football stadium. I was either five or six years old when we moved to Robeson Street (I can't recall whether it was late 1942 or early 1943.) and we lived there—my mother, father, and sister Willene, who had been born on Dick Street, and I—until I was eighteen.

The twelve years I spent on Robeson Street were my formative years. That is where and when I came to understand the world. World War II was brought home to me because we took in roomers. Soldiers passed through Fort Bragg by the thousands, as they waited to be sent "overseas." Many of them brought their wives and small children, and there was a serious housing shortage. Fayettevillians were encouraged to rent rooms to soldiers and their families, and we rented rooms to a number of couples, but only one with a child. As I recall, the child's name was Jackie, and he was about two. One day my three-year-old sister decided that she should show Jackie the town and, without saying a word to anyone, headed downtown with him. Before long, both children were missed, and no one had any idea where either one was. We all looked high and low throughout the neighborhood and called everybody we could think of. My mother and Jackie's mother, too, were frantic. Finally, the telephone rang, and a cashier at the Carolina Theater informed my mother that my sister and a little boy were there, demanding to see the show! I am not quite sure how the cashier knew to call my mother, but probably my precocious sister had given her our telephone number. At that time our telephone numbers in Fayetteville had only four digits, and I still remember ours to this day—2940. Even though Willene was only three, I have no doubt she knew our number.

The two mothers were so happy to have the children back that there were no spankings administered. When asked why she had done such a thing, Willene innocently and nonchalantly answered that Jackie had been in Fayetteville for sometime now and that she thought it was time for him to get out and go somewhere. It was from Jackie's parents and other renters, like Smitty (whose real first name I can't recall, since we never called him by it) and Alice Smith, his wife, that I learned about the worlds from which they had come—Washington state, Virginia, New York, and other places that escape my memory now. In retrospect, it was not a bad way for a boy of seven or eight years to learn about the world beyond Fayetteville. I remember, even at that early age, longing to see such places as Virginia and New York, and even faraway Washington state. Eventually I did—Virginia and New York by age thirteen, but Washington state only in my later years.

Our house at 216 Robeson was only three or four blocks from Hay Street, which was lined with a fair number of "joints" where soldiers went on "payday" to celebrate, usually by getting "higher than a Georgia pine," as the expression went. Some of the soldiers, once inebriated, began looking for trouble. There were fights aplenty, and some of the soldiers wandered into neighborhoods and peered into people's windows. On more than one occasion I remember neighborhood menfolk apprehending soldiers and other "peeping toms" and holding them until the police arrived. Sometimes the offenders were roughed up before the police appeared on the scene.

One particularly ugly incident involving liquored-up soldiers took place in Fayetteville during the war. The most notorious nightspot in town was called the Town Pump. On 4 October 1942, at the infamous Donaldson Street establishment, two sergeants, Herman W. Patterson and John N. Cash, got into a fight. The military police arrested the two men and placed them in a car. Hundreds of soldiers gathered around the MPs' vehicle and began shaking it. To break up the mob, Fayetteville police officers, who had been called in to back up the MPs, fired tear gas at the soldiers. One shell that fell near the door of the nightspot was kicked inside. Soldiers inside rushed into the street, but the authorities, thanks to the tear gas, were able to restore order, in spite of the fact that an estimated 2,000 soldiers were ultimately involved. Donaldson Street was cleared, and Sergeants Patterson and Cash were hauled away and charged with disorderly conduct, inciting a riot, and resisting arrest. This incident was highly embellished by locals who spread stories that machine-gun fire had been used to restore order and that a number of businesses in the area had bullet holes in their second-story windows and walls when the smoke cleared. This gave townspeople something to talk about and enlarge upon for years. I heard the story several times and was among the many who came to believe that the incident was far more serious than it really was. The truth is that there were so many disturbances at the Town Pump that they all got lumped together in city lore into one super riot that never actually happened.

The less-rowdy soldiers stayed away from the downtown dives and sought more civilized entertainment at the USO, an annex of which was located just a couple of blocks from our house. At the USO there were music and dancing and fraternizing between the townspeople and the soldiers. I, along with my neighborhood pals Tommy Stanton and Chesley Grimsley, knew the USO in a way that the adults who frequented the place did not. We used it as our secret hideout by crawling under the building until we got to the area where the stage was located. That area of the building featured a high platform inside, thus creating what amounted to a raised ceiling underneath. It was like a large room, and we could stand up and walk around without hitting our heads. Many were the times that we crawled on our stomachs to reach this secret place of refuge. There we sat and talked or walked around and talked, usually conversing about things we knew little about. In our naiveté we even talked about persuading girls to crawl under there with us, for we were sure we would know what to do with them once they were there! We had heard just enough about sex so that we thought we knew all about it.

While the war raged and soldiers came and went, I started to school in the fall of 1943 at Haymount Elementary School, located about five or six blocks from my house. I walked to school and quickly learned "the shortcut," walking behind the high school and taking some back streets that came out just in front of my school. My first-grade teacher was Mrs. Cobb, a kind and patient lady, who guided me gently through my first year, after concluding that I was a headstrong but imaginative little fellow. I spent my second year at Haymount and part of my third, but hardly had I begun the third grade when the school authorities did some redistricting and transferred me to Central School downtown. At Central I became known for a number of things, not all of them admirable. I became a pretty fair softball player, but never up to the level of my two heroes, William Olmstead and Danny Underwood. Both of them were bigger and stronger than I was, and both regularly hit homeruns over a very high fence in the outfield. For a long time I thought that the two of them were the only boys my age who could clear the fence regularly until Phil Harris showed up to play in a tournament involving all of the city's elementary schools. During batting practice, Phil hit balls over the fence with the ease that William and Danny did. As best I can remember, that was the first time I ever saw Phil, but later I would go through high school with him and know him from then until now. Not a big, strong boy, I never had the strength to clear the fence the way that William, Danny, and Phil did, but I could place the ball well and wound up hitting a lot of singles and doubles. Until I was a sixth grader, though, I had to arrive at school very early in order to be picked for a team, since I was younger and only an average player. Being early was not a problem for me, because I apparently came into the world as a punctual being. My mother swore that I was the first one at school on the day that I entered the first grade and that I was never late for school or anything else ever after.

My strongest area at Central was academics. I was considered one of the smartest students in my grade, but as a third and fourth grader I showed my violent temper from time to time, often getting into fights and some-times causing my teachers great frustration. One particular incident occurred when I was in the fourth grade. I have regretted what happened on that occasion ever since. My teacher was a very dedicated lady named Georgia McCaskill. Miss McCaskill loved all of her students, but I was her pet. She gave me the leading part in a class play. We practiced without costumes for weeks until a day or two before the play was to be performed. When she brought out my costume I hated it so much that I told her I would not play my part, if I had to wear the costume. As I recall, the costume was a pale blue and white cape with a shiny, satin finish, and it looked like something a girl should wear. I refused to wear such a sissy-looking garment. Crushed, my teacher started crying and became angry. The next day I reconsidered and offered to go ahead with the part, but she would not let me. I had hurt her feelings so badly that she got someone else to play the part, even though my replacement hardly knew the lines. Needless to say, my days as her pet were over. Miss McCaskill did not deserve to be disappointed the way I disappointed her, and in later years I wished many times that I had not been so mean. She was truly a fine teacher who ultimately suffered much sadness in her life. I can still hear her reading those stories from Greek mythology to us after lunch everyday.

During my year in the fourth grade—at least that is my recollection of when it happened—I came down with my first case of puppy love, as the adults called it. I, on the other hand, was sure that it was the real thing. Since the first grade I had secretly had girlfriends—Joanne Bullard in the first grade and Evelyn Fisher in the second—but I had not been smitten as I was in the fourth when I became enamored with Carol Smith. There were other pretty girls in our class—Inez Owen and Peggy Averitte, for example—but Carol was, at least to me, the prettiest of all. Carol lived on Campbell Avenue, near where I had once lived on Dick Street. It was a long way from Robeson Street, and it was not fashionable for boys my age to have a girlfriend and admit it openly. I needed an excuse to go all the way down to Campbell Avenue, and fortunately I had one. A classmate named Talmadge Martin lived on Dick Street, about three or four blocks from Carol's house. Talmadge and I liked to skate, so every afternoon that I was allowed to go to Talmadge's I grabbed my skates and headed for his house. He had his eye on Carol, too, and before long we were skating by Carol's house to see if she was at home and if she wanted to skate with us. We spent many an afternoon skating on the sidewalks of Campbell Avenue, Nimocks Avenue, and Dick Street. There were other kids who skated with us, but time has removed their identities from my memory. Even so, I can still see in my mind's eye the three of us—Talmadge and me and especially Carol skating down those sidewalks. We often rested by sitting down on the ground to look for four leaf clovers. I was in love, but I didn't dare tell anybody. I guess it became obvious, though, when I gave Carol my scout ring. My mother was upset with me for doing this and made me ask Carol to give the ring back. Whether it embarrassed her to do so or not, I don't know, but Carol returned the ring to me. To be honest, I forgot about the ring incident until Carol reminded me of it over a half century after it happened.

In the fifth and sixth grades I settled down some, began to control my temper better, and made excellent grades. Always a curious boy, I noticed that everyday, before our fifth-grade teacher, Miss Nita Highsmith, led the class in Bible reading and prayer, Bernice Fleishman left her seat and went into the hall until the devotional was over. Then Miss Highsmith would send someone to tell Bernice that she could come back in. One day my curiosity could contain itself no longer, and I audaciously asked why Bernice left the classroom everyday just before the devotional. Miss Highsmith answered that she was Jewish. I knowingly responded with an "Oh," as if I knew what being Jewish meant! At age ten or eleven, I had heard people speak of Jews (not always approvingly), but I had absolutely no idea of what their religion of Judaism was all about until years later.

My final year at Central School was perhaps my most memorable. Reaching the sixth grade meant that you were somebody at Central, for it was from the ranks of the sixth graders that the school safety patrol was selected. The safety patrol helped the younger children cross the street safely and helped to put them on the school bus after school. I was made captain of the patrol, and Danny Underwood was lieutenant. We were in charge of directing the other members of the patrol. On the shoulder crossover-strap that we patrolmen wore, we proudly pinned a silver badge indicating our exalted status as members of the safety patrol. I don't recall how the others felt about all of this, but I thought I was pretty important, and I still have that badge to this day.

Also in the sixth grade, one member of the class was chosen as the outstanding student of our class. That person received a silver cup with his or her name inscribed on it. I knew that my chances of being awarded that cup were quite good until I had a slight run-in with our sixth-grade teacher, Miss Alma Easom. I have forgotten what we clashed over, but she gave me a B in deportment, the only grade other than A I received all that year. When I saw it on my report card, I feared that my chances of receiving the cup were gone, but Miss Easom apparently reported to our principal, Mrs. Souders, that the B was not for an academic grade and that I should be awarded the cup as the outstanding student of the sixth-grade class. My mother and father were proud, but nobody was prouder than my maternal grandparents, who were sure that I would one day be president of the United States! When my mother told my grandfather about my honor, he said, "Well, they couldn't have picked a better boy."

One last observation about my years at Central. It was during that time that I became acquainted with the YMCA, which was located just two blocks from the school. As a fifth and sixth grader I went there nearly every afternoon after school, usually with my buddy Ronald Simpson. Ron and I swam almost everyday, after which we would play checkers or ping-pong. Sometimes we played basketball, as both of us were on a church-league team representing First Baptist Church. I don't think Ron's enthusiasm for basketball was quite as intense as mine. He was a thoughtful kid who had more serious things on his mind—like chess. As a result of his encouragement, I, too, learned to play chess, and I enjoyed playing it for a number of years. Eventually, however, I went on to other things, but Ron maintained his interest in chess and became a master chess player who traveled widely to play in tournaments in later years. After high school I would cross paths again with Ron when we were both at the University of North Carolina in Chapel Hill. In the interim he had served a tour of duty in the United State Air Force, while I had married my high school sweetheart, Judy McIntosh, and had become the father of a daughter, Cindi, who was about three at that time. To this day—more than five decades after grammar school and more than thirty years after our days in Chapel Hill—Ron and I remain in contact with each other. I have stayed in closer touch with him longer (at least on a regular basis) than with any other friend from my early school years.

Upon leaving Central School and going to junior high school, all I had to do was walk a block behind my house, and I was at the old Alexander Graham School, where I attended the seventh and eighth grades. There I became acquainted with kids from all over Fayetteville and began running around with Billy McLeod, a short boy with red hair, which he always wore in a crew cut. Billy was loads of fun, but he was as mischievous as they come, and he and I sometimes found ourselves getting into trouble, usually with one of our teachers. We both should have been flogged for tormenting several idealistic women who were dedicated to educating us and making something out of us. While we gave the women teachers hell, it was an entirely different story with our homeroom teacher, Coach Mike Spann. The coach had played professional football with the Detroit Lions, and there was not a boy in school who dared do anything but snap to attention when Coach Spann called his name. Though doing so was frowned upon in later years, the coach kept a paddle in his desk, and those who misbehaved were called to the front, told to bend over, and were struck in the rear by this powerful man. If the coach was riled up, one of his swings could lift you off the floor, as well as sting like being attacked simultaneously by a dozen bumblebees.

I think it was during my junior high years that I learned some things about responsibility and doing what was expected of me. Ever since the age of ten I had worked in a grocery store across the street from my house. I earned ten dollars a week during summers and five dollars a week during the school year. When school was in session, I went in after school on school days and then worked all day on Saturdays. On one occasion we were dismissed from school early so that we could go to the county fair. I went with my buddy Billy McLeod, and we were having so much fun that I stayed too long and did not make it to work on time. When I finally arrived at the store, the owner, Pryor Gibson, told me to go on home, that he did not need me. I took that to mean that I had been fired and resolved not to return. My mother made me go back the next day and apologize. When I did, Mr. Gibson told me that I was not fired and that I could return to work. However, he made it clear that I was never to be late again without calling or letting him know ahead of time. I learned a lesson. I was happy to keep my job, for it had enabled me to purchase my first bicycle at age ten. Costing fifty dollars, I paid for the bicycle monthly until I had paid the entire amount all by myself. This gave me a tremendous sense of pride. After working for Mr. Gibson for over a year, I went to work at another grocery store about two blocks from home. Whether at Gibson's or the other store, my job description was the same—stocking shelves, delivering groceries, and sweeping the floor. In other words, I was a "flunky" or a "gofer." One of my neighborhood friends was an older boy named Frank Kelly. His father delighted in teasing me. He liked to come into Gibson's Grocery, look at me in all seriousness, and say, "Boy, do you think you will ever amount to anything?" I wish Mr. Kelly were around today so that I could tell him that I never amounted to very much, but that I did go beyond sweeping floors in a grocery store!

After my days of working in the grocery store ended, I started going out to the ballpark at night to see Fayetteville's professional Class B baseball team play. Our team was the Fayetteville Athletics, and it played in the

Carolina League. I got a job at the ballpark, starting out as a ball boy. I chased down foul balls and returned them to the field of play or to the general manager. I was admitted to the game free and was paid the whopping sum of one dollar per game. Later I became the batboy and actually traveled with the team to some of the out-of-town games. For this service my salary was doubled to two dollars per game, but I would have done it for free. To this day I remember many of the players—Billy Harrington, Ray Berns, Dick Schoonover, Joe Aliperto, George Suder, Johnny Miller, Pete Brozovich, Mike Kume, Len Matterazzo, Tony Naples, Laddie Phillips, and Frank Camerata. Frank was good enough to show me around his home city of Philadelphia in the summer of 1950, when I went with my paternal grandparents to visit my aunt and uncle who lived there. It was a heady experience at age twelve and thirteen for a boy to be in the company of such men as these players and their manager, Tom Oliver, and to be privileged to see the legendary baseball figure, Connie Mack, on one occasion. The players were not always complimentary in their remarks about Fayetteville, but to me, my hometown was a fine place to be. By this time I had traveled to places like Virginia, Florida, and even the northern cities of Philadelphia and New York, and I was always glad to "get back home" to "Fedvul."

During my Robeson Street years I met someone who would become a surrogate member of our family. Georgella Wells was a large black woman of about eighteen years of age when she started working for my mother. Eventually she worked for other members of our family as well, particularly my mother's oldest sister, Aunt Mary. Georgella loved us all as if we were her relatives, and she marveled at me because I could go to the movies and tell her everything that I saw and heard. And she enjoyed telling my sister and me about the movies she saw. Though uneducated, Georgella had a natural intelligence that was remarkable. To this day I am convinced that if she had been part of a later generation and could have been lucky enough to have parents who would have encouraged her to be somebody special, she would have gone far. In spite of her lack of sophistication, she demonstrated a good understanding of the human condition and was quite perceptive in handling problems. And she could be quite amusing. My maternal grandfather lived with us the last nine years of his life, and he and Georgella had some humorous conversations. John Harrison Herring, Sr., or "Pa," as we grandchildren called my grandfather, was constantly telling us around the time of his birthday each year that his impending birthday would be his last. When he turned 79, Georgella told him that we would have to have a huge celebration the following year when he would reach the 80 mark. Pa quickly replied that he would not be there next year. "Where you goin', Mr. Herring?" Georgella asked. "To the graveyard," he replied without hesitation. Twelve months later, the day before his eightieth birthday, Georgella reminded Pa of their conversation the year before. She said, "See, Mr. Herring, you said last year you wouldn't be here for your eightieth birthday, and your birthday will be here tomorrow. So you are going to be 80 after all." He shot back, "The day's not over yet."

After I married and moved away from Fayetteville, I kept up with Georgella, even though she stopped working for my mother, except on rare occasions. I would go to see her at her home ever so often. She always was delighted, and she showed great love for my wife, my children, and me. And she always loved my sister Willene every bit as much as she did me. I remember hearing about Georgella's death, and I was immensely saddened by it. Before going into her last surgery, which she would not survive, she told someone who was with her to tell "Mrs. Margan" (She always pronounced our name as if it were spelled with an "a" instead of an "o.") and all the family that she loved us. Many members of my family used the "N-word" without hesitation, whenever they referred to black people in general, but I cannot remember a single one of them ever using it when referring to Georgella. As did many Southerners, my family—I regret to say—looked down on black people as a race, but there were individual members who were accepted, appreciated, and even loved, as Georgella was. Eventually I learned to view such an attitude as nonsensical and wrong, but I was among the few from my family who did. To this day I will tell the world and anyone in it that Georgella was one of the finest human beings I have ever known. The fact that she never had the remotest chance of realizing her potential is a tragedy.

Having grown up in this Southern town called Fayetteville, I am convinced that racism is not inherent in us—us meaning the human race. We are taught to be racists by our elders, and they learned it from theirs. One generation passes it along to another until it is embedded in the culture and is thus expected of everyone. When I was not around adults, I expressed no resentment toward black people. I loved Georgella and Annie Mae, and I did not mind playing with black boys who lived a few blocks from my neighborhood. I remember one occasion during my years on Robeson Street when I learned racism from a prominent member of our community. He was the superintendent of city schools, Mr. Horace Sisk. One Saturday morning a number of white boys went over to the high school football field located a block behind my house, just down the hill from the junior high, with the idea of playing some pick-up baseball. We found black boys already there and already playing. We did not try to run them off. They had only a few players, and someone proposed that we join ranks, choose up sides, and play. The black boys found this acceptable, and that is what we did. We were having a splendid time until a heavyset, bald-headed man burst on the scene in a rage. I knew who he was, but he proceeded to tell us that he was the superintendent of city schools. First, he ran the black boys off and told them that the school property was for whites and that they had their schools on the other side of town. Next, he called all of us white boys together and gave us hell for degrading ourselves by playing with black boys. Until he told me that, I did not know I was degrading myself. I thought I was simply playing baseball with other boys, but now I knew that if I dared to play with boys who had a dark skin, I was somehow lowering myself. After all, I had it straight from the school superintendent. Since he ran the city schools, I assumed he ought to know.

I regret to say that I would not question this ridiculous and immoral nonsense from then until I was in college, when I finally saw racism for what it is—shortsighted and wrong. Through it all I somehow rationalized that Georgella and Annie Mae were different, not to be equated with other black people.

One's culture can easily wrap a person in chains of ignorance and prejudice, chains that are not always easy to break. There came a defining moment in my life, however, when I realized that racism and the system of segregation it perpetuated was totally wrong. It was when I was in college. President Eisenhower had sent troops into Lebanon. I was a senior at Baylor University and was not interested in being pulled out of school and put in the army. Even so, I received a notice to go from Waco, Texas to Dallas, Texas to be examined for the service. At the time appointed, I boarded a bus with others who had been notified. About two-thirds of the young men on board were black, the other third white. We arrived in Dallas and were examined in the morning, but we did not finish before lunch. The sergeant in charge gave us directions to the café at which we were to eat lunch. We were each allowed fifty cents for the meal; anything over that, we paid for ourselves. Several of the black guys were in front of the group and reached the café first. They went in and came out instantly, whereupon some of us wondered if we were at the wrong place. Then we learned that blacks were not served inside. Their lunches would be handed to them through a back window, after which they could find a place in the parking lot to eat. Even a fool could see the injustice in this situation, even if the policy of segregation had been drilled into him for years. Those black fellows were being examined for the same army I was. All of us might possibly go into the army and be sent overseas to fight and perhaps die for our country—a country in which a black person did not have the right to sit down in a restaurant and eat his lunch! I saw the wrong in segregation as I had never seen it before. It struck home, and I resolved that I would never again treat a black person any differently than a white person. I would never again be a party to prejudice and the mistreatment of black people, and I would form a friendship with a black person I liked as readily as with a white person.

That was 1958, three years after I graduated from high school. Meanwhile, I had had some interesting experiences during my three years at the old Fayetteville High School on Robeson Street and my final year at the new Fayetteville High School on Fort Bragg Road, which, eventually, was renamed in honor of Governor Terry Sanford. My old temper was still with me, but I had steadily gained more control over it through the years. Still, it would sometimes get me into trouble. I had said the wrong thing to an upperclassman on one occasion, and he kept trying to pick a fight with me. Since he was bigger and stronger than I was, I backed off, but I told my cousin, Charles Cox, about the bully. Charles was four years older than I was and was well known at Fayetteville High. After all, a few years before this, he and two or three of his friends had skipped school one day, had come to school (the one on Robeson Street) on horseback, and had ridden their horses through the halls of the school. Imagine what the people in the building thought when they heard that commotion. After going out the door at the other end, the riders split up, riding off in different directions. But not for long, for the police caught up with them in short order. This was my daring cousin who, upon being told of my experience with the bully, decided to go to the school and confront him on my behalf. He did, and he told the guy that he needed to pick on somebody his own size and that he had better stop picking on me or he, Charles, would be back to settle matters with him.

That ended the threats by that particular bully, but my troubles were not over. I had a knack for creating trouble for myself. My last fight was during my sophomore or junior year, when I knocked out a classmate and a friend of his knocked me out. I got into other trouble as well. I defied my freshman English teacher, Mrs. Florence Bogart, about a week before the end of the school year. When it appeared to Mrs. Bogart that class members were neglecting our reading assignments, she surprised us by giving a pop quiz one day. I had neither paper nor pencil. I borrowed a pencil, but could not borrow any paper. I asked Mrs. Bogart if I could step right outside the door and get some paper out of my locker. She said, "No." I told her that I had no paper. She said, "Borrow some." I explained that I had tried and that no one had extra paper. "Write it on your shirt, then," she said. That angered me, and so I arose, went to my locker, got some paper, and returned to my seat, where I quickly faced her fury.

Although I was sporting a 99 average in her class, Mrs. Bogart threw me out of her class, told me I could not take her final exam, and advised me that I would fail freshman English unless the other freshman English teacher, Miss Ronnie Lee, admitted me to her class. Miss Lee did indeed admit me, exempted me from the final exam, and passed me with an A. Over the next couple of years I took two years of Spanish and senior English with Miss Lee, who, in all of my formal educational experience (close to twenty years altogether), was, perhaps, the most outstanding teacher I ever had.

All in all, we were blessed by being students at Fayetteville High School, for we had some fine teachers, among whom were some genuine characters like Assistant Principal J. Warren George, an earnest man who was determined to pound Algebra into our heads. The antithesis of the excitable Mr. George was our dedicated Civics teacher, Thomas Templeton, who, the more serious he became, lowered his voice until he was actually whispering at times. I well remember the day that Joseph Stalin's death was announced. Mr. Templeton went to the main office on an errand. When he returned, he looked pale and began to whisper. After we asked him several times to raise his voice, we finally made out that he was saying, "Stalin is dead." We had some excellent teachers, and no public high school could have had a more dedicated and professional principal than Sam Edwards. A serious man, Mr. Edwards was also a man of real substance who insisted on academic excellence at his school.

Fayetteville during my high school years seemed what it had always been—an army town where Fort Bragg soldiers came to get drunk and raise hell on payday. Only reckless citizens went downtown on payday night, and even those looked straight ahead as they walked, lest eye contact with a soldier might be interpreted as staring and as an insult that could easily end up in a fight. I guess I was one of the reckless, since I was often downtown on payday night, for at age fourteen I went to work at the Colony Theater, and we were open for business every night of the year. The theater was packed on paydays and payday nights. Occasionally there was trouble with a soldier who had had one or two beers too many or with someone who slipped liquor into the theater and got plastered in his seat before passing out or throwing up on the floor. Happily such incidents were rare in the nicest theater in Fayetteville. The manager was Mr. Hazel Ponton, but the person who really ran the place was his assistant, Miss Delores Kelly, a heavyset lady with a beautiful face and a charming manner. Yet, she was a strict employer who kept a watchful eye on me, as well as my fellow ushers, Ernest Mutzberg and Billy Beard. If we appeared less than serious in carrying out our work, she was quick to let us know about it. I worked for her until I was sixteen, and then one day Mr. Thomas Hood, who was vice president of the Commercial and Industrial Bank (right next door to the theater), asked me if I would be interested in working at the bank. I jumped at the chance and soon found myself a member of the bookkeeping staff, ably led by Orie G. Hudson, whom we all called "Miss Orie."

Since I already had a job at the bank when I became a senior in high school, I decided to get credit for my work by enrolling in the Distributive Education class conducted by David K. Tally. The class consisted largely of getting class credit for working and making some reports to Mr. Tally about my work at the bank. Mr. Hood, who had arranged for me to be hired, had my future all mapped out. He thought I would train to be a banker, starting as a bookkeeper, moving up to teller, then to loan officer, and finally to a higher executive position. After all, he was behind me, as was the bank president, Mr. Graham Bell, whom I knew because his son Graham and I had gone to Sunday school together since around age five. The man just under Mr. Hood was Wilbur Beard, and he, too, seemed to like me and push me toward a career in banking. "Miss Orie", one of the most wonderful people I ever knew and the best boss I ever had, was also in my corner, and almost everyone in the bank liked me. My banking career, however, got derailed because, when I was seventeen, I "got religion," as people used to say.

From the start I was an overly zealous convert. It was during my junior year in high school, when I was seventeen, and I was soon annoying people at work and school by buttonholing them and asking them if they had been saved. My conversion came about because of my association with an older young man named Dick Bene (pronounced Benny but originally Benay, as Dick was always careful to explain), whom I had met at First Baptist Church and at the YMCA. Dick's father was a minister, and eventually Mr. Bene accepted a call to the Mt. Gilead Baptist Church in Seventy-First Township, located between Fayetteville and Fort Bragg. There was a revival meeting at Mt. Gilead, and Dick persuaded me to attend. There I fell prey to the persuasive pleadings of a fiery preacher from South Carolina named Y. Z. Gordy and answered the altar call. I had a humdinger of a conversion experience and soon attached myself to some of Fayetteville's earnest evangelicals who regularly held services at the hospitals, nursing homes, and jails of the city. Among my new friends were Al Bean, Frank Turner, and the family of J. Pat Lee, a layman who sponsored the Cool Spring Mission and was a close friend of every evangelist who had ever passed through Fayetteville. Mr. Lee and his wife Katie had three daughters and a son. His daughter Frances was a missionary, and his daughter Ruth was a dedicated Christian teacher. Ruth was among those of us who conducted services around town, and we were all very close friends. They were wonderful people, the epitome of sincerity, but all were thoroughgoing Fundamentalists and somewhat scornful of those who did not believe the Bible to be literally true in every particular. I, too, held those views at the time, and it would take years of education to make me understand that faith is truly that—*faith*. Religion is based far more on faith than on fact, but for the devotees of a religion, what they take on faith becomes fact to them. In other words, in their minds it becomes very difficult to separate what is actually fact from what they take on faith.

Ruth Lee, who was certain that every word in the Bible was fact, had attended and graduated from Bob Jones University, once labeled the "Buckle on the Bible Belt" in a widely circulated magazine article. She persuaded Frank Turner to go there, and Frank persuaded me. Although I soon rebelled against the dogmatism and dictatorial atmosphere of Bob Jones and left there after a year and a half, I did become a Baptist minister and remained one for about five years. I finished my college training at Baylor University and then attended Southeastern Baptist Theological Seminary for a year. As minister of education and assistant pastor of a Baptist Church in Durham, North Carolina, I became disenchanted with the ministry when I saw deacons of the church stand in the church door and forbid black people to enter. When those who were denied entry asked for me, I went to the front door and told them how sorry I was that they had been prevented from entering the church. This angered some of the deacons, and people who had been my friends for several years turned on me. Once exuding friendship and love toward my wife, my daughter, and me, they now either ignored me or told me that they wanted nothing further to do with me. Some in the church, however, were supportive enough not to hate me, but few approved of my stance that segregation was unchristian.

The general attitude of the church's people did much to bring on my disillusionment with the kind of Christianity that could not transcend a flawed culture that insisted on segregation. Because of this I decided to leave the ministry and become a history professor. Thus, in 1962 I resigned from the church to attend full-time the graduate history program at the University of North Carolina in Chapel Hill. There I eventually earned my master's and Ph.D. degrees. Soon after receiving my master's I entered upon a teaching career that spanned thirty-three years in the college classroom. While teaching in Martinsville, Virginia at Patrick Henry College, the school where I began my career, I finished my Ph.D. degree in 1967 and was formally awarded it in June 1968. Thirteen years before this I had left the banks of the Cape Fear for Greenville, South Carolina and later for Waco, Texas, but fate had brought me home to North Carolina, and there, twenty-five or so miles north and slightly west of where the Cape Fear flows by Fuqua-Varina, I completed my formal education. And, once again, I headed west to teach on the banks of another river—the Brazos—in central Texas. There had been but three Morgans—Judy, Cindi, and I—when I had gone to Patrick Henry College in 1964 to teach. Upon our departure four years later there were four, our son Brian having entered the world in 1966 during my teaching stint in Martinsville. When Brian was two we swapped a picturesque view of the Blue Ridge Mountains for the big, blue sky and hot, hot sun of Brazos County, a place we would call home for five years. That is how long I was a member of the faculty at Texas A&M University.

Though I was a very long way from the banks of the Cape Fear, most of my kinfolks and my wife's parents still lived in Fayetteville, and we returned regularly to visit. Then, during the 1970s, the place that I had always called home—"Fedvul"—made national news when Jeffrey MacDonald was charged with murdering his wife and daughters, and Velma Barfield was indicted for poisoning at least four people and tried for her life for murdering one of them. Because of the Vietnam War, Fayetteville had already been labeled "Fayettenam." Now, because of MacDonald and Barfield, my hometown was referred to occasionally as the murder capital of North Carolina, and many other horrible murders were soon to follow.

Chapter 1

A Century Ends, Another Begins: The Last Hanging and the First Electrocution

Any calendar expert will tell you that the nineteenth century ended just past the stroke of midnight in the year 1900. There was no zero year in the beginning, and, since a century is a hundred years, a century is not over until the *end* of its hundredth year. Thus, Fayetteville, along with the rest of the world, watched the nineteenth century end on the last day of year 1900. The small river town, known by the name of Fayetteville since 1783, had seen some interesting developments during the nineteenth century and, before that, during its eighteenth-century beginnings as Campbellton and Cross Creek. Now it was on the verge of even more significant developments, as the nineteenth century was set to expire.

Looking back, it is interesting to note that one of the town's early founders, Farquhard Campbell, was found guilty of assisting the British in 1776. Though sent up north as a prisoner on parole (meaning he was restricted in his movements but not incarcerated), Campbell later returned home and was able to reestablish himself politically and socially after the Revolutionary War. He even won election to the North Carolina Senate and served in that body from 1785 to 1793. Campbell's last year in the state senate was the year when the Fayetteville Independent Light Infantry, the second oldest military unit in the United States that still exists, was formed. Men in that unit would participate in the War of 1812, the Spanish American War, and the Pershing Expedition into Mexico in 1916. Even more significant than the creation of the FILI was the fact that in 1789—four years before that military unit was established—North Carolina, after turning down the United States Constitution some months previously, had ratified the controversial document in Fayetteville. Thus, ever since, Fayetteville has been able to glory in the distinction of bringing North Carolina into the Union.

Although no Fayettevillian has ever been elected president of the United States, some of its natives have held high office, and the town has enjoyed many other distinctions. For instance, native son James C. Dobbin served as secretary of the Navy in the administration of Franklin Pierce (1853–1857). Among the "other distinctions" was the capture of the town in March 1865 by Union Army General William T. Sherman. The general's purpose was to take over the Confederate arsenal located there. Sherman succeeded, and his troops destroyed that facility.

A distinction of a vastly different kind was that an area called Tokay, just north of Fayetteville, was once famous as a wine production center. The Tokay vineyard was part of the estate of Colonel Wharton J. Green, a farmer, writer, and congressman. The famous vineyard had up to a hundred acres of bearing vines and produced dry red and dry white wines and sweet red and sweet white wines. The estate and its vineyards fell victim to Fayetteville's expansion in the twentieth century, and Tokay eventually became a residential area.

I begin the story of twentieth-century Fayetteville on a personal note. The year 1900, the last year of the nineteenth century, was the year in which my maternal grandparents, John Harrison Herring, Sr. and Mary Jane Deal, took their marriage vows in Fayetteville. My grandfather, a working young man of age twenty-one, could not afford a house, and so he and my grandmother set up housekeeping in the house she had lived in since she was eleven years old. My great grandfather, Andrew Jackson Deal, had built the house on Mechanic Street in 1890, at a time when the location was considered a good distance from downtown. Grandpa Deal was still living in the house when he died in 1909, and so was my grandmother living in it when she died forty-five years after her father's death. This house, at which I spent many pleasant hours as a boy, was sold after my grandmother's death, and my grandfather came to live with us, as noted earlier. Meanwhile, in the house on Mechanic Street—between 1900 and 1954—my grandparents produced and reared seven children; my mother, Bessie, was their sixth child. I remember the house as a frequent gathering place of the Herring clan, a place where all of us met on Christmas day, except my Uncle Charles and his family. Because they lived in faraway Jacksonville, Florida, they did not come until summer vacation, when we all gathered together again to be with them.

Enough nostalgia. Back to 1900, when the tiny-but-active little town of Fayetteville stood on the brink of a new century, not knowing that its character would soon be changed forever. The development that would alter the little town the most and give impetus to turning it into a much larger town was the decision by the federal government during World War I to establish "Camp Bragg" on the rolling sand hills and amidst the pines and scrub oaks ten or so miles to the west. That would happen before the second decade of the new century ended. Once it happened, Fayetteville would never again be the same place. Very early a pattern would be established of soldiers receiving their pay and making their way into town in search of a good time. From time immemorial soldiers have associated a good time with wine, women, and song, and for a price there were people in Fayetteville and Cumberland County who were eager to oblige the pleasure seekers in khaki uniforms.

Prior to "Camp Bragg's" emergence amidst the scrub oaks, there were other developments—highly important ones, too. Railroad connections already opened Fayetteville to the outside world via the Atlantic Coastline Railroad. As the iron horse came, the steamboats went, slowly disappearing from the Cape Fear. Local travel was still by horseback and on foot, and horses could always be seen around the Market House. Horse-drawn wagons carried baggage up and down Hay Street to the various hotels. Just before the turn of the century, in November 1900, Southern Bell Telephone Company announced that it would have Fayetteville connected to all parts of the United States within a few months. Fayetteville was on the move, but it was still a small town of less than seven thousand residents.

In the first month of the new century, January 1901, the town received notice that one of its famous sons, who was perhaps infamous in the minds of most white Fayettevillians, had died. That highly publicized native was a Methodist minister named Hiram R. Revels, and he was a black man. What distinguished him was that he had represented Mississippi in the United States Senate, and he was one of the first two blacks to serve in that body, the other being Blanche K. Bruce, also of Mississippi. Revels, a mulatto, found his political opportunity during the halcyon days of Radical Reconstruction—1865–1877. Those days were short-lived, as a conservative reaction during the last two decades of the nineteenth century brought forth Jim Crow laws in all Southern states, laws that would make second-class citizens of African Americans. Not only would black people be prevented by Jim Crow laws from holding public office, they would be denied the right to vote and be compelled to endure the indignities of segregation for decades to come. Yet, Jim Crow laws would not come to Fayetteville and Cumberland County for a while. The 1900 U.S. census listed 3,823 "white native voters," 40 "white foreign voters," and 2,362

"Negro voters." Soon enough, however, the rights of blacks would be phased out in Fayetteville and Cumberland County, just as they were already being phased out in other places in the South.

Oh, that first decade of the twentieth century in Fayetteville! The old was desperately trying to hang on, while the new was energetically trying to break forth. There were so many exciting developments. A sensation was created when Wade T. Saunders, in 1902, drove the first gasoline automobile down the dirt streets of Fayetteville. Some claimed that it was the first automobile driven in North Carolina. The vehicle, which would run ten to twelve miles per hour, had cost $1,200. Saunders's "gas buggy" had no muffler and was thus noisy enough to frighten horses and mules, since it could be heard from several blocks away. Peace-disturbing or not, the automobile was a sign of things to come. Machines would soon carry people more and more, while horses and wagons would be used less and less for that purpose. Fayetteville soon had steam-powered trolleys running up and down its main streets and then motor cars powered by forty horsepower gasoline engines. The latter were replaced in 1908 by electric-powered trolleys offering a ride for a mere nickel. In 1916 the trolley system was shut down. More and more automobiles were making their appearance.

As the automobile emerged as the transportation of the future, the steamboat gasped at one last breath of life. In 1902 the steamer called "The City of Fayetteville" was completed in Jacksonville, Florida for the Fayetteville and Wilmington Steamboat Company. Two years later the U.S. district court appointed Carolina Trust Company of Raleigh as receiver for the company, which had gone bankrupt. Steamboats on the Cape Fear would soon be gone forever.

A new day was dawning, and for many this meant an improvement in their quality of life. Grade schools opened in September 1903, schools that can be called public, since they were paid for by public taxation for the first time in the town's history. Education was becoming possible for all children—white children at least. In April of that same year free postal delivery began in Fayetteville, and it was extended in September to rural areas surrounding the town. Perhaps some of this was linked to the prosperity that prevailed, for cotton was bringing the very good price of eleven cents a pound. The farmers and merchants along the Cape Fear had money in their pockets—more money than they had had since before the Panic of 1893. Much of the cotton that was fueling the economy of the town and county was sold under the Market House in the center of downtown Fayetteville.

The citizens of Fayetteville were obviously civic-minded, as they tried in schizophrenic fashion to glory in their Confederate past and be good Americans simultaneously. In 1901 the town's Ladies Monument Association entered into a contract to erect a monument to Confederate soldiers. That monument soon made its appearance, and for many years it stood in the middle of St. James Square where Green, Grove, Ramsey, and Rowan Streets converged, forcing all automobile traffic to drive around it. I cannot count the number of times that I either rode around or drove around the Confederate soldier who stood blocking four streets. Eventually, increased traffic made circling the square a luxury that a modern Fayetteville could no longer afford. The monument was moved over to stand in front of the John A. Oates residence, which stood on the corners of Grove and Ramsey Streets. Traffic that had previously been slowed by the monument came to be controlled by modern stoplights. Within a month of the time that Fayetteville ladies contracted to erect a Confederate monument, Fayette-villians joined the national mourning for slain United States President William McKinley, who had been shot twice in the abdomen by an anarchist named Leon Czolgosz at the Pan American Exposition in Buffalo, New York. A few years later, in 1904, the residents of Fayetteville invited President Theodore Roosevelt to visit the town during his Southern tour, but Roosevelt passed up the opportunity to visit the growing little city that sprawled out westward from the banks of the Cape Fear.

Although "Teddy" Roosevelt passed up an invitation to stop in Fayetteville, other dignitaries made their appearance from time to time. The famous bandleader John Philip Sousa and his band performed for Fayetteville's citizens in 1902. The applause of the appreciative audiences who heard the performances of these famous musicians was long and loud. Five years later some people of the city were treated to a speech by William Jennings Bryan, the "Boy Orator of the Platte," who had already failed to win the presidency of the United States, as the Democratic Party's nominee, in the elections of 1896 and 1900. Bryan spoke to the Women's Civic Improvement Association in Fayetteville.

Even though Fayetteville was no metropolis, it was not exactly some backwater town either. After December 1902 it was lighted electrically by the new municipal electric light plant. This development led to considerable celebrating, for nine years earlier the town had attempted but failed to establish electrical lighting. Fayetteville also had a college, the Fayetteville Colored Normal School, established in 1877. While having only 135 students in 1902, it would grow and eventually become Fayetteville State University. Begun as a school to train black teachers, it would, before the twentieth century closed, become a full-fledged university, granting degrees to people of all races.

In 1904 Fayetteville got its second hospital with the building of St. Luke's. Two years after its erection, St. Luke's obtained an X-ray machine, a somewhat remarkable development, since X-rays had been discovered by German physicist Wilhelm Röntgen just a few years earlier (1895). Thus, in 1906 Fayetteville had its first X-ray machine, but that was not what was most talked about that year, for so many other things happened. In March a fire ripped through fifteen buildings on Hay Street, and one of them was Highsmith Hospital. Perhaps the most talked about item was the Market House, for there were some who wanted to sell it to make way for a new United States Post Office. Two leading men of the town, J. H. Myrover and Charles G. Rose, would have none of it. To save the landmark, they rallied the town's citizens to protest the proposed sale, and the Market House survived.

Spirituous liquor was another hot topic of conversation during the first decade of the twentieth century in Fayetteville. Although the town and county were dry, there was still a big demand for strong drink. In October 1906 the Cumberland County Medical Society petitioned the state legislature to repeal the section of the county prohibition law that permitted druggists to sell "prescription whiskey." Doctors contended that they were "harassed beyond endurance" for whiskey prescriptions. The legislature honored their request in March 1907. Even so, in 1908 the matter of prohibition emerged again, and there was a statewide vote. A majority of the state's one hundred counties voted to continue prohibition. Cumberland voted with the majority, and the selling of alcoholic beverages remained unlawful in Fayetteville.

Through all of these developments the *Fayetteville Observer,* the town's sole newspaper, thrived and reported the news. In spite of suffering heavy damage from a fire in 1908, the *Observer* managed to continue publication. One gentleman offered the opinion: "I believe *The Fayetteville Observer* would be issued if its editors themselves had to stand on their heads to set type with their toes." The year 1908 was an event-filled year. Not only did the town's only newspaper almost burn down, Fayetteville got its first woman doctor. She was Irene Thornton, a native, who was a graduate of Baltimore College of Medicine for Women. A couple of months after this happy development, toward the end of summer, the city received its heaviest rainfall in seventeen years, and the water level of the Cape Fear reached more than seventy-one feet. The town was flooded almost to the Market House, and small bridges washed away. The Clarendon Bridge at the end of Person Street, which was the only bridge crossing the Cape Fear out of Fayetteville, was made of wood, and it almost gave way, as floodwaters rushed up against it. The bridge had wooden sides, and its destruction by the rapidly flowing floodwaters hitting against them appeared certain.

My grandfather Herring often told how concerned public officials called upon my great-grandfather, Grandpa Deal, for advice on how to save the bridge. Grandpa Deal was an engineer and builder of many Fayetteville bridges. According to the story my grandfather told, Grandpa Deal, who was 76 years old in 1908 and who would die the next year, was rowed out in a boat to assess the situation. When asked what could be done to save the bridge, he said, "Knock the sides out of the bridge and let the water run over the bottom." The sides were somehow removed (I don't know how), and the bridge bottom survived. The sides were rebuilt, but in 1909 the bridge was destroyed by fire and was replaced by a steel bridge. As best I can remember, my grandfather never told me how people crossed the river while the new steel bridge was being built, but I imagine ferry boats were temporarily used.

Besides the flood of 1908 and the ravaging of Clarendon Bridge by fire in 1909, Fayettevillians had other things to talk about as the first decade of the twentieth century moved toward its end. The Coca Cola franchise in Fayetteville was held by Charles Dietrich Hutaff, and in 1909 he obtained a patent on an "ingenious" bottle washer. It was heralded as an innovation far ahead of other such devices. The new bottle washer appeared long before my day, but, as a boy, I passed the Coca Cola Bottling Company many times. I even went inside once. I cannot remember why. I never met any of the Hutaffs, as far as I can recall. Yet, I heard them mentioned quite often. And for some reason, all the kids knew where the Coca Colas were made, as well as the Pepsis. The Pepsi Cola Bottling Company in Fayetteville did not receive its charter until late in 1910. Its first owners were James S. Hall, J. J. Hall, and T. G. Bullard. Other trivial matters for discussion in the last year or two of that first decade was the construction of a new post office on Hay Street, and the purchase of a Cadillac touring car in 1910 by Dr. J. F. Highsmith, a prominent local physician.

On the religious scene there were developments, too. Two of Fayetteville's foundation churches were rebuilt and dedicated—Hay Street Methodist and First Baptist in 1908 and 1910 respectively. For those who were looking for something new and more unconventional in religion there was a big meeting at Falcon, just north of Fayetteville, in August 1910. About 4,000 attended what was reported as a "sanctification-unknown tongue" gathering. The Pentecostal Holiness movement had gotten under way in California a few years earlier, and charismatic religion had made its way eastward to Fayetteville in a very short time. Falcon soon became a center for religion of that sort. It featured Christians receiving a "second blessing," meaning that they went beyond mere salvation to sanctification, which often resulted in the person speaking in an "unknown tongue." Purportedly this unknown tongue was the language of the Holy Spirit. The Baptists and Methodists were apparently satisfied with salvation and good deeds, for I have never encountered one of them who spoke in an unknown tongue—not even among the most zealous members of those denominations.

Religious excitement was not alone in shaking up the Fayetteville area in the last years of that first decade, for there was a dramatic shooting in town on 23 February 1908. That Sunday morning, Sam Melvin, alias Sam Murchison, an illegitimate black man who sometimes used his mother's name and sometimes his father's, arrived in Fayetteville from Parkton, a small community fourteen miles south of Fayetteville. Soon after his arrival he "began to tank up on mean whiskey in the Dross Neck section near the train station." He shot one black woman and then shot at another. He shot other blacks later in the day and shot at still others. When he threatened a black woman named Ida Johnson, she ran to secure the help of Police Chief James Herbert Benton. The chief ran to assist her, and Melvin (or Murchison) "shot him full in the face." Benton, who was fifty-two years old, died immediately.

When Melvin was arrested and taken to jail, about a thousand citizens gathered there with intentions of lynching him. Governor Robert Glenn ordered Fayetteville's FILI to duty to protect the accused killer. The troops were commanded by "Major Vann" and Captain N. H. McGeachy. Later tried and convicted, Melvin was sentenced to death by hanging. That sentence was carried out at the Cumberland County Jail. Before being hanged, the doomed man made a statement, blaming his misdeeds on whiskey and pleading, "I hope everybody will forgive me as their Lord has." The hangman's noose did its work on 16 April 1908, and Sam Melvin went to meet his maker. Two years later in 1910 another black man in another county forty miles down the Cape Fear would become the last man to be hanged by the state of North Carolina.

In 1910 the last state execution by hanging was one of two significant developments along the Cape Fear. The last execution by that means affected all of North Carolina, while the other was limited to Fayetteville and Cumberland County. On 17 March 1910 the *Fayetteville Observer* reported the execution, which had been carried out on 11 March: "After spending a restful night in his cell at the county jail in Elizabethtown, Henry Spivey, a Negro, the last man in North Carolina to hang, walked boldly to the gallows in the jail yard."

As noted above, Elizabethtown is approximately forty miles downriver in Bladen County. How the reporter of the *Observer* knew that Spivey's last night on earth was restful, I have no idea. Anyway, the report noted further that Spivey, while waiting to hang, put out his hand to the sheriff to show that it was steady. The convicted man carefully observed the guards as they adjusted the rope. He declined to make a statement. No relatives or friends were there to see him hang. At 12:09 p.m. the trap was sprung. In ten minutes, Spivey was dead. Why had Spivey been sentenced to death by hanging? He had been convicted of killing his father-in-law, shooting him after calling him to his front door.

Fayettevillians were quite aware of and interested in Spivey's execution, and they took note, too, of another execution that soon followed. Within days of Spivey's death at the end of a noose, Walter Morrison, another black man, became the first man to die in North Carolina's new electric chair at North Carolina's Central Prison in Raleigh. Morrison's execution had already been postponed five times because of the "incompleteness of the electric chair." The man's crime was criminal assault on "a Croatan Indian woman." There were calls upon Governor Claude Kitchin to commute Morrison's sentence to life in prison, but the governor declined, and North Carolina moved from hanging people convicted of capital crimes to electrocuting them.

More attention was probably given—at least it was in the local newspaper—to the two executions than to the elections held that year. Toward the end of 1910, in the November elections, Cumberland County chose a new sheriff, who outpolled his opponent more than two to one—

1,770 votes to 862. The new sheriff was Neill Hector McGeachy (pronounced McGayhay), and he would remain the "high sheriff" of Cumberland County for an amazing forty years. Not until the end of 1950 would Sheriff McGeachy leave office, and that was by his choice. I never met Sheriff McGeachy, but I heard about him and read about him often during my boyhood. His name was uttered in almost reverent tones. I didn't know that there was any other sheriff in all the world. I suppose I thought he was the sheriff of the world.

Members of my family knew Sheriff McGeachy. My mother's oldest brother, John H. Herring, Jr., once told me why, in his mind at least, the sheriff was unbeatable in any election. Uncle John claimed that if any residents in Cumberland County were in trouble—particularly if there was a death in the family—the sheriff showed up at their door to offer his assistance. If they needed groceries, the sheriff saw to it that they got groceries. If they needed transportation, he sent a car to provide it. Thus, whatever Cumberland County residents who had suffered a tragedy needed, they got, courtesy of the sheriff. He was everybody's friend. Though he always did his job when it required bringing in criminals, he was usually not even disdainful of those he arrested. Apparently he thought it was his job to arrest them, not judge them.

Although not born in Fayetteville, N. H. McGeachy resided there a number of years before being elected sheriff. He was born in Robeson County on 9 June 1870, the son of Alexander and Ann McNeill McGeachy. His grandfather, Hector McNeill, had been sheriff of Cumberland County at the end of the Civil War. His family could trace its beginnings in North Carolina back to 1793. McGeachy arrived in Fayetteville in 1888 with his widowed mother. Five years later, in 1893, he was a private in the FILI. By 1898 he had risen to the rank of first sergeant in the military unit, and he was numbered among the two companies of soldiers from Fayetteville that served in the Spanish American War. He served with distinction and rose to the rank of captain.

On a more social note, in 1903 McGeachy was the escort for Miss Mary W. Cameron who got the third highest number of votes for Carnival Queen. The future sheriff made himself visible to the folks of Fayetteville, and it paid off for him at election time in 1910.

Five years after becoming sheriff, in December 1915, McGeachy married Kate McArthur. Always an active member of the community, the sheriff was a member of the Knights of Pythias, a deacon at the Presbyterian Church, and years later a large stockholder in the Prince Charles Hotel Company. He lived on Gillespie Street, just a few blocks from the Market House.

The sheriff's son, Hector, was a lawyer in Fayetteville and for a while served in the state senate. While I never met Sheriff McGeachy, I did meet Hector on one occasion, and I seem to remember that my mother said she went to school with him. Sheriff McGeachy was quite proud of Hector and on one occasion observed that he had never had the experience of testifying against a defendant represented by his son. He said he hoped it would never come to pass: "I dread the day it happens, because Hector is a good lawyer and he'd probably win the case."

Sheriff McGeachy assumed office in December 1910 and vacated it in December 1950. He had spent half of his eighty years as sheriff of Cumberland County, and he had never had to enter a second primary in seeking the Democratic nomination. It was a source of immense pride to him that he had helped many "down-and-outers" get back on their feet. He died at his home on Gillespie Street in September of 1956.

When McGeachy became sheriff in 1910, the federal census of that year recorded a population of 2,206,287 for North Carolina. Sheriff McGeachy's job was to uphold the law among the 35,284 citizens of Cumberland County. Perhaps there have been other sheriffs who have kept a firm grasp on their office for forty years, but not in Cumberland County and not anywhere else that I know about.

So the first decade of the twentieth century ended for Fayetteville and Cumberland County, the final year highlighted by the last state execution by hanging and by an election that would have an impact on the area for four decades. During the years 1901 through 1910 Fayetteville had taken its first steps toward breaking into the modern world, and additional progress lay before it.

Chapter 2

The Decade in Which Fort Bragg Arrived on the Scene, 1911–1920

According to the U.S. census of 1910, Fayetteville entered the second decade of the twentieth century with a citizenry numbering 7,405. In 1911, my father, David Taft Morgan, Sr., was born, but not in Fayetteville. Instead he entered the world in the little town of Four Oaks, forty or so miles to the north of Fayetteville in Johnston County. Not until my father was nearly grown would the Morgan family pick up and move to Cumberland County, first to Seventy-First Township and finally to Mason Street in Fayetteville. In 1935, when he was twenty-four years old, my father would marry my mother, who was twenty at the time. So far, my dad has not figured prominently in the story, but I will say more about him in a subsequent chapter.

This second decade was crucial in Fayetteville's future, not because the Morgan side of my family moved there (that would come much later), but because those years brought forth one of the most significant developments in the town's whole history. The cause was the Great War of 1914–1918, later to be renamed World War I; the development was the founding of Camp Bragg in 1918. Afterward the camp would receive the enhanced designation of Fort Bragg. It was named for native North Carolinian General Braxton Bragg of Civil War fame. There will be far more about this all-important development below.

The decade got off to an inauspicious beginning with an outbreak of hookworm cases in September 1911. That month, Dr. B. W. Page, head of the Hookworm Commission, reported that he treated 556 cases of hookworm in the county in a single week. Hookworm, of course, was a problem that plagued the entire southern United States at that time, and it is obvious that the lower Cape Fear region of North Carolina did not escape the problem. Seven more years passed before the area was troubled again by another epidemic. In 1918 North Carolina, along with the entire nation, suffered the worst flu epidemic in American history. Thousands across the state and nation succumbed to "Spanish Influenza." Strangely enough,

Mayor James D. McNeill claimed that Fayetteville was not as hard hit as other places.

In spite of hookworm and the flu, life went on along the Cape Fear, and Fayetteville witnessed some interesting political battles. The perennial issues of prohibition and woman's suffrage were resolved, but only temporarily in the case of prohibition. In June 1911 the so-called "Near Beer Bill" passed the General Assembly and went into effect the following month. It prohibited the sale of any beverage containing alcohol in North Carolina. Four years later, in 1915, the legislature reinforced that law with the Liquor Act of North Carolina, which prohibited the shipment of liquor to the state and the brewing of malt therein. The battle against alcohol appeared to be settled once and for all in 1919 when the Eighteenth Amendment to the United States Constitution outlawed the manufacture and sale of "intoxicating liquors" nationwide. Ceremonies in North Carolina—punctuated by the tolling of bells—proclaimed the death and burial of John Barleycorn. But John, as it turned out, refused to stay dead and buried, as the Twenty-First Amendment in 1933 prepared the way for his resurrection after the "Roaring Twenties" had proved that Prohibition simply did not work.

The woman's suffrage issue was settled more definitively than the matter of prohibition. Fayetteville never gave the advocates of a woman's right to vote much support. Although there were women in the town who supported it, there was a strong antisuffrage sentiment in Fayetteville. The first public addresses on the subject were made by outsiders. In January 1914 Congressman and Mrs. William Kent of California offered their views in support of suffrage, as did Mrs. John Rogers, Jr. of New York. There was little mention of the matter again until the Nineteenth Amendment, ratified in 1920, gave all American women the right to vote. There would be no attempt to repeal that amendment.

Besides politics, Fayettevillians had the weather to talk about during the decade of the nineteen teens. The deepest snow since 1899—nineteen inches—fell on the city in March 1914. Another thirteen years would pass before Fayetteville would be blanketed in that fashion again. More threatening than an abundance of snow was an earthquake, which rocked the Cape Fear region in March 1916. Shocks from that powerful act of nature were felt in six southern states. Although the earthquake shook Fayetteville, the town apparently suffered little damage.

Still, life went on apace, and a variety of pastimes were available to Fayettevillians and their neighbors. The LaFayette Theatre opened its season in 1912 with the production of the play called *Mutt and Jeff* and announced its future attractions: *Introduce Me*, *Alma*, *Where Do You Live?*, *Bohemian Girl*, and *Merry Widow*. There were baseball games to watch, and none other than the famous athlete Jim Thorpe had played for money on teams in Rocky Mount and Fayetteville during 1909 and 1910. Because of this, Thorpe was declared a professional in 1913 and stripped of medals and honors he had previously won in the Olympics. Thorpe was already recognized as one of the greatest athletes in the world when he was knocked from his pinnacle for being a professional. Another athlete whose fame and glory lay yet before him blew into Fayetteville in 1914. He was there training with the Baltimore Orioles. In a baseball game at the Cumberland County Fairgrounds on Gillespie Street in Fayetteville, he hit his first professional homerun, a towering shot that traveled more than 400 feet. That hitter was none other than George Herman Ruth, a young man of eighteen years, who was given his celebrated nickname of "Babe," a little more than a mile from the banks of the Cape Fear River. As everyone knows, the Babe, as he was universally known, became one of the greatest players in baseball history, and Fayettevillians saw him launch that heralded career.

Fayetteville was branching out in others ways, too. In 1913 some national recognition accrued to the town when Major E. J. Hale, publisher of the *Fayetteville Observer*, was appointed U.S. minister to Costa Rica. That same year a local attorney named Donald F. Ray was commissioned to organize a Boy Scout troop in the city. Four years later a Red Cross chapter was formed. The coming of both of these organizations indicated that Fayetteville was joining the mainstream of American society, and Major Hale's appointment gave the city at least a small measure of national prominence. The life of city residents would become even more tied to the nation's destiny with the decision to establish Camp Bragg the year following the establishment of its Red Cross chapter.

Even so, Fayetteville, economically speaking, was still just as much a part of the South as it had ever been. Just a few years earlier farmers around Fayetteville had relied on cotton and had prospered. The introduction of a mechanical cotton picker in the area about 1912 suggested that the prosperity based on cotton would expand. However, the problems with transporting local cotton to outside markets was dramatized in 1913 when the steamer "City of Fayetteville," carrying 236 bales of fiber, sank at Wilmington. As a result of this economic catastrophe, state agriculture officials urged Cumberland County farmers to grow more tobacco and less cotton. They soon did, and within a few years, tobacco joined cotton as one of the main economic staples of the area. In February 1914 2,000 acres of tobacco were planted in Cumberland County, and the Planter's Tobacco Warehouse opened in Fayetteville. At that time tobacco was bringing seventy-six cents per pound. More tobacco, more warehouses, and higher prices were soon to follow. Years later, as a boy growing up in the area and traveling about, I noticed that to head south or east out of Fayetteville one looked upon one cotton field after another, while one saw mostly tobacco fields if he traveled north or west from town.

As the economy along the Cape Fear became dependent on tobacco as well as cotton, there were visible signs of economic growth in Fayetteville. New businesses kept emerging. In 1914 the Kress Store, which I later came to know as Kressie's as a child, opened at the corner of Hay and Maxwell Streets. It was, of course, part of a national chain of "five and ten" (-cent) stores. No store goes back deeper into my memory than that one, and there is still a picture of it in my mind's eye, looking the way it looked when I was about nine or ten years old. Three years after the Kress Store opened its doors, two Jewish merchant brothers, Jacob and Kalman Stein, opened a men's store near the Market House. A few years later Kalman and his son, Bernard Stein, established the landmark store known as the Capitol, less than a block from the Market House. In future years, when the Capitol established a branch store in Eutaw Shopping Center, my mother went to work there, remaining with the store until she retired. The Stein brothers opened their store in June 1917. Two months later C. D. Hutaff announced that his Coca Cola Bottling Company was preparing and selling Coca Cola in bottles ready to drink. All indications pointed to a Fayetteville moving rapidly into the modern world.

No other development of the nineteen-teens, however, would impact the future of Fayetteville in a greater way than the establishment of "Camp Bragg." That happened, it is clear, because of World War I. The Great War changed Fayetteville forever, beginning with the Selective Service Act of May 1917, which compelled young Cumberland County men ages 21 to 30 years to register for the draft. Even before that, however, the people had taken note of the war as it raged in Europe. Knowing that the United States might be dragged into the war, the citizens of Fayetteville put on an elaborate Independence Day observance on 4 July 1916. Many, perhaps, expected America to go to war, and, besides, Fayetteville already had soldiers from the FILI in Mexico as part of the "Mexican conflict." Actually, that "conflict" was in reality the Pershing Expedition, the limited objective of which was to capture the marauding Pancho Villa, a Mexican revolutionary who had committed crimes in the United States in order to promote his political fortunes in Mexico.

The first sign that the United States military was moving to within less than a dozen miles of the banks of the Cape Fear came in August 1917, when General Leonard Wood, one of the nation's most heralded general officers, visited Fayetteville to inspect two potential sites for a military camp. Less than a year later, in July 1918, the U.S. War Department announced the selection of the Fayetteville area as the site for the nation's "largest military camp yet located." The camp was to be a base for the purpose of practicing artillery. While still searching for the exact site, Colonel E. P. King, a staff member with the Army's chief of artillery, and geologist T. Wayland Vaughan stopped for a Coca Cola in Manchester, a sawmill village in northern Cumberland County. Both men liked the rolling sandhills and the piney woods there and recommended the area. Following up on their recommendation, Major General William Josiah Snow, chief of artillery, came, inspected, and concurred. Probably none of the three men realized that they were laying the foundation for one of the most important army posts in the world. Before long, the earth of Cumberland County would shake mightily and frequently, not from earthquakes like the one in 1916 but from the big guns of the U.S. Army. Everyone who grew up in Fayetteville after 1918 knew what it was like to feel the earth shake beneath his or her feet and to watch the plaster walls crack in their houses when the big guns boomed. And they boomed rather frequently. As a result, people eventually discontinued using plaster in the construction of their houses and turned to drywall, which did not crack so easily.

To build Camp Bragg, the U.S. government brought in 900 Puerto Rican construction workers. In 1919, when their job was done, they left for home. The camp was soon designated a permanent base and renamed Fort Bragg. Also in 1919 the "flying field" at "Camp Bragg" was established. It would eventually be named Pope Air Force Base. Near the end of 1919, in December, none other than General John J. Pershing himself arrived to inspect the troops at the fort, and after that he delivered an address to Fayetteville citizens at the Market House. A few months after Pershing's visit, Congress, in February 1920, would appropriate $1,173,000 to expand Fort Bragg.

The town was changing rapidly, and the establishment of Fort Bragg had much to do with that. In September 1919 a former resident named William H. Powell returned to Fayetteville after an absence of six years. He claimed that he would not have known where he was if he had been left in a place where he could not see the Market House!

Meanwhile, the Armistice of 11 November 1918 had brought the worst war the world had yet known to its bloody end. Fayettevillians had been enthusiastic supporters of the American war effort. There was a huge patriotic rally at the LaFayette Theatre in September 1918, a rally that featured Private Joseph Foley as the main speaker. The Germans had dared to use deadly mustard gas in the conflict, and Private Foley was a survivor of a German mustard gas attack. He and other speakers urged Fayetteville residents to buy War Savings Stamps and Bonds to defeat the merciless "Huns," a term of utter derision by which the Germans were popularly known.

Even though the people of Fayetteville did their part to support the war effort, they were surely pleased when the destruction ended. The city's sons had fought in foreign fields, and the winter of 1918 had brought coal and wood shortages to residents on the home front. On the other hand, a beneficial result of the war was that the Cumberland County Jail was briefly empty in the summer of 1918 for only the second time in the county's history.

The coming of Fort Bragg to the vicinity of Fayetteville eventually gave rise to an interesting question: Was Fayetteville a peaceful little town with only a nominal amount of crime before the founding of Fort Bragg, or was there a fairly normal crime rate in the area already? This is one of those questions that will never be answered to everybody's satisfaction. Nobody ever came right out and told me during my growing-up years that Fort Bragg was responsible for most of my hometown's crime, but from comments by the adults around me that impression became embedded in my mind. I always assumed that if Fort Bragg would go away, most of Fayetteville's crime would vanish like smoke in a whirlwind. Now that I am older and hopefully more knowledgeable about the ways of the world, I have a different slant on the matter. There is no doubt that human beings will be human beings, and they are constantly subject to failure with regard to acceptable behavior. Evidence abounds that a goodly number of

Fayettevillians had an affinity for strong drink, and ladies of easy virtue plied their trade among Cumberland County men long before anybody thought about soldiers being stationed in the area. For instance, in January 1915 some Fayetteville residents petitioned the city's Board of Aldermen to take action against the "red light district," and they were not talking about traffic signals! And, surprisingly, in the early years of Fort Bragg, the first post commander complained about his soldiers being corrupted by civilians in the town and county.

In all probability there was *more* crime and certainly more murders after Fort Bragg was established. A reasonable explanation is that more people means more crime. Most citizens, civilian and military, are law abiding; as a rule, only a small percentage of both are not. An increase in population means that there are more criminals to perpetrate crime, but the percentage of criminals will likely stay about the same. Some soldiers wanted to drink and go a-whoring, and there were citizens in the area who were ready to capitalize on that. Oftentimes outsiders also showed up around payday to capitalize. Drunken soldiers meant more fights, and more fights sometimes led to killings that were often spur-of-the-moment crimes of passion. And it was not always drunken, disorderly, and provoked soldiers who killed; sometimes it was a local citizen or citizens, and they were not always from the dregs of society, as will shortly be brought to light.

The decade of the teens ended with an incident that highlights the work of Sheriff McGeachy. On 21 May 1920, in the Fayetteville suburb called Massey Hill, a black woman and a white woman got into a fight. The black woman was the daughter of a mill worker named George Hobbs. After the confrontation, at least two white men went to Hobbs's house. They were met with gunfire. When they fired back, the Hobbses headed for the barn. In no time at all, word spread, and a mob formed.

The sheriff's office was called, and deputies Herman Butler and W. G. Moore were sent to the scene. Both were shot and fatally wounded when they approached Hobbs's barn. This provoked the mob to set Hobbs's house and barn on fire, but Hobbs escaped in the darkness. Sheriff McGeachy arrived on the scene and attempted unsuccessfully to restore order. Eventually Hobbs surrendered to the sheriff and was secretly taken to the state prison in Raleigh. If he had been taken to the Cumberland County Jail, it is entirely likely the mob would have broken him out and lynched him. In the end Hobbs accepted a plea bargain, pleading guilty to second-degree murder. He was sentenced to two-to-twenty years in prison. The fact that he was not given life in prison or even the death penalty indicates that there was probably so much confusion surrounding the incident that the authorities could not determine the exact circumstances that led to the deaths of the two deputies.

Thus, the decade of the teens ended in violence, and there was a great deal more violence on the way in the years to come. Sometimes it was connected with soldiers stationed at Fort Bragg, but often the fault lay with locals who were longtime residents. So it was with regard to two highly publicized murder cases of the 1920s—both packed with drama.

Chapter 3

Whiskey and Murder during the Roaring Twenties

The 1920s was the decade when the United States tried an experiment called Prohibition. Herbert Hoover, one of the presidents during that decade, called Prohibition the "noble experiment." Whether noble or not is debatable, but there is no doubt that the experiment produced widespread violence, and people fighting over buying and selling whiskey often resulted in murder.

So it was in Cumberland County during the first year of the new decade. Al Pate was reputed to be among the bravest and most popular deputy sheriffs that the county had. A raid on a whiskey still made his wife a widow and his four children fatherless. On the night of 22 July 1921 Pate joined Sheriff McGeachy, fellow deputy Bill West, and three other officers in a raid on a whiskey still near Godwin, just a few miles north of Fayetteville. Upon the approach of the sheriff and his men, three men ran from the still. The six officers proceeded to confiscate the still and then drove off from the site carrying it in the sheriff's car. Shots rang out! The bullets barely missed the sheriff and West, while one struck Pate in the right side near the waist. As the bullet passed through, it severed a main artery. McGeachy took Pate to Dr. J. A. McLean, who informed the sheriff that his deputy had died immediately after being hit. From the doctor's office, McGeachy took Pate to Rogers and Breece Funeral Home, where he was to be prepared for burial.

Al Pate was a well-loved man. The Reverend Joel Snyder performed the deputy's funeral service at the First Baptist Church, where Pate was a deacon. By all accounts his was one of the biggest funerals ever held in Fayetteville up to that time.

What of the man who shot him? That man, who was hardly more than a boy, was David Marshall Williams, the son of J. Claude Williams, a former county commissioner. Young Williams, called "Marsh" by his family, was more than a little strange. His older brother, the Reverend J. Mack Williams, was convinced that Marsh was insane and would testify to that at his trial. In retrospect, it is clear that Marshall Williams definitely marched to the beat of a different drummer. Though convicted of a murder he denied committing, Williams would spend nearly eight years in prison before being pardoned in 1929 by Governor Angus McLean. While an inmate, he would invent the M-1 carbine, a weapon that helped the United States win World War II. Eventually, he would become known to the world as "Carbine" Williams. The famous actor James ("Jimmy") Stewart would play this troubled genius in a 1952 movie based on Williams's life. The world premiere of that movie was shown at the Colony Theater, where I was an usher. I was there for that much-ballyhooed event. I saw Mr. Williams, his wife, and his son David, the only time I ever saw Williams. Although Stewart was not there for the occasion, actor Wendell Cory was. Cory played the part of "Captain Peoples," the warden who secured Williams's parole. I saw all the hoopla. Williams spoke and introduced his wife and son. Cory spoke. What an occasion! I saw a real movie star close up; I saw a world-famous man who was hailed as a genius and a genuine hero. The movie, which I saw several times, was terrific. How could it have been anything else with Jimmy Stewart playing the lead role? To say the least, it was a dazzling experience for a fifteen-year-old boy. How could I have known then that some of it wasn't true? How could I have known that Hollywood had taken some of the liberties for which it is so notorious? Not until many years later did I discover the truth about David Marshall ("Carbine") Williams.

Marshall Williams was born on 13 November 1900 into a respected family near Godwin, which sits near the east bank of the Cape Fear between Dunn and Fayetteville. As a boy, Williams was fascinated with guns, building his first pistol at the age of ten. At his trial in 1921 family members testified that Williams had a history of doing crazy things with firearms. When Marshall was sent off to Blackstone Military Academy, he was soon in trouble for stealing guns and shipping the stocks home. He was expelled. With misgivings, Marshall was allowed to marry in the hope that it would change him. When testifying at his son's trial in October 1921, J. Claude Williams was asked why he had not gone to the authorities and reported some of the crazy actions of his son. Like any father, Mr. Williams said, he loved his son and hoped and prayed that he would change. Emotion overcame the distraught father, and he burst into tears. Even so, Mr. Williams denied knowing that his son was running a still and said he would have reported it to Sheriff McGeachy, if he had known. He also denied a report claiming that he said he would spend ten thousand dollars to get his son out of "killing Pate."

The events following the shooting of Deputy Al Pate (not federal agent Jesse Rimmer, as the 1952 movie had it) and leading up to the trial of Marshall Williams make a dramatic story. After Pate was killed, Sheriff McGeachy went to Williams's home and told his wife that her husband should give himself up. The next morning young Williams was handed over to the sheriff by his father and his uncle, Columbus McClellan. McGeachy took the suspect to "some unknown jail for safekeeping." About a week later Williams went before Recorder James C. McRae for a preliminary hearing, and McRae bound him over for trial before Judge John H. Kerr without bail. J. Claude Williams immediately hired a legal firm from Dunn—John C. Clifford and N. A. Townsend—to defend his son. He soon added to the defense team Fayetteville attorneys John G. Shaw, Duncan Shaw, D. M. Stringfield, and V. C. Bullard. Marshall Williams's lawyers were judged by the press to be the "strongest array of legal talent this section of the state affords."

During the preliminary hearing it was noted that there was no eyewitness to the shooting, and thus the case was based on circumstantial evidence. The evidence included sworn and signed affidavits by Sheriff McGeachy and Randal (also known as "Ham") Dawson, a black man who had been at the still with Williams before the officers arrived on the scene. Dawson claimed that Williams admitted to him that he, Williams, had done the shooting and bragged that when he shot he didn't miss. Williams's black cohort said he was telling the truth "as certain as Jesus died." Williams insisted that he did not shoot Pate and that Dawson was lying. Both men were indicted by a coroner's jury. Pate's popularity prompted arguments for having the trial moved to another county so that the men could be sure of receiving a fair trial. That there was some cause for alarm is indicated by the fact that Williams was held until trial, not in the Cumberland County Jail, but in the Hoke County Jail in Raeford, some twenty miles west of Fayetteville. Even so, the trial was not moved out of Cumberland County.

The Williams defense team was up against a tough judge in John H. Kerr of Warrenton. When the judge addressed the grand jury on 28 August 1921 he said: "I cannot say what other judges will do, but for me, let them come before me on a second offense of toting pistols and other crimes, and they just as well kiss their wives and family goodbye, because I am going to send them away for a long time."

Williams's trial commenced on 11 October 1921. He was charged with first-degree murder. The strategy of Williams's lawyers was to argue that their client was insane and could not be held responsible for what he had done. A number of experts and "former school teachers" testified that Williams was "mentally unsound" and not responsible, if in fact he had shot Deputy Pate. Even family members made similar observations. J. Mack Williams, the preacher brother from Missouri, testified that he had warned his father, J. Claude Williams, in 1919 that Marshall was paranoid and might kill his father, mother, or wife, and burn the house down. "You are sitting on dynamite and don't know it," Mack warned the family physician, Dr. McLean. Also, Marshall Kornegay, Williams's maternal grandfather, claimed that insanity ran in the family. One of Marshall's uncles, said Kornegay, had the same "mania" for firearms and finally killed himself with a shotgun.

All of these defense witnesses contradicted the experts from the State Hospital for the Insane, who had been put on the stand by the prosecutor. Those experts claimed that Williams was "subnormal" but that he certainly knew right from wrong. Dr. R. A. Allgood, the county coroner, asserted that Williams's intelligence was not up to that of "boys his age," but he clearly knew right from wrong.

The fate of Marshall Williams was handed to the jury on 15 October 1921. After forty-five hours of deliberation the jury hung at 11 to 1— eleven for sanity and one for insanity. Twelve for sanity would probably have landed Williams in the electric chair. As it was, a mistrial was declared. I was always told by my father that the man who hung the jury was Alton Spears, a man whom I knew from sometimes attending the Mt. Gilead Baptist Church. My father once told this to me in Mr. Spears's presence, and Mr. Spears did not deny it. I have no reason to doubt it, but I have no other confirmation that it is true.

With the mistrial, Williams was returned to the Hoke County Jail to see what the state would do next. When the state announced its intention for a retrial the next month before Judge Henry P. Lane, Williams pled guilty to second-degree murder and was sentenced to thirty years in prison. He left for state prison on the morning of Saturday, 26 November. Sheriff McGeachy, nearly every man's friend, allowed Williams's father to accompany him and allowed Williams to stop by home and say goodbye to his wife and mother.

As for Ham Dawson, he was found not guilty, a decision that provoked Williams. The owner of the raided still insisted that he did not shoot to kill, but Dawson did. According to the convicted man, he fired only once, while Dawson fired four times. Interestingly enough, the all-white jury believed the black man and not the white man in this case—a remarkable development in view of the fact that the Ku Klux Klan was being revived at this time and blacks were being lynched from time to time throughout the South. But Dawson went free, while Williams went to prison.

Less than eight years later Williams would walk away from the Caledonia Prison farm with a full pardon, thanks mainly to Captain H. T. Peoples. In the meantime, he had resumed his interest in guns, inventing while incarcerated a breach-loading mechanism that would not jam. Williams also made a demonstration model of what would become known as the M-1 carbine, a weapon that would eventually bring him praise from such noteworthy military men as Generals Douglas MacArthur and Mark Clark. Upon returning home to Godwin, Williams continued his inventions and ultimately held at least fifty patents. In 1971 his workshop was taken to the North Carolina Museum of History and put on display.

Marshall Williams was nationally famous by this time, but his health failed. Strokes took a toll on his body and mind. In 1972 he was admitted to Dorothea Dix Hospital in Raleigh, a facility for the mentally ill that was popularly known throughout North Carolina as "Dix Hill." There Williams died of pneumonia in January 1975 at age 74.

The Williams trial took place sixteen years before I was born, but I feel some connection with it because I knew some of the people who were involved in it. First, there was James McRae, the judge of Recorder's Court, who bound Williams over for trial. I knew of him nearly all my life, and I knew his children, Jimmy and Betsy McRae. Betsy, as Elizabeth McRae, gained a measure of fame as Gomer Pyle's girl friend on the Gomer Pyle television show. Judge McRae, as he was known when I first remember hearing of him, dispensed justice in Fayetteville for many years. Then there was Alton Spears, whom I knew personally. While I had no dealings with Williams himself, I saw and spoke to him on that one occasion in 1952, and my uncle, Gilbert Herring (my mother's youngest brother), did have some dealings with him.

Uncle Gilbert fought in World War II in France, Germany, and Austria. When the war ended, he sent home a number of German rifles and shotguns. One of the shotguns, a sixteen gauge, was a fancy two-barrel shotgun with a .22 Hornet rifle barrel underneath the two shotgun barrels. There were two sights on the gun for use in shooting the .22 Hornet. One was a regular notched sight, while the other was a peep sight that lay on top of the gun in between the shotgun barrels. It had to be flipped up for use. Not knowing quite how to sight the rifle barrel in, Uncle Gilbert told a friend, a deputy sheriff, about it. This friend happened to know Marshall Williams, or "Carbine," as everyone was calling him then, and the deputy took my uncle out to meet Williams. The great inventor was in his shop working when the two men arrived. Uncle Gilbert explained that he was not sure what to do about the sights for the .22 Hornet barrel. Almost without a word, Williams threw open a little window, pointed the gun at a target outside the shop, and, using the notched sight, put a bullet in the dead center of the target. He then reloaded, flipped up the peep sight, and fired again. The second bullet struck a mere fraction to one side of the hole made by the first bullet. Williams then handed the shotgun to my uncle and said that the sights were just fine and that his advice was not to mess with them.

Uncle Gilbert had another occasion to be in Williams's presence. My uncle was a member of the FILI, and "Carbine" Williams supported that independent military unit with financial contributions, fairly sizable ones, I have been told. On one occasion, the commander of the FILI decided to honor Williams for his support by holding a banquet and making the famous inventor the honored guest. The wine flowed freely at the banquet, and Williams became intoxicated. According to rumors, he was frequently intoxicated. After a number of glasses of wine, Williams apparently got bored with drinking, and when more wine was poured, he pulled out a .45 pistol and broke the glass, splattering the wine in all directions. Thinking that Williams wanted a different kind of wine, the commander of the FILI poured him a glass of a different variety. Again Williams pulled out his pistol and broke the glass, thereby making another mess. As a young man Williams had marched to a different drummer; as an old man he obviously did the same. While his murder trial is obscure compared to the trials of Jeffrey MacDonald and Velma Barfield, he remains one of the most famous people the Cape Fear region around Fayetteville has produced.

In spite of the violence that erupted at the site of Williams's still in the summer of 1921, the year had not started out on a particularly violent note.

Then—all of a sudden—all hell broke loose, as that summer saw far more violence than was ordinary for the area. In August 1921, just before the Williams case was tried, Judge Kerr presided over the trial of a black man named James Hart, who had assaulted a woman named Bessie Hair with the intent to rape her. During a struggle to subdue her, Hart was scared by a dog barking. Thinking someone was coming, he fled the scene. He was easily identified and soon apprehended, for, in the struggle with Mrs. Hair, the sack Hart had over his head came off. Hair's ability to identify her assailant made his capture just a matter of time. At trial he was found guilty and given five years on the county roads. Judge Kerr informed Hart that he had missed being electrocuted only because a dog barked.

There was still more violence as the summer of 1921 gave way to autumn. While Marshall Williams sat in the Hoke County Jail awaiting his day in court, there was a murder just north of Fayetteville at the falls of the Cape Fear. On September 25 Sheriff McGeachy received "a startling telegram" from Linden. Deputy W. E. Hunnyecut wired him: "Negro shot and killed. Come at once and bring coroner." McGeachy and coroner Dr. R. A. Allgood headed for Linden. There the sheriff found that, during a card game, a black man named Waddell had been gunned down by another black man named Covington. Violent crime definitely seemed to be on the rise in Cumberland County in the summer of 1921.

Nothing has been said yet about any violence emanating from Fort Bragg or crimes committed by soldiers from that post. Indeed, it was the base commander at Fort Bragg, Brigadier General Albert J. Bowley, who was alarmed because of crimes being perpetrated by civilians in Fayetteville and Cumberland County. In August 1922 he personally appeared before the Cumberland County grand jury and declared that he would put Fayetteville "off limits" to his soldiers, unless the city got rid of its bootleggers and prostitutes. He observed that Fort Bragg's monthly payroll was about $150,000, most of which was being spent on liquor and women.

Perhaps the increasing crime and violence along the Cape Fear was a mere reflection of the national picture. The establishment of Prohibition had spawned hordes of bootleggers who sought to make money off those who meant to have whiskey whether it was legal or not. Competition among the bootleggers led to rivals killing one another. Chicago was the nation's number one hot spot. There the notorious Al Capone, raking in an estimated two million dollars a week by selling illegal booze, sought to eliminate his competitors. Similar battles went on in various places throughout the country. North Carolina had its share of bootleggers before Prohibition became a national law, for the state had long been dry, at least legally speaking, and thus escaped the extreme violence associated with Chicago. But on a much smaller scale, whiskey stills and what they produced led to an increase in violence and death in the Tar Heel State and in Cumberland County. Crime news was so ubiquitous that in April 1925 the *Fayetteville Observer* announced that it would observe a fifteen-day moratorium on reporting crime.

Meanwhile, ordinary life went on in Fayetteville during the decade of the twenties. With the rest of the nation, Fayetteville and the surrounding area entered upon economic boom times. New businesses were among the indicators of this economic expansion. There were new banks, new clothing stores, new restaurants, new theaters, new hotels, and some of the old businesses grew larger. In 1926 the National Bank of Fayetteville opened on Hay Street in a building that was ten stories high. At that time and for many years afterward, it was the tallest building in town. Four years later Branch Banking and Trust Company opened, also on Hay Street. While the National Bank of Fayetteville gave way to First Citizens Bank and Trust Company, which occupied the ten-story building (along with various other offices) when I was a boy, Branch Banking and Trust Company has expanded enormously and remains a gigantic financial institution under the name BB&T.

Among the new clothing stores was the Capitol, which opened in 1921. Kalman Stein would later pass this landmark store on to his son Bernard, who would own and run it and branches of it for the rest of his life. In October, Ed Fleishman and his brothers opened a new dollar store, selling men's clothing primarily. The clothing business in Fayetteville was rapidly falling into the hands of Jewish merchants, while most of the new restaurants belonged to Greeks. Among the new stores not owned by Jews was the Woolworth 10-cent variety store that opened on the corner of Hay and Anderson Streets in 1923.

A growing city needed new places of entertainment, and more theaters were soon opening their doors. In October 1927 the Carolina Theater opened for business on the corner of Pittman and Hay Streets. The first movie it showed was a silent film called *The Unknown*, starring Lon Chaney, an actor I saw in several horror films at the same theater some years later. Fayetteville really moved uptown in 1930 when the Broadway Theater opened about four blocks down Hay Street toward the Market

House and announced that it would show "all talking pictures." Years later, my mother's first job outside the home was at the Carolina Theater, where she worked as cashier. Later, when her manager, Leon Gibson, moved down the street to manage the Broadway, my mother followed him and became one of the cashiers there. It was during the 1920s that what might be called the restaurant "craze" was combined with the interest of Fayette-villians in the theater. Going out to eat at one of the Greek restaurants and then taking in a movie became the thing to do for a goodly number of the town's citizens.

Other signs that Fayetteville was on the move was the expansion of the LaFayette Hotel by an additional fifty sleeping rooms in 1923 and, in March 1925, the opening of the Prince Charles Hotel, a huge seven-story structure. Briefly the Prince Charles was the tallest building in town until the bank building a few blocks down the street topped it by three stories the next year. Adding to the excitement caused by the opening of the Prince Charles was that the front of the building was scaled the same month it opened by George C. Polley, a man calling himself the "Human Fly." Another hotel, the Millbrook, opened in 1930 on Market Square in the old Highsmith Hospital building, which stood beside the bank building. Highsmith Hospital had moved to a new building on Haymount Hill four years earlier.

The opening of new hotels and the expansion of the LaFayette came about because more and more people were visiting the city, and the city's own population was growing substantially. It was announced in September 1923 that a new record had been set for home building in town and that the average price of a home was $6,750. Meanwhile, Fayetteville's Board of Aldermen had, in May, advocated extending the city limits, which would boost the city's population from around 8,000 to nearly 20,000, but that was not done. Even so, the area's population was clearly on the upswing. Moreover, the numbers at Fort Bragg, which was officially designated by that name in September 1922, were also growing steadily. During the decade of the twenties those stationed at the post nearly tripled, going from 1,091 to 3,169. This explains, in part, the demand for new housing, since, presumably, some who were stationed at Fort Bragg preferred living in town to residing on the base. At the end of the decade, Cumberland County's population had climbed to 45,000.

More people, more businesses, a growing town were all in keeping with what was happening in American society. It was the "Roaring Twenties," but there is little indication that Fayetteville was roaring as much as the big cities were. In fact, there was strong reaction in town against the raucous goings on in the North. In September 1922, Ku Klux Klan members marched up Winslow Street distributing handbills threatening "evildoers." While the Klan has traditionally been associated with being racist and anti-Semitic—which it surely was—it was also self-righteous and puritanical, and its members were intent upon imposing their moral values on American society.

While these self-appointed guardians of Christian morality crusaded for purity, Fort Bragg was trying to keep step with the fun being enjoyed by the rest of society. In April 1922 the Annie Oakley Western show was performed on base, but when, in September 1923, the Bragg authorities allowed a show called "Cuddle Up" to be presented, the mayor of Fayetteville revealed a sanctimonious, Puritan streak when he lashed out in condemnation. He said that the show should be called "Cover Up" and that the chorus girls should cover up or "put out the lights." Then he issued a warning that nothing "indecent or unclad gets by in Fayetteville." This pharisaical mayor was H. M. Robinson who, three months earlier, had issued a stern warning to "flirts." "Flirting is an evil which will incur penalties," he threatened. He warned that he would fine or send to jail anyone found guilty of flirting. Obviously, the Puritan magistrates who presided over seventeenth-century Massachusetts would have found Robinson to be a man after their own hearts. No doubt hooded Klansmen found him highly acceptable in Fayetteville during the twenties. Could he have been one of them?

One wonders why the puritanical mayor was not incensed over the increasing enforcement of Jim Crow laws in Fayetteville during the twenties. Those racist statutes brought rank discrimination to African Americans, who made up about half of the city's population. Adding to the racial animosity engendered at the time was the showing at the Rose Theatre in 1924 of the infamous movie entitled *The Birth of a Nation*. This epic film, produced and released in 1915 by D. W. Griffith, celebrated the Ku Klux Klan, an organization the film portrayed as saving the South from the anarchy of black rule by reuniting Civil War enemies "in defense of their Aryan birthright." When it was released in 1915, *The Birth of a Nation* was the most expensive film ever produced up to that time, costing more than $100,000. Unfortunately, the extremism and racism it applauded received a positive endorsement from President Woodrow Wilson who pronounced it to be "so terribly true." Of course, Wilson, who did not leave the presidency until 1921, had demonstrated his own racism while in office by segregating blacks who worked in government posts.

In spite of all that a racist president, an extremist mayor, and discriminatory laws could do to dampen spirits, the decade's rage for fun and, especially, jazz were not impeded along the Cape Fear. At the heart of jazz, of course, were African-American musicians, and Fayetteville produced a notable black group called the "Jazz Hounds." The group's vocalist was Rosabelle Wright of Blount's Alley. Furthermore, a good sign that Fayetteville had experienced a little too much Puritanism came in 1926, when the Board of Aldermen scrapped the city's Blue Law. A new law went so far as to permit the sale of soft drinks, ice cream, and other goods on Sunday—except during the hours of 10:00 A.M. and noon. Still, a number of ministers in the area complained about the theaters, insisting that they were keeping people from attending church. Obviously, they were referring to midweek services, since theaters were not allowed to open on Sunday in Fayetteville until near the end of 1940, and that was done by a court order.

All things considered, the year of years in Fayetteville during the 1920s was 1927. On 2 March 1927, the city was blanketed by the biggest snowfall in twenty-nine years. Well over twenty inches fell, as the twenty-inch mark was reached by noon. Telephone and telegraph services went down, trains were delayed, schools were closed, and people were advised to remain at home because of dangerous road conditions. Only a few cars attempted to drive down Hay Street through the snow, which accumulated up to the doors of the vehicles. My mother was twelve years old at the time of the deep snow of 1927, and I remember hearing her talk about it a number of times when I was growing up during the 1940s. She never mentioned, as far as I can recall, that Mother Nature dealt Fayetteville another blow seventeen months later, in 1928, when heavy rain brought September flooding that closed the Cape Fear River Bridge. Floods occurred far more frequently than did snows measuring two feet deep, and so it was always the snowstorms that came more readily to the minds of the people along the Cape Fear.

The month of May brought Fayettevillians something other than a huge snowstorm to discuss. Hundreds of the city's citizens gathered in front of the *Fayetteville Observer*'s office late in the afternoon of 21 May, following an Associated Press flash that a young aviator named Charles A.

Lindbergh had flown solo across the Atlantic Ocean between New York and Paris. In his monoplane, named the "Spirit of St. Louis," Lindbergh had left New York on 20 May without a parachute or a radio, preferring additional gasoline instead of devices that might make his flight safer. Carrying only sandwiches and water, he fought fog and drowsiness before landing at Le Bourget Field near Paris thirty-three and a half hours later. He had flown 3,600 miles alone, thus enabling him to claim a prize of $25,000, which New York businessman Raymond Orteig had offered to the first person who performed a nonstop, solo flight between New York and Paris. Lindbergh captured the imagination of the nation and became a genuine national hero. His feat did more to stir official and popular interest in aviation than any flying feat had before. Important people soon predicted that passenger flights would become commonplace because of what Lindbergh had done. A state bank examiner named John Mitchell urged "every municipality" in North Carolina to establish a "flying field."

Deep snow and a solo transatlantic flight gave Fayetteville much to talk about, but nothing prompted animated conversation quite so quickly as another murder, and the city was soon abuzz on 9 June. That was the day Kenneth O. Boone and Mae Belle Phillips went to trial, charged with the first-degree murder of Frank McLaurin. Mrs. Phillips was the first woman in seventy-seven years—since way back in 1850—to stand trial for murder in Cumberland County. Because she was a defendant in a capital murder case, choosing a jury proved difficult. For days people filled the courtroom, but 10 June was the day of days, a day when the largest crowd ever to appear in a courtroom in the county showed up. That was the day that Dr. R. A. Allgood took the stand and introduced into evidence the skull of the victim! It was reported in the *Fayetteville Observer*, "Many stood on seats and window sills to get a better view as the expert witness pulled the human skull from a black handbag."

Frank McLaurin, a twenty-six-year-old mechanic and the father of several children, apparently died on either 18 or 19 January 1927. McLaurin's widow testified that she had last seen her husband alive on January 18, when he had left her home on Branson Street in the company of Kenneth Boone, who lived on Winslow Street. The mechanic had failed to return home, whereupon Mrs. McLaurin called Boone who told her that he had left her husband in front of the New York Café on Hay Street. Later Boone changed his story and told her that McLaurin would probably be found dead with a gun beside him, but he denied knowing anything of the mechanic's whereabouts and suggested forming a search party. Boone was regarded as McLaurin's best friend, and, interestingly enough, served as a pallbearer at his funeral when McLaurin's body was finally found.

Boone had suggested that McLaurin might be found off the Cumberland Mills Road, and he was finally found about six miles from there. The young mechanic was discovered lying on his left side, pistol in hand pointing toward his face—shot through the temple and the back of the head. There was a wound over his left eye and three small wounds on his forehead. The 38-caliber pistol had been fired only once, having one empty chamber. Two sisters, Alice Spry and Nellie Cameron, found the body and went for help. Sheriff McGeachy was called. The investigation that followed led to the indictments against Boone and his alleged accomplice, Mae Belle Phillips.

It was a dramatic trial, and a hot one, too. So bad was the heat in the courtroom that the twelve men on the jury were allowed to remove their coats. Six did. Fifteen lawyers—seven for Boone, three for Phillips, and five for the state—tried the case, which produced a myriad of conflicting stories by the witnesses for both the prosecution and the defense. Kenneth Boone, who ran a tire business on Gillespie Street, doubtlessly paid a fortune for the seven attorneys he hired to defend him. One of them was James Pou, a renowned defense attorney from Raleigh. Given the wild stories his client told, Pou and his six cocounselors must have done a magnificent job.

Besides having McLaurin's body exhumed and introducing his skull into evidence, the prosecutors put two witnesses on the stand who offered what appeared to be damning testimony against Boone. First, the prosecutors introduced the skull to show that McLaurin's skull had been fractured from a hard blow to the head, in addition to his having been shot. Both Dr. Allgood, the corner, and Dr. J. H. Highsmith, one of the town's most respected physicians, testified that a blow and not a bullet had fractured McLaurin's skull. Hence the need to show the jury the skull. The defense strenuously objected to the display, but the objections were denied by the judge. Dr. Allgood testified that, in his opinion, McLaurin was severely incapacitated by the blow but alive when he was shot.

Second, the state called its two star witnesses to the stand. They were a black man named Will Priest and a white man named C. H. Savage, who ran a "filling station" on Lumberton Road. It was alleged that one could fill up with both gas and bootleg whiskey at Savage's station. Priest, who apparently worked for Boone or hung around his shop, testified that Boone, Phillips, and McLaurin were drinking at the shop and got into an argument. Boone got angry and hit McLaurin in the head with a wrench. When McLaurin collapsed, Boone said he did not mean to hit his friend hard enough to kill him. Mae Phillips then remarked, "The ___ ___ ___ ___ I'll kill him." Later, Priest contended, Boone took McLaurin out on the Cumberland Mills Road and killed him, after which he offered Priest ten dollars to bury him. Priest, claiming to be frightened, ran home, but Boone went to him later and threatened to kill him if he talked. Pou, doing his job brilliantly, pointed out lies and inconsistencies in Priest's story.

Savage, who was openly identified as a "rum runner," was, at the time he gave testimony, an inmate in the Atlanta Penitentiary. He testified that Boone, Phillips, McLaurin, and "a Negro man" stopped at his filling station on 18 January. The Negro man, of course, was Will Priest. Savage stated that Boone bought a pint of whiskey and a ginger ale and that McLaurin was in the back seat with his head leaning on Priest's shoulder. Already, Priest had testified that Boone had hit McLaurin in the head with a wrench. Savage further testified that when the party left they turned off the main road and drove down a road leading to where McLaurin's body was ultimately found. Moreover, Savage himself, he testified, later went down the same road to retrieve some whiskey he had hidden. While looking for his whiskey stash, Savage heard gunfire. Upon looking in the direction of the gunfire, he saw two people near a pine tree who proceeded to run and jump in a car. He became frightened and fled, losing his hat in his haste. When shown whiskey and ale bottles found near the murder site, Savage affirmed that they looked like the ones he had sold to Boone. Lawyer Pou tried but failed to shake Savage's testimony.

After the testimony given by Savage, the state rested, and the array of defense attorneys went to work. They argued that McLaurin committed suicide and that the testimonies of a "rum runner" and an ignorant Negro were not credible. On 13 June Kenneth Boone took the stand in his own defense. He denied having any part in the death of McLaurin. He stated that, at about 11:30 a.m. on 18 January, he had taken McLaurin to the pine tree where the mechanic was found dead. Supposedly, McLaurin was to meet a woman there and Boone was to return that afternoon to pick him up. Somehow the tire dealer—he claimed—forgot about going back until Mrs. McLaurin called to inquire about her husband's whereabouts. When Boone finally went back to get McLaurin, Priest went with him. They found

McLaurin dead, presumably a victim of suicide. Boone admitted that he told Priest to keep his mouth shut because of the circumstances, but he denied going to Savage's place on the Lumberton Road. He claimed that McLaurin had asked him, Boone, to get the mechanic a pistol and that his friend had alluded to committing suicide. Furthermore, Boone denied seeing Mrs. Phillips at the time of the incident and said he did not take her for rides at night, as the prosecution claimed. Newspaper accounts indicate that Boone was tripped up badly by the prosecutors on cross-examination.

Suddenly, on 14 June, the defense rested without calling Mrs. Phillips to the stand, perhaps because flaws in her character might have been brought to light and prejudiced the jury. Although little is known of her, what is known suggests that she was far from a virtuous woman. Most likely her attorneys did not want to risk having her cross-examined. Thus, arguments to the jury began at 2:00 p.m. on 15 June. Three days later, on the evening of Friday, 18 June, the jury delivered a verdict, finding Boone and Phillips "not guilty." Both defendants collapsed when the verdict was announced. According to the *Fayetteville Observer*, "Seldom, if ever, has a more dramatic scene been enacted in a courtroom in Cumberland County." Boone crumpled up and fell backwards in his chair. Mrs. Phillips "gave way and dropped as the tension snapped." During the elation and congratulations, Boone's wife fainted.

That trial took place ten years before I was born, and I suppose that I have no right to second-guess the jury, the members of which heard all the testimony. Even so, looking back on the event through the eyes of the newspaper reporters who also heard the evidence, one can't help but wonder about the verdict—especially in view of Boone's miscues during his cross-examination. What it got down to was that the jury believed Boone's testimony and did not believe the testimonies of Priest and Savage. How they rationalized away McLaurin's fractured skull, which Dr. Allgood contended was caused by a blow and not a bullet, we will never know.

To my knowledge, the only person connected with the trial that I ever remember meeting was Dr. Allgood, who had been practicing medicine in Fayetteville since 1915 and who served on the side as coroner for many years. Reese Alexander Allgood was born in Pickens, South Carolina and finished medical school at the University of Maryland before setting up his practice in Fayetteville as a young physician in his mid-twenties. His home was a sprawling house that sat on a hill overlooking Bradford Avenue on one side and Branson Street on the other. It was not more than six blocks from my house on Robeson Street, and I went by it on foot, on my bicycle, and in a car hundreds of times. His office was located on Market Square for many years. My mother took me to that office to see Dr. Allgood a time or two during my sickly childhood, but I scarcely remember him. He certainly never discussed the McLaurin (or Boone/Phillips) trial with me. I wish I could ask him today what he thought of the verdict. I can't, of course, because he left Fayetteville in 1954 to return to his hometown in South Carolina, and, since he was born in 1889, he presumably died years ago.

Even more than I wish I could ask Dr. Allgood what his reaction was to the trial's outcome, I wish I could ask one or more of the jurors how they arrived at a "not guilty" verdict. The information I have, though it is admittedly incomplete and was examined long years after the fact, directs me to a different conclusion.

Thus, the 1920s was a time when bootleg whiskey brought two high-profile murder trials to Cumberland County, although one of them produced a perplexing verdict. Between McLaurin's death in January and the Boone/Phillips trial in June, the deep snow of March fell. It appears that some snow of a different sort—manufactured verbally by attorney James Pou—might have blinded that jury in June, thus resulting in the not-guilty verdict. After the alleged murder of Frank McLaurin, the deep snow, Lindbergh's solo flight across the Atlantic, and the dramatic murder trial of Kenneth Boone and Mae Belle Phillips, the last three years of the decade were fairly uneventful, except it should be noted that one of Fayetteville's own was elected to the United States House of Representatives in 1928. He was Jerome Bayard Clark, and he would remain a House member for twenty years. Although Fayetteville could take pride in having a Fayette-villian in Congress, Clark was not a flamboyant member of the House and did not bring much national publicity to his hometown during his tenure. Oddly enough, the hero-to-be and the man to bring much fame to Fayette-ville was the same man who had been convicted of murder in 1921. When Marshall Williams, who had served less than eight years for killing Al Pate, left prison with a full pardon in 1929, no one knew that he would later emerge as an American hero.

Most of what happened along the Cape Fear in 1928, 1929, and 1930 was tame compared to what had happened during the previous seven years. There was another flood in 1928, but the Cape Fear had overflowed its banks numbers of times before. Nobody paid much attention when the Fayetteville Police Department got a bloodhound in June 1928 in hopes of catching some people who had committed numerous robberies in the city. Nor did people do more than chuckle when Luis Spero, in June 1929, received a suspended sentence for blocking traffic on Hay Street with his donkey. The stock market crash of 1929 was hardly noticed in Fayetteville, but in 1930, the last year of the decade, the LaFayette National Bank was forced to close. Before long other businesses would close and textile mill workers would go on strike. The Great Depression would cause the Roaring Twenties to come to a whimpering end, as economic stagnation laid its blighting hand on the land along the Cape Fear and all across the nation. Life would go on, of course, and whiskey and murder would not vanish from the scene, but the frivolity of spirit that had characterized the 1920s was replaced by somber reflection and a high regard for three square meals a day.

Chapter 4

Depression and Murder: The 1930s

Wall Street fell in the autumn of 1929, as a selling frenzy sent stock prices plummeting. People had been so exuberant during the boom years of the twenties that no one seemed ready to concede that there might be an end to it all. One economist had talked of stocks reaching a permanently high plateau. How wrong he was! The old saying that what goes up must come down was borne out dramatically on 24 October 1929, when more than thirteen million shares of stock exchanged hands on the stock exchange. Panic set in, and on 29 October sixteen million shares were traded. The value of many stocks sank so rapidly that they quickly became worthless. This financial crash of unprecedented proportions heralded an economic depression of similar proportions, but the Great Depression, which was yet to come, began slowly. President Herbert Hoover assured American citizens that the economy was sound. Over and over he uttered assurances that had about the same value as the stocks that had been wiped out in the crash. He said that prosperity was hovering just around the corner so many times that people joked about it by saying something like, "Don't forget, prosperity is *Hoovering* just around the corner." Meanwhile, a fourth to a third of American workers were losing their jobs.

Fayetteville scarcely noticed the stock market crash, but as the Depression began to deepen and spread across the nation, the people along the banks of the Cape Fear suffered in the same way that people did elsewhere. The most visible sign of trouble in Fayetteville by the summer of 1931 was that the National Bank of Fayetteville, which was housed in the tallest building in town, became defunct and was sold at auction. In general, the banks were hit particularly hard, but there were personal bankruptcies as well—many of them. Before long, homeless people walking the city streets was a common occurrence. Four female vagrants were run out of Fayetteville in early February 1933. The divorce rate doubled, and there was a drastic increase in the number of people arrested for public drunkenness. The worst of the despair lasted about two years. By February 1933 there were some signs of a slight economic upturn, as banks reopened and automobile sales increased. People apparently had enough money to do a little gambling, since Sheriff McGeachy declared war on slot machines and other gambling devices in January 1934. In less than six months fifty-six persons were indicted for violations.

The Depression did not hurt all people equally, of course. Some people had little or nothing to lose. One black woman, years later, explained that her family had a garden and ways of preserving meat and that they did not suffer as some others did. She noted, "We had no money to lose; we had been eatin' and we went on eatin.' " The same was not true of the mill workers at Victory Mill. In June 1932 thirty men from the mill marched on the sheriff's office declaring that they had to have food immediately for their families, who had been surviving mainly on blackberries. A leader of the group, M. F. Butler, reportedly said, "We don't want to do anything wrong because we are law abiding people, but we are desperate and we are liable to do anything before we see our wives and children starve to death." Temporary relief was provided by Aldermen J. P. Lee and Donald McQueen, who secured a quantity of food for the men and their families.

I was not yet born when those thirty hungry men got help through the efforts of two compassionate Fayetteville aldermen, but twenty-five years later, one of those men, Mr. J. Pat Lee, and I were close personal friends. I mentioned him and his family earlier. He was one of the most generous and caring people I ever knew. If you needed something and he had it, it quickly became yours. He spent his life helping people. I remember many things about him. He was a devout Christian first and foremost, and he befriended most of the evangelists who came to town, but not the healers and advocates of speaking in the "unknown tongue." Most of those he befriended were Fundamentalist in their theology, and I am sure some of them must have wondered why Mr. Lee was so fond of the writings of E. Stanley Jones, a Methodist preacher whom most considered to be an outright liberal. Whatever anybody else thought of Mr. Lee, I thought then (and I still do) that, if I ever knew a thoroughly honest and good man, J. Pat Lee was that man. He demonstrated it in 1932 when he helped feed hungry mill workers and their families, and I saw him demonstrate it many more times during the years that I knew him.

The efforts of Pat Lee and Donald McQueen were admirable, but not enough, for times were very bad. Even after President Franklin D. Roosevelt replaced Hoover in the White House on 4 March 1933 and launched his famous New Deal, there was labor unrest, for conditions had not improved much in the mills. In August and September 1934 textile workers struck all over the nation, and again Sheriff McGeachy came under pressure. In Cumberland County three or four mills closed down for a brief time. When the mills reopened, the sheriff and his deputies showed up to protect workers who wanted to go back to work. The officers were jeered by the strikers. Some strike sympathizers hurled a bomb into the Puritan Mill, causing the Parkton Company of the National Guard to be called to duty. Sheriff McGeachy and his men obviously were too few in number to prevent the violence that erupted from pent-up emotions. After some weeks the strike was finally settled, and by 27 September the situation at the mills was about back to normal.

The labor unrest in 1932 was clearly caused by the Depression, which had taken food out of the mouths of workers and their families. In all likelihood the strike of 1934 was caused in part by Depression hardships *and* the new president's sympathy with organized labor. Labor wanted a better deal, and Roosevelt believed they deserved one. Why not use that as leverage against the mill owners? The workers saw what they believed was an opportunity to make gains, and they seized it. Organized labor asserted itself during the decade of the thirties and, supported by a sympathetic federal government, won numerous victories. The story is told about an unidentified striker of that period who was asked why he was such a strong supporter of President Roosevelt. The worker replied, "Franklin D. Roosevelt is the only man who has ever been in the White House who would agree with me if I told him my boss is a son-of-a-bitch."

Along with the human misery and despair and labor violence of the thirties, there was plenty of crime. As in the past, much of that crime was alcohol-related. Upon the recommendation of President Roosevelt, Congress repealed the Volstead Act in 1933, thus ending national Prohibition and returning the decision of whether or not to allow the manufacture and sale of intoxicating beverages to the individual states. In November 1933 the voters of North Carolina decided to hold on to prohibition, except for beer, which had been legalized statewide in April of that year. Almost immediately, Steve Fasul made application for the first beer license in Fayetteville. However, in February 1935, the sheriff and city police, who stubbornly opposed the sale of alcoholic beverages, announced their intention of making Cumberland County the "Sahara Desert" of North Carolina where alcohol was concerned. Apparently the authorities along the Cape Fear had failed to learn the major lesson taught by the enactment and unsuccessful enforcement of the Volstead Act, namely, that enforcing prohibition was impossible. In 1937 the state backed away from prohibition in favor of ABC stores, which sold liquor under the control of the North Carolina ABC (Alcoholic Beverage Control) Commission. After the voters of Cumberland County gave their approval for such stores, one opened in Fayetteville in September. Those who expected state-controlled liquor to end bootlegging in North Carolina were soon disappointed. The moonshine trade went on apace in Cumberland County, in spite of the fact that a person could now purchase whiskey legally. The reason was simple. Swamp-made corn whiskey was cheaper. It sold for sixty cents a pint on weekdays and seventy-five cents on Sundays and holidays when the ABC store was closed. Why abandon the tried and true, when the new, legal stuff cost more? Many citizens of Cumberland County had a longstanding relationship with their friendly bootlegger.

Along with the free flow of whiskey, legal and illegal, prostitution was on the rise, probably due in part to the expansion of Fort Bragg during the twenties. Again, however, it was not soldiers alone who sought the services of Cumberland County's ladies of easy virtue. According to my uncle, who passed the years of his early manhood during that time, every curious male in the county knew where "the whorehouse" was located. And, with increased prostitution, there came an increase in the number of people afflicted with syphilis. In Cumberland County, and indeed throughout North Carolina, there were reports of an alarming number of cases in January 1931. However, the Cape Fear region apparently had more than its share of those cases, for it was reported in 1937 that the county's venereal disease clinic was the second largest in the state.

People who went to jail for drunkenness, gambling, and prostitution in Fayetteville and nearby Hope Mills spent their days of incarceration in squalid surroundings. In March 1938 the Cumberland County grand jury told Judge Marshall T. Spears that Fayetteville's city jail was "filthy and inadequate for proper sanitation of prisoners" and that the Hope Mills Jail was "a disgrace to any civilized community." There were no derogatory reports about Sheriff McGeachy's jail.

As bad as times were along the Cape Fear during the thirties—depression woes, labor strikes, drunkenness, and prostitution—there were positive developments, too. One Fayetteville native made his mark in the world, as did a couple of other former residents. In November 1931 native-son Frank Porter Graham became the president of the University of North

Carolina. Years later Graham would go on to represent North Carolina in the United States Senate.

A year after Graham went to Chapel Hill, a famous artist from Fayetteville, Elliott Daingerfield, died, and people across the nation who appreciated art mourned his passing. Though born at Harper's Ferry, Virginia, Daingerfield moved to Fayetteville with his parents when he was two years old, spending nineteen years there before going off to New York. His art, including his religious subjects—*Madonna and Child, The Child of Mary*, and *The Holy Family*, among others—was prominently exhibited there. Following his death at his home in New York in 1932, Daingerfield was brought back to Fayetteville and interred at Cross Creek Cemetery.

During the last year of the decade, 1940, Fayetteville could take pride in another "former resident" (but not a native) named Carson Smith McCullers, whose novel *The Heart Is a Lonely Hunter* was published that year and went on to become highly acclaimed as a literary classic. Although born and reared in Columbus, Georgia, McCullers moved to Fayetteville with her husband Reeves McCullers in 1938 and finished writing her famous novel while there. The couple lived first on Rowan Street and then on North Cool Spring Street. Both of them hated the small-town South in general and Fayetteville in particular, but McCullers used the setting of Fayetteville and Fort Bragg for her second novel, *Reflections in a Golden Eye*. When not at her typewriter, Carson McCullers often walked the streets of Fayetteville in strange garb, talking to various people, particularly African Americans. She thoroughly disliked what she regarded as the racist attitudes of Fayetteville citizens, and those citizens thought that "the McCullers girl" was "a queer duck." Almost as soon as this twenty-three-year-old phenomenon got her second advance on royalties for *The Heart Is a Lonely Hunter*, she and Reeves packed up and left for New York, hoping never to have to live in a small Southern town again. Much of Carson McCullers's life after that, until the time of her death in 1967, was characterized by serious physical and psychological problems and some bizarre behavior at times. Still, Fayetteville claimed her as a literary celebrity who had once lived there, even though she had held the town in contempt, and the town had regarded her with suspicion. Since I was born on Cool Spring Street about a hundred and fifty yards (across Person Street) from the house in which the McCullers couple lived, I can only wonder if my mother, while strolling me down Person Street in 1939 or 1940, ever spoke to the strange young woman from Columbus, Georgia. At some juncture, as a toddler, could I possibly have looked into the eyes of one who was destined for literary fame and personal tragedy?

Publicity about Graham, Daingerfield, and McCullers enhanced Fayetteville's image, as did the city's being visited by some of the most famous people in America. One of the biggest events of the dismal decade was a visit in November 1931 by the famous woman aviator, Amelia Earhart. In 1927 the people of Fayetteville had joined with the nation in celebrating the solo flight of Charles Lindbergh across the Atlantic. Four years later they celebrated the most famous woman pilot in America. Ms. Earhart had flown across the Atlantic with two male pilots in 1928 and had subsequently founded the Ninety-Nines, an international organization of women pilots. She arrived in Fayetteville on 11 November 1931 to appear in the American Legion Armistice Day air show that took place at a field off the Raleigh Road, a few miles north of Fayetteville. As her part in the air show she flew an "autogyro," a precursor of the helicopter. The huge crowd, which watched her hold the flying machine almost stationary in the air, was thrilled. That Earhart's appearance was considered an event of mammoth proportions was demonstrated by the fact that the schools in the area were closed, along with the offices at the courthouse and most of the town's stores. When Ms. Earhart rode through the streets of downtown in an open car, she was greeted at the Market House by an enormous crowd that applauded and cheered her.

A year after her appearance in Fayetteville, Earhart made a solo flight across the Atlantic, flying from Newfoundland to Londonderry, Ireland. In 1937 she set out with Fred Noonan, her navigator, in an attempt to fly around the world. She didn't make it. Somewhere in the South Pacific her plane went down, and no one has ever found out what happened to her and Noonan. Gone but never forgotten, Amelia Earhart had received in 1931 one of the warmest and most enthusiastic welcomes Fayetteville ever gave a visiting celebrity—not equaled or surpassed until President Roosevelt's visit in 1941.

Earhart was not the only famous person to grace the streets of Fayetteville during the 1930s. In 1934 the nation's first lady, Eleanor Roosevelt, paid a surprise visit, and in 1936 her husband, Franklin D. Roosevelt himself, passed through on a train. Hundreds of Fayettevillians lined up along the railroad tracks to get a glimpse of the president as his train passed through. Two other celebrities who came to town were Governor Clyde Hoey and New York City mayor, Fiorello LaGuardia.

Hoey arrived in October 1937 to address a convention of the American Legion. He and the legionnaires gathered on Person Street at the bridge that crossed the Cape Fear River. There the governor and the legionnaires dedicated the bridge to the memory of the sailors and soldiers who had been killed in World War I. Apparently little was made of LaGuardia's visit in July 1939. Nor was much attention paid to General George C. Marshall's visit to Fort Bragg in November of the same year, for he was not yet a national hero. America's participation in World War II lay two years in the future, and Marshall's great fame was tied to that conflict and its aftermath.

There were significant developments in education during the lean years of the thirties. In April 1935 school superintendent Horace Sisk proposed that a twelfth grade be added for high school. That soon became the new norm, and five years later there was a new high school. The new school on Robeson Street cost $195,000 to build. Lauded as the most modern high school structure in the state, it had a huge auditorium with 1,100 seats, a "beautifully draped stage," and "ideal acoustics." It was hailed as a convention site in newspaper reports, which asserted that Fayetteville could now accommodate any convention, "no matter what the size." I spent three of my four years of high school in that building and thought it was a building for the ages. Now I look back and realize that it was used as a high school for only fourteen years and was razed long before the twentieth century reached its end. I lived at 216 Robeson Street in the shadow of that building for twelve years. I first saw my wife, Judith Lynn McIntosh, in its halls and fell in love with her at first sight. I was fifteen; she was fourteen. She did not know that I had been smitten for another year or so, however. That building, in whose halls Cupid dazzled me, will always be seen in my mind's eye, though it has long since vanished from the scene. On that site at century's end stood the new Highsmith-Rainey Hospital.

This "new" Fayetteville High School was not the only building that attracted attention during the decade. In September 1940 the huge Veterans Administration Hospital was dedicated on Ramsey Street. It was destined to become in future years one of the largest facilities of its kind in North Carolina.

The Cape Fear region had always had its share of reli-gion—Presbyterians, Baptists, Methodists, and other religious folks were numerous. Most of the area's citizens who affiliated with a church were Protestants, of course, but it should be noted that Fayetteville had long had a Catholic presence. In December 1931 St. Patrick's Catholic Church, reputed to be the oldest Catholic church in North Carolina, celebrated its first century of existence. A little over seven years later, in March 1938, the church moved into a new building on the corners of Bradford and Arsenal Avenues, where it maintained a quiet existence. I recall being in that church only once or twice. In 1952 my cousin, Lillian Cox, married William Long of Richmond, Virginia there, and I was an usher, along with Lillian's brother, Charles. The church still stands in 2002 and still maintains its quiet existence in a city dominated by Protestants.

During the hard times of the thirties a real estate tycoon emerged in Fayetteville in the person of Dr. R. L. Pittman, a prominent physician and businessman. In 1935 Dr. Pittman bought the LaFayette Hotel, and the following year he purchased the Woolworth Building. To add to his real estate empire, he bought the Prince Charles Hotel, Fayetteville's largest, in May 1940 for $300,000 and added seventy-five rooms to it in September. All of these properties were in addition to Pittman Hospital, which Dr. Pittman also owned. I saw this man many times, and I walked and drove by his mansion on Hay Street more times than I can count. I knew his son Raymond on sight, and I was aware that his daughter was the wife of Dr. Wade Parker. As far as I know, I never saw Mrs. Parker, but I saw Dr. Parker many times, and I remember the huge white house in which the Parkers lived. It sat just beside the Pittman mansion, which, for many years, was the most imposing house in the city.

In spite of the fact that times were hard and money was in short supply during the thirties, life went on, and by the end of the decade the economic picture looked a little brighter. World War II, the great economic pump primer, was already going on in Europe and Asia, but the United States would not be dragged into it until December 1941. What had changed the economic situation up to that time was President Roosevelt's heralded New Deal. In 1933 more than 300 unemployed workers in Cumberland County got jobs in the relief programs sponsored by the Civil Works Administration, or CWA, one of the many New Deal "alphabet agencies" established to create work for people. Upwards of a hundred Cumberland County men joined the Civilian Conservation Corps (CCC), working on road construction at Fort Bragg and in various soil and conservation efforts. Several CCC units were located at Fort Bragg in 1938, including two of the few all-black companies. The Emergency Relief Administration (ERA) found many jobs for people in local governments—jobs ranging from supervisors, to clerks, to janitors. As late as April 1940 hundreds of workers were involved in projects sponsored by the Works Progress Administration (WPA), assisting in the paving of streets, the landscaping of grounds at the new high school, and construction at Fort Bragg. Within a year or two all of these federal, make-work jobs would pass away, and the Depression itself would become yesterday's nightmare, as our involvement in World War II would bring an end to unemployment and infuse the American economy with a steady stream of money. Also helping to put money into the economy, while simultaneously providing some income for the elderly and disabled, was the new Social Security Act that President Roosevelt had signed into law on 14 August 1935. In December 1936 the Social Security office in Fayetteville reported that 3,822 citizens in the area had registered for benefits under this new federal program. The New Deal was definitely providing much-needed assistance to many, while trying to pull the nation from the depths of the Depression. World War II would complete the job that the New Deal began.

Since we were not yet in the war in 1940 and hoped desperately to stay out of it, Fayettevillians were still focused on less serious matters. Where to eat out? Charles Gordon had helped with that a little in 1937 by opening the new Rainbow Restaurant. This added another option to the several Greek restaurants that had sprung up during the twenties. After dinner there were various movie theaters to which people could go. The blockbuster film that the nation was abuzz about in late 1939 was *Gone with the Wind*. That epic movie, which starred Clark Gable and Vivian Leigh, finally arrived in Fayetteville in March 1940. It opened with much fanfare at the Carolina Theater. Still, it was not available to viewers on Sunday, since the city ordinance against Sunday showings was not declared invalid by a judge until November of that year. In the minds of many it was about time for Fayetteville to act like an important city and behave like most of American society. After all, by the time the biggest of all movies yet made had ended its run in town, Fayetteville could boast of a population that was just under 18,000, and there were thousands more just a few miles away at Fort Bragg. The city named for LaFayette was no longer just some little cotton-mill town on the west bank of the Cape Fear. World War I had started it down the path to state and national prominence, and World War II would propel it on to that destination.

The coming of Fort Bragg to Cumberland County brought with it additional pressure to legalize liquor in an area where legalization had been consistently resisted, at least by the authorities and the churches. Many argued that legalized liquor would bring more crime and violence. Perhaps so, but it has already been demonstrated that alcoholic beverages, largely in the form of moonshine whiskey, had always been available in the county and that most citizens had little trouble finding a friendly bootlegger. In the last chapter it was shown that the two notable murder cases that grabbed the spotlight along the Cape Fear during the twenties were directly related to whiskey—at a time when alcoholic beverages were prohibited by law. That liquor sometimes bred violence was obvious—whether the alcohol was legal or illegal. Yet, the authorities used Fayetteville's next sensational murder case to blame the violence on legalization. In the next-to-last year of the decade, a young man who was nine days away from his twenty-second birthday shot and killed a Fayetteville policeman. That young man was drunk on *legal* alcohol.

On 16 March 1939 Fayetteville policeman Willis Genes was killed with his own gun while trying to arrest the twenty-one-year-old son of local dentist Dr. L. G. Hair. The Hairs lived in a big house on Person Street, not a mile from the Cape Fear. The shooting occurred in that house and was committed by Lenward Hair.

The following story emerged from testimony given at the trial. Lenward Hair, the oldest of Dr. Hair's four sons, was drunk on the night of March 16. He hired a taxi, driven by C. R. Bagwell, to take him home. Upon arrival, "young Hair" told Bagwell that he had no money and that the cab driver would have to go with him into the house in order to get his fare. When the two men reached the back porch, Hair attacked Bagwell, striking the cab driver with his fists and then a pipe or some piece of metal. Bagwell fled the scene and went to the Fayetteville police station to report the incident.

Desk Sergeant J. J. Maloney said that the mother of the accused called and that it was only after her call requesting them to come that policemen were dispatched to the Hair home to arrest Lenward. Officers Charles Godwin, Willis Genes, and Frank Johnson showed up at the house, whereupon Lenward fled to a bedroom upstairs. When the officers entered the house, Dr. Hair told them that Lenward was upstairs and that they would have to go up and get him. The three of them retrieved the young man and started downstairs with him. It was reported that Lenward "entangled his feet" in the stair railing. While the policemen were trying to release him, a pistol shot was fired, wounding Johnson in the leg. Hair and the three officers then tumbled down the stairs together, and four more shots were fired. One of the shots creased Godwin's scalp, while another one entered Genes's back near the waistline, "ploughing upwards through the body and lodging near his heart. He died almost instantly." All of the evidence indicated that, in the confusion, Hair had pulled the gun from Genes's holster and started firing, but neither of the two surviving officers could swear that they saw that happen. In other words, they were not able to say with certainty how Hair got possession of Genes's gun, although the *Fayetteville Observer* had reported on 18 March that Lenward had "jerked" the gun from Genes's holster.

Hair was finally subdued and taken, not to the Fayetteville city jail, but to the county jail. There he was held without bond pending a coroner's inquest. Genes was taken to Pittman Hospital, where he was pronounced dead on arrival. Frank Johnson was taken to Highsmith Hospital for medical attention, while Godwin was treated at Pittman.

At the inquest three weeks later, the coroner's jury, after deliberating less than five minutes, ordered Lenward Hair held without bond for investigation by the grand jury. The *Observer* reported on 27 April that Hair's trial would begin on 3 May. Hair was arraigned on 2 May before Judge J. J. Burney of Wilmington and charged with first-degree murder. Solicitor F. Ertyle Carlyle, later the longtime congressman for the Seventh District of North Carolina, read the charges. Judge Burney ordered a special venire of seventy-five men to supply jurors for the trial. Also on the judge's docket at the same time was one Marvin Strickland, who, like Lenward Hair, awaited trial for murder.

Hair's trial got under way, according to schedule, on 3 May. Jury selection moved slowly, with nine jurors being seated by noon. Only ten were accepted after 112 members of the regular panel and 75 from the special venire had been called, but finally twelve jurors and an alternate were selected, and the trial began. It was expected to last a day and a half. Rumors circulated of a possible deal between the defense and the prosecution, and it was asserted by certain "courtroom attachés" that the state would not seek the death penalty.

As it turned out, the trial was of short duration. The prosecution put C. R. Bagwell on the stand to testify about his run-in with Hair over the cab fare on 16 March. The widow of Willis Genes was called to the stand, perhaps in an effort to play on the heartstrings of the jurors. Dr. Wade Parker of Pittman Hospital identified the bullet that killed Genes, and a fellow doctor, who examined Genes's body, said that the entry wound appeared to have powder burns around it. Officer Godwin testified that, as a result of the scuffle and the gunfire on the stairs in the Hair home, Genes fell to the bottom landing of the stairway, raised up and said, "Boys, he got me," and then fell back down.

Defense attorneys tried for an hour to break Godwin's testimony. All they could get him to say was that the officers did enter the home without a search warrant, but they had obtained Dr. Hair's permission to enter and to go upstairs after Lenward.

The prosecution's case was strong, maybe even airtight. This appeared to be the case, in spite of the fact that Lenward's parents gave testimony that contradicted that of the police. Mrs. Hair denied calling the police station and asking them to come to her house. Dr. Hair said he saw Frank Johnson hit Lenward in the head with a blackjack as the policemen were taking him downstairs. Mrs. Hair claimed that her son's head was injured and required first aid. The Hairs also contended that six shots were fired—not five, as the police claimed. Dr. Hair insisted that he saw Lenward and Godwin struggling over the pistol that fired the shots. The Hairs were obviously trying to create a self-defense scenario, but there was little indication that the jury was being persuaded.

If young Lenward Hair was convicted on first-degree murder, he would surely go to the electric chair, for the death sentence was mandatory. Consequently, after the lunch recess on 4 May, his attorneys "tendered a plea of guilty to second-degree murder, and the plea was accepted by Solicitor Ertyle Carlyle." Judge Burney delayed passing sentence until testimony was offered that might bear on the degree of punishment. On both days of the trial, the courtroom was packed, as it had been each day in 1927 during the Boone/Phillips trial.

On 5 May Judge Burney sentenced Lenward Hair to ten-to-twelve years in Central Prison for the murder of Willis Genes. He called it the "saddest case I ever heard" and blamed it all on liquor. The judge was echoing what Hair's defense attorneys had said when they entered their plea of guilty to second-degree murder. The defense team told the court that their client had "admitted being intoxicated beyond power of reason or possession of his faculties." Judge Burney then asserted that seventy-five percent of all murder cases were caused "by the influence of whiskey." In their pleas for mercy for Hair, the defense attorneys, playing to Judge Burney's prejudices, blamed everything that had happened the night of 16 March on "the legalization and sale of intoxicating beverages." Nobody seemed to remember that bootleg whiskey had been readily obtainable in Cumberland County almost forever. Illegal whiskey had led to murder in 1927; in 1939 it was legal whiskey. What was the difference? From what I know about Lenward Hair, he would have been drunk that night on bootleg whiskey, if he could not have bought liquor legally. Moreover, in 1940, just about a year and half after being sentenced, Hair would be paroled, only to get drunk again and to kill again in 1947.

Judge Burney was busy the day he sentenced Lenward Hair, for, on the same day, he dealt with the murder case of Marvin Strickland, a black man from Wade, a small town north of Fayetteville. Strickland had been indicted when his friend Julius Lee died of injuries sustained when a pickup truck in which the two men were riding "tore down a barricade and turned over several times." The surviving man pled guilty to involuntary manslaughter and was given a two-year suspended sentence by the judge, provided he would remain on good behavior for five years and pay court costs. Strickland's sentence seemed appropriate, given the fact that Lee had died in a crash that was more accidental than anything else.

Whether or not Lenward Hair received justice or mercy with his relatively brief sentence is open to debate. It is clear that officer Genes was not killed out of premeditation. On the other hand, he was a police officer killed in the line of duty by a man who was being placed under arrest. Such an act usually carries a stiffer penalty than does simple second-degree murder, and one could argue that Hair killed Genes out of anger, not merely because he was drunk and out of control. There can be no doubt that Dr. Hair did everything in his power to keep his son out of the electric chair. Rumor had it that Sheriff McGeachy, a longtime friend of Dr. Hair's, provided the dentist with a list of the jurors prior to the trial, presumably to enable Dr. Hair to persuade them to acquit his son or at least to have mercy on him. In itself, the short sentence of ten-to-twelve years given to Hair raises questions, but the young man's quick parole suggests exertion of powerful influence or payola.

As far as I know, I never laid eyes on Lenward Hair. On the other hand, I have heard about him since I was a small boy. My mother went to school with him, and I heard her recount stories about Hair's temper tantrums at school. My uncle knew Hair, and he has told me that Lenward would fight over the least offense. For instance, one of Lenward's friends was thrown out of "the whore house" one night. Lenward, who was drinking, took offense, went to the door, caused a scene, and beat up several people who were associated with the house of ill repute. Lenward Hair was apparently a consummate "bad ass." I remember my uncle telling me that on one occasion a man hit Lenward in the head with a baseball bat. Only momentarily dazed by the blow, Hair took the bat away from the man and almost beat him to death with it.

No pun intended, but hair-trigger tempers ran in the Hair family. Stories were told about "Old Dr. Hair," as many people called him. I remember seeing him a couple of times as a child, when I visited his dental office on Market Square. On one occasion, I had an abscessed tooth that needed to be pulled. Dr. Hair's second son, Stacy, was a dentist in practice with his father, and it was Stacy who pulled my tooth. Because of the abscess, the Novocain had no deadening effect on the tooth. It took several people to hold me down, since I kicked and screamed as young Dr. Hair performed the extraction. Although Dr. Stacy Hair seemed to be a mild-mannered man, unlike his father and two of his brothers, I have been told that he, too, could lose control on occasion. And, as for "Old Dr. Hair," he was known to have a propensity for pulling and brandishing a knife when he was angry with someone. A source that knew the family told me about Dr. Hair's pulling a knife at a party on one occasion and slashing at a man. Fortunately the knife only grazed the man's stomach, but cut through his belt. The man filed charges, and the police went to serve Dr. Hair with a warrant. When he heard why the police were there, the old dentist instinctively reached into his pocket. Knowing Dr. Hair's reputation for knife wielding, one of the policeman said something like, "Dr. Hair, I have known you all my life, and I don't want to hurt you. But, if your hand comes out of your pocket with a knife in it, I will kill you where you stand." Dr. Hair slowly withdrew an empty hand from his pocket. In all fairness to the Hairs, I cannot verify the stories about their knife wielding. Although told to me by a source that knew the family well, such accounts would still be considered hearsay in a court of law.

Again, in fairness, there are some positive things to be said about the Hairs, even Lenward. By all accounts he married a nice, refined woman. The couple had a daughter who was born around the time her father killed Willis Genes. When I was in Miss Nita Highsmith's fifth grade class at Central School (1947), this daughter joined our class. She was smart, attractive, quiet, congenial, and as sophisticated as any child I ever knew. In fact, she was more sophisticated than the rest of us. That is saying a great deal, because, generally speaking, I went to grammar school with bright, cultured boys and girls. We weren't big city, but we weren't country either. Some of my classmates even accused Lenward Hair's daughter of "putting on airs" because of her sophisticated demeanor. I went to school with her for seven years, and I never heard of her losing her temper. She was an excellent student, and she went on in her education to become a physician. She always seemed to be a loner during the years we were in school together, and upon graduation in 1955 she faded away, failing to remain in contact with any of her classmates, as far as I know. Mrs. Mickey Thompson, the daughter of Willis Genes, asserted in a telephone conversation with me that Lenward's daughter abandoned Fayetteville because of embarrassment over her father's reputation, even though her mother continued to live there. The fact remains, however, that I have never heard anything but good reports on Lenward Hair's wife and daughter, including his other two daughters whom I never knew. Upon asking my source about this, he simply said, "Women make strange choices sometimes. I am living proof of that!"

In the spring of 1939, when the citizens of Fayetteville were talking about Lenward Hair and the fatal shooting of Willis Genes, there were serious developments in the wider world. It was around this time that Mussolini invaded Albania. Three years earlier he had attacked the backward African nation of Ethiopia and taken it over. No one knew yet that in a few more months Adolph Hitler, Mussolini's Fascist ally, would invade Poland and thereby ignite a world war. The people of Fayetteville, like most Americans around the nation, were still working to pull themselves out of the Depression with the help of Roosevelt's New Deal. There were some who firmly believed that spiritual renewal or an old-time revival meeting was the only hope for the country. That is why evangelist Fred Brown from Tennessee was in town. He was preaching a revival at a place called the Tabernacle at the same time that the grand jury indicted Lenward Hair for murder and while Hair was being held without bond in the county jail. Brown would come and go in Fayetteville for years to come. He was a bosom friend of the J. Pat Lee family, and, during the mid-1950s, I came to know him through them. Brown, who was a thoroughgoing Fundamentalist, was a powerful preacher, though not flamboyant like many of the evangelists who passed through. He was a good man, and many Fayettevillians responded to his call "to repent and be saved." I spent considerable time with Fred when he preached a revival meeting at the First Baptist

Church in the mid-1950s. Although Brown had nothing to do with it, as far as I know, Lenward Hair later became a member of that church.

In the months after Hair was tried for murder and went off to serve his time—brief though it turned out to be—at Central Prison, people along the Cape Fear became concerned over bigger events. The war Hitler started by invading Poland widened in the spring of 1940, when the German dictator overran the Scandinavian countries, the Low Countries, and finally France. Europe was slowly being turned into a Nazi empire. How long could the United States sit by and watch that process go on? President Roosevelt wanted to intervene immediately, but he did not have the support of the American people, who seemed to be frozen in an isolationist mode. Still, Roosevelt, knowing that we could not stand aside indefinitely, slowly got the nation ready for the inevitable. Fort Bragg would figure prominently in the war picture, and Fayetteville would have to go along for the ride. Once more war, as it had in 1918 and following, would stimulate the local economy and push a growing city into even greater growth, much faster than would ordinarily have been the case. More soldiers visited Fayetteville than ever before in the next few years, and they whooped it up in the city's many dives before heading across the Atlantic or Pacific. Some, of course, would never return. Thus, the 1930s ended as they had begun—in an atmosphere of uncertainty.

Chapter 5

War and Murder: The 1940s

In 1941, as the decade of the forties began, the United States was not at war, in spite of the fact that war had raged between China and Japan since 1937 and between Germany and much of Europe since 1939. Still, only the most imperceptive of our society could have held out any prospect for continued nonbelligerency in the closing months of 1941. President Roosevelt clearly favored China in Asia and Britain in Europe. After Germany overran nearly all of Europe except Great Britain, the president wanted desperately to help the British, since he perceived Hitler as a threat to peace everywhere. His hands were tied, however, because of a series of Neutrality Acts passed during the thirties and because of the American public's short-sighted commitment to isolationism. Having been disappointed by the results of World War I, Americans generally wanted to sit out this new war.

When nothing stood between the dangerous Nazi dictator of Germany and the United States except Great Britain and when Britain seemed to be faltering under the relentless pounding of the German *Luftwaffe*, our president resolved to help the British however he had to do so—with or without the good wishes of Congress and the American public. Our official policy was that of neutrality, but Roosevelt began to take actions that belied that policy. As early as 3 September 1940 he transferred fifty naval destroyers to the British in exchange for ninety-nine-year leases on some naval bases in the Atlantic. In March 1941 he persuaded Congress to pass the Lend-Lease Act, which provided for lending or leasing arms to the British and later to the Russians, when the Soviet Union was invaded by Germany in June 1941. Then to make sure that the arms picked up by British cargo ships in the United States made it safely home to Great Britain, he ordered our Navy to escort the ships and shoot German submarines on sight. Roosevelt gave lip service to our official policy of neutrality while flouting it by his deeds. Moreover, in August 1941, Roosevelt met with Prime Minister Winston Churchill of Britain on board the U.S. cruiser *Augusta* off the coast of Newfoundland. The two leaders formulated and announced the broad postwar aims of the two countries in the famous Atlantic Charter. All of these developments pointed toward

American entry into the war as soon as a belligerent nation committed a serious enough provocation. Japan, an ally of Germany, provided that and more by attacking the U.S. naval base at Pearl Harbor in Hawaii on 7 December 1941. In a matter of days the United States was at war with Japan and also Japan's European allies, Germany and Italy.

Meanwhile, at Fort Bragg there was lots of movement. Only the most unaware in Fayetteville could have failed to see that our country was headed for war. Because of the region's proximity to and connection with Fort Bragg, it should have been clear that the Cape Fear region was going to be directly and deeply affected when we entered the conflict. Actually, in July 1940, almost a year and a half before the Japanese attack on Pearl Harbor, our government decided to make Fort Bragg the nation's largest Army training post. In September of that year the Selective Service and Training Act was approved, providing for the registration of all men 21 to 35 years of age for a draft. This was the first peacetime draft in American history, and it called for the selection of 2,000,000 men to be trained over a one-year period. When Roosevelt called upon Congress eleven months later to extend the bill for another eighteen months, there was great reluctance to do so. In the House of Representatives the bill passed by just one vote—203 to 202. Recruits began pouring into Fort Bragg in the last half of 1940, and the base's population jumped from 6,000 to 20,000 in a matter of a few months. By June 1941 it was reported that there were 67,000 men on the base. The first Cumberland County trainees had been inducted in December 1940.

Even this limited preparation for war was frowned upon and resisted by isolationists until 7 December 1941, the day the Japanese launched their sneak attack on Pearl Harbor. The next day President Roosevelt told Congress and the nation that 7 December 1941 was "a day that will live in infamy" and asked for recognition that a state of war existed between the United States and Japan. Congress, of course, complied—almost unanimously. A few days later, Germany and Italy, honoring the Tripartite Agreement they had made with Japan, declared war on the United States. Fort Bragg became a very important place because of the war, and Fayetteville felt the effects. Very early the city was caught up in the frenzy that accompanies the prosecution of a war.

On 8 December about sixty soldiers joined arms at the Market House, and began singing "California, here I come" and varied the words here and there to "Yokohama, here I come," and "Fujiama, here I come." The preparations that Roosevelt had undertaken and carried forth for well over a year were now seen as the actions of a wise head of state and commander in chief. The credibility of diehard isolationists, in Congress and out, declined precipitously.

Fort Bragg, already the nation's foremost Army base, assumed even greater importance as a military installation when the headquarters of the Airborne Command was transferred there in March 1942 from Fort Benning, Georgia. Bragg could now boast of being the home of the 82nd Airborne Division, and men jumping out of airplanes on the military reservation became as common an occurrence as the booming noise of its big guns during artillery practice.

So many soldiers pouring into Fort Bragg caused a housing shortage in the area, as was noted earlier. Rent prices were jacked up. There were warnings to landlords not to overcharge, and, beginning in 1942, a government agency called the Office of Price Administration (OPA) made a strong effort to ride herd on such matters. I recall being puzzled when my boyhood friend Frank Kelly told me that the rent on his house, which was just a block down the street from ours and was made of brick, was only twenty dollars per month, while the rent on our house, which was made of wood, was thirty-five dollars. Why did we have to pay more? The answer was that we moved to 216 Robeson Street *before* the OPA stepped in and froze rents. The Kellys were fortunate enough to move in after the rent on their house had been set by the government agency. Price controls extended beyond rent prices to the prices of many retail items sold in stores. There were those who ignored the OPA and overcharged, and some who did were caught. For instance, in January 1944 forty Fayetteville retailers were cited for price violations by this watchdog, government agency.

Controls over rent in defense areas and over some retail items were not by any means the only controls established by the government. Rationing of many items started right after Christmas in 1941, beginning with automobile tires and then being extended to coffee, sugar, gasoline, meat, fats and oils, butter, cheese, and processed food. Ultimately, even shoes were put on the ration list. The first ration books that were distributed to citizens provided coupons for sugar and coffee with a separate book for gasoline. All rationing ended in November and December 1945, except for sugar, which continued to be rationed until June 1947. As a six-, seven-, and eight-year-old boy I was sometimes sent to the Corner Market on the corner of Russell and Winslow Streets with ration stamps. Since we did practically all of our grocery buying there, we were friends with the Crooms, who owned the store. Somebody at the store would tip off my mother that sugar or coffee or some other rationed item would be coming in the next day. As soon as the store opened the next morning I went with the required number of stamps and the money that was needed to pick up the rationed item or items. This was a regular occurrence, and I remember it as if it were yesterday, in spite of my being only a young boy at the time. I still recall my mother saying on those occasions, "I want you to go to the store for me. Some sugar came in, and I don't know when there will be anymore." Then she would admonish me to look both ways before crossing the street and to make sure a train was not coming when I crossed the railroad tracks on Winslow Street. Believe me, I did remember. I sometimes pretended I was Superman, but not when a train was coming!

In 2002 I drove by what once was the Corner Market. Above the front door of the building was a sign that read "Cloud 9" and "Entertainment." Needless to say, Cloud 9 does not sell groceries. Alas, the Corner Market, like my boyhood, is a thing of the past.

Along with the rationing of the war years came numerous air-raid blackouts. When the air-raid sirens sounded, we pulled down the shades, turned out all lights in the house, and huddled together in the darkness, talking and wondering aloud how long it would be before the German bombs would start falling or the siren would sound again so that we could switch the lights back on and continue what we had been doing. After going through numerous air-raid warnings without any bombs falling, this became a ho-hum experience with which we all grew impatient. I remember thinking "Not again!" many times. Still, for as long as the war lasted, when those sirens sounded, all houses went dark, street lights went off, and car lights were turned off. Fayetteville became an invisible black spot on the map, as block wardens patrolled in the dark to make sure nobody even struck a match to light a cigarette.

Possible penetration of American airspace and the bombing of Fort Bragg and Fayetteville were not the only fears confronting us. People who had any ties with Germany, Japan, and even Italy sometimes came under suspicion, and people conjured up images of saboteurs among us. The relocation of many Japanese families on the West Coast is an oft-told tale, but many people are probably unaware that a much smaller version of this xenophobic phenomenon occurred along the Cape Fear. In March 1942 FBI agents, assisted by local officers, searched the homes of registered aliens in Cumberland County for contraband articles—guns, cameras, and shortwave radios—which aliens were forbidden to possess. The raid was disappointing, since it turned up only one shotgun and a single meat cleaver and resulted in no arrests. Even so, many people still believed that there were fifth colonists lurking among us and urged vigilance.

Besides the ration books and stamps, the air-raid blackouts, and raids on suspected fifth columnists, with which we all became so familiar, everybody—even school children—were encouraged to demonstrate their patriotism by finding scrap metal and taking it to one of the many scrap metal piles in town. Eventually, the piles were picked up, and the metal was sent to be recycled for the war effort. Then we started all over again. Collecting tin cans and other metal sometimes resulted in kids being admitted to the movies free on Saturday. Along with the encouragement to round up scrap metal, we were urged to buy war bonds, or savings stamps if we couldn't afford a war bond. As I recall, the cheapest war bond was $25, which, to me, was an astronomical sum. However, all of us could request a book in which to paste savings stamps, and the stamps could be purchased for twenty-five cents each. If we bought one or two stamps per week, we could eventually fill up the book and turn it into a $25 savings bond. I remember buying some stamps, but I cannot remember whether I ever filled up my book or not.

One thing I do remember about those years was the seemingly perpetual absence from home of my dad. He drove a bus, sometimes hauling draftees from some distant place to Fort Bragg. Since I was only four years old when the war started, it was not until after the war that I would really get to know him. He was a large man. Although he stood only six feet tall, he had a big frame and some of the biggest hands I ever saw. He wore a size 13 ring. He was the best-natured person you ever met, unless you crossed him. I quickly learned not to do that. I only remember him giving me one whipping, but I vividly recall him slapping me on a couple of occasions, when I did not do what he told me. A slap from his huge right hand sent you reeling across the room. After being swatted a couple of times, I feared him and carefully avoided antagonizing him.

Dad was movie-star handsome, and he loved to have a good time. His initials were "D.T.," and some of his buddies labeled him "Double Trouble." After the war he stopped driving a bus and worked driving a laundry truck and then a bread truck before becoming a car salesman. He continued to sell cars for the rest of his life. Unfortunately, binge drinking cost him many a job, and he moved from one dealership to another. Although I loved him for his many good qualities, by the time I was ten years old I came to resent him for his periodic binges and for neglecting my mother, my sister, and me. The bad side of my dad was not apparent to me until after the war, and I recall asking my mother many times during those years where he was and when he was coming home.

One of the vital parts of the war for all of us who lived or served along the Cape Fear was the periodic visitation of the nation's famous entertainers and sports figures. To boost the morale of the soldiers and help take their minds off the prospect of shipping out to Europe or the Pacific, some of the nation's most popular celebrities made their way to Fayetteville and Fort Bragg to appear before the men waiting to go to war. Among those who graced the Cape Fear area with their acclaimed presence were stripteaser Gypsy Rose Lee, heavyweight boxing champion Joe Louis, and cover girl Jill Falkenburg. The celebrities most enthusiastically received, however, were Mickey Rooney and Betty Grable, particularly Grable. Before there was Marilyn Monroe, there was Betty Grable, and it is likely that more soldiers (and civilian men, too) had a picture of her in a bathing suit than any other woman up to that time. As a wartime pinup girl, Grable probably remains the most looked at and drooled over woman of all time. Grable arrived in Fayetteville by train in August 1942 with the USO Camp Show. In a blue evening gown she dazzled ten thousand soldiers in her appearance at the 9th Division's amphitheater at Fort Bragg. She also visited men in Fort Bragg hospitals, dined with men in the mess hall, visited numerous units on post, and performed on the radio show "Fort Bragg Cavalcade."

Eight months before Grable's sensational arrival, Mickey Rooney, in January 1942, was greeted at the Fayetteville train depot by a host of fans. Not accompanying him as he stepped down from the train was his movie-star wife Ava Gardner, who had left the train in Wilson, North Carolina to visit her mother. City and military police escorted Rooney to the Prince Charles Hotel, as his fans followed, crowding into the lobby and beating on his door. They calmed down when they were told that the movie idol would speak to them later in the lobby, but he sneaked out of the hotel without speaking to the crowd and headed to Fort Bragg for his appearance before the troops.

Over the next four years other celebrities visited Fayetteville and Fort Bragg. It was not until January 1944 that the "intellectual stripteaser"

Gypsy Rose Lee entertained the troops on the post. That same month heavyweight-boxing champion Joe Louis fought a three-round exhibition with Corporal Bob Smith, a former Golden Gloves champion. As popular as Louis was, he lost the spotlight that night at Fort Bragg to Corporal Sugar Ray Robinson, the uncrowned welterweight champion, who fought a two-round exhibition with Corporal Jimmie Edgar, the seventh-ranked welterweight. Robinson, who moved as quickly and gracefully as a cat and unleashed lightning fast punches, overshadowed the slower, more powerful Louis. The soldiers who watched were more impressed by speed than power on that occasion.

Wars do not go on forever, not even the biggest and most destructive war in the history of the world. In retrospect, we were at war for only a short time—late 1941 to August 1945, less than four years. That is not how it seemed to me at the time. To a young boy who heard about war constantly—especially after starting to school in 1943—it truly seemed like the war would indeed last forever. I just came to expect that the war would go on indefinitely. Following the D-Day invasion in June 1944 people began to express optimism and to say that the war was winding down. It was just a matter of time before Hitler would surrender. By September 1944 preparations began to be made in our area for the expected celebration of Victory in Europe Day, but the war dragged on through the winter and the next spring, and it was not until May 1945 that news of victory was announced. President Harry Truman, who had ascended to the presidency following President Roosevelt's death less than a month earlier, made the official announcement. The city's mayor, J. Scott McFadyen, announced that Fayetteville businesses would close for the day, and churches opened their doors for prayer. The mood along the Cape Fear was simultaneously one of reserve and exuberance. Some wept, some laughed, some danced around and shouted, and people hugged and congratulated people that they didn't even know. As an eight-year-old boy I remember jumping up and down on our front porch while cheering.

There was more cheering and celebrating in August when the Japanese surrendered on the fourteenth of that month. Sirens sounded, car horns blared throughout the day, and Fayettevillians once more celebrated in the streets. Victory services were held at the Hay Street Methodist Church, but the church was too small to hold the overflow crowd. A few days later, on 17 and 18 August, Fayetteville merchants closed their businesses to celebrate the end of the war. In the course of the war more than thirty men from

Cumberland County had died on the battlefields of Europe and Asia. And now the killing was over for both area residents and Americans in general. No wonder there was widespread rejoicing and sincere thanksgiving.

With the war over, the rationing of cheese and shoes was brought to an end in September, and the government announced that all rationing would soon end. Everything but rubber tires and sugar were removed from the rationing list in November, and on 31 December tires were taken off the list. Not until 11 June 1947 did the government announce the end of sugar rationing. In addition to the end of rationing, soldiers were discharged as fast as possible from the service. By June 1946 the Fort Bragg Separation Center had discharged 250,000 military personnel. Furthermore, President Truman, the month before, had signed an order authorizing the expansion of the Fayetteville Veterans Administration Hospital from 246 beds to 435 beds, no doubt partly as a consequence of the war and because of the facility's proximity to Fort Bragg.

The most egregious aspect of the war was, of course, the battlefield losses of American men and women—321,999 dead and about 800,000 wounded, captured, or missing. Even the unexpected death of the nation's thirty-second president on 12 April 1945 at Warm Springs, Georgia could not overshadow such appalling losses. Still, Roosevelt's death cast a cloud of gloom over the entire nation. Few American presidents have been more popular or well loved than this victim of polio from Hyde Park, New York. He was a man of compassion, a man with a huge heart, and a man with whom the average American identified. I will never forget watching grown people weep on the streets of Fayetteville after hearing the news that our president was dead. People appeared to be dazed, unbelieving, as the town appeared—at least to me—to be engulfed in silence until the man who had worked so hard to pull us out of the Great Depression and had heroically led us to victory in World War II was laid to rest in Hyde Park.

Although the decade of the 1940s in Fayetteville was more about World War II than anything else, life did go on much as it had in the past. Crimes continued to be committed, and the consumption of alcohol increased. Again, there were some sensational murder cases. Famous people continued to come to town from time to time, and the firearms genius, David Marshall Williams, continued to bring forth innovations in weaponry. Even before we entered the war, Williams went to San Diego, California in January 1941 to demonstrate for Marine Corps officers a weapon he had built at his shop in Godwin. It was a .22-caliber machine gun that could fire from 700 to 1,800 rounds a minute. Of course, the weapon that won him his greatest recognition was the M-1 carbine, which millions of soldiers carried into battle in World War II.

Crime in Fayetteville was related mostly, as in the past, to drunkenness and prostitution. In May 1942 the Town Pump, which boasted that it had the longest bar in the nation, opened at 211 Donaldson Street. As noted earlier, this nightspot became the scene of a big riot later that year. Alcohol consumption and prostitution always seemed to go hand in hand. In June 1942 it was reported that there were more women than men in Sheriff McGeachy's jail, and most of them had been arrested on the charge of prostitution. Drunkenness and prostitution were not the only crimes, of course. Because of the shortage of rubber brought on by the war, there was an alarming increase in the theft of automobile tires and bicycles.

Just as the war ended and people began looking forward to a return to normal times, Mother Nature again dealt the city a damaging blow. Hard, continuous rain sent the Cape Fear River and area creeks rushing over their banks in September 1945. The river itself reached a stage of 68.9 feet, and the overflowing waters crept gradually up Person Street almost to Liberty Point, just a block from the Market House. Many city streets were blocked by water, and people were driven from their homes. I was only eight years old, but I have vivid memories of people paddling boats down city streets, and I walked past the Market House down Person Street, coming as near as I dared to Liberty Point, so that I could see how far the Cape Fear had risen. As I recall, I did it on a school day, since schools were closed so that their auditoriums and cafeterias could be used as places of refuge by flood victims who had to leave their homes. When the rain finally stopped, the flood waters receded faster than they had risen, and the city began to dry out, just as it had done several times after the floods of the past.

Many bad things happened during the forties, but there were also many positive developments and moments of glory. As indicated above, famous people continued to visit Fayetteville. In March 1941 President and Mrs. Roosevelt were paraded down Hay Street before they visited Fort Bragg. Not since the appearance of Amelia Earhart ten years earlier had downtown Fayetteville seen such a crowd, and this one was even larger than the one that assembled for the famous woman aviator. Six years after the Roosevelts came, in April 1947, General Dwight D. Eisenhower, chief of staff of the Army and commander of Allied Forces in Europe at the end of World War II, toured Fort Bragg, accompanied by his wife Mamie. Of course, they had to be paraded down the streets of Fayetteville in an open convertible, and Scott McFadyen, who had been elected to a fifth term as mayor in May 1945, rode with them. School children and adults stood along the curbs and watched as they passed. I was among them, standing on Hay Street, just across from the Colony Theater. No one knew, as we watched him pass by, that six years later General Eisenhower would become president of the United States.

The war had brought thousands of new people to Fayetteville and Cumberland County, and many of them stayed. By June 1950 the population in Fayetteville reached 34,605, just about double what it had been in 1940. The county's population climbed to 95,799. When the city schools opened in September 1950, a record number of 4,986 students were in attendance. All of the new people who now lived in the area required more businesses and services of all kinds to meet their needs. And those businesses and services gradually appeared. Daily air passenger service began in and out of Fayetteville in August 1945, and in 1947 Piedmont Airlines scheduled regular flights to and from the city. Dr. M. B. White-head, an optometrist who had opened his practice in Fayetteville, became the first eye-care professional in town to fit people with contact lenses in July 1946. Although I took no notice of this at age nine, I heard much about Dr. Whitehead later. I attended high school with Priscilla Whitehead, the doctor's daughter, and have seen her regularly through the years at our high school class reunions. A month after Dr. Whitehead began fitting contacts, Tide Water Power Company began selling propane fuel to people in the area. Clearly more and more services were becoming available to Fayette-villians, as modernity made its way into their lives.

The Cape Fear area also saw an enhancement of culture and an expansion of entertainment opportunities. Early in 1941 the Civic Orchestra and the Community Concert Association was formed. In a special election held in November 1945 local voters approved a proposal to support the Cumberland County public library system with tax money. As regards entertainment, the Hamont Theater opened in July 1941 with the feature film *Gallant Sons*, starring Jackie Cooper. The new theater had 600 seats, with twenty of those being designated as "love seats." When I was growing up I saw many movies at the Hamont, and many teenagers turned some of the seats into "love seats" which were not officially designated as such! When the theater opened, admission prices ranged from ten to thirty cents.

Later in the decade a new kind of theater called the "drive-in" appeared. The first one opened for business on the Fort Bragg Road in April 1947. A year and a half later a second one began operating on the Lumberton Road. This meant that boys old enough to drive could take their dates to one of the drive-in theaters and make mad love in their cars while ostensibly being there to see the movie. Needless to say, many did exactly that. "How did you make out with your date at the drive-in?" was a question often asked among teenage males.

At approximately the same time this new form of entertainment became available to Cape Fear area residents, sports took on a new significance in Fayetteville, when Fayetteville High School won a couple of state football championships. The city also got a professional baseball team. The high school football team was called the Bulldogs, and they won the state championship in 1947 by defeating Central High School of Charlotte 39-0. Emerging as a local hero for this heralded achievement was Coach Bill Dole, who led the Bulldogs to twenty-one wins and one tie during his two-year tenure. I can't remember the circumstances, but I met Coach Dole on one occasion. From the little I can recall about the time I was in his presence, he was a gracious and humble man. A number of his players became heroes, too, but the two receiving the most publicity were William E. "Nub" Smith and Howard Cheshire. In recent years one of Smith's teammates from the championship team told me that Smith stands out in his mind as the greatest high school football player he ever saw. Nub was not from Fayetteville; he was from Alabama. He followed Coach Dole to Fayetteville to play for him. Upon graduating from FHS, Smith went to Wake Forest College. Great accomplishments on the gridiron were expected of him there, but he was kicked out of school for personal reasons. I was told many years after the fact that those reasons involved a waitress who worked at a café just off the Wake Forest campus. Smith eventually returned home to Alabama and became a deputy sheriff in St. Clair County until his death near the end of the 1990s. I remember clipping his obituary out of the *Birmingham News* and giving it to that teammate who admired him so much that he thought he was the greatest running back in Bulldog history.

When the Bulldogs won the championship again in 1948, Smith was gone. It was Howard Cheshire who stood out above his teammates this time, although there were other heroes, too. Leon Dale comes to mind. I did not know either Cheshire or Dale, except on sight. I knew Ray Cheshire,

Howard's younger brother, very well. Ray, too, was a fine athlete. After high school he became a fervent, evangelical Christian and went off to study at Dallas Theological Seminary, one of the most evangelical and Fundamentalist citadels of theology in the nation. During those years I was of a similar theological persuasion, and Ray and I were fairly close friends. I also knew Leon Dale's younger siblings. The Dales lived on Winslow Street, just three blocks from where I lived on Robeson, and I sometimes played with the Dale kids.

But back to the 1948 championship. Fayetteville won the Eastern AA championship by beating Wilmington High School 34-0 on 12 November and then waited to see who the opponent from the west would be. Burlington and High Point High Schools had the same number of wins, and both claimed to be the Western AA champions. Finally, they played each other to settle the dispute, and Burlington won. Fayetteville and Burlington played in Winston-Salem for the state title. Cheshire made several great runs that night, but it was Dale who took the ball from the twenty-one-yard line into the end zone for the winning touchdown. Ray Green kicked the extra point, and Fayetteville ended up winning 14-13.

Coaching Fayetteville to two successive state championships made Coach Dole a hot commodity, and he soon left Fayetteville for the college ranks. He went to what became East Carolina University, but in those days was known as East Carolina State Teachers College, which most everyone shortened to ECTC. Some fine coaches followed Dole as head football coach at Fayetteville—Chuck Clements, Clyde Biggers, and Buddy Luper. None of them, however, ever won two consecutive state championships.

Some players on Bulldog teams during the fifties would stand out, but not nearly to the extent that the members of the state championship teams of the late forties did. I think of two linemen of the fifties in particular— Frank Turner, who went to East Carolina to play for Coach Biggers, when Biggers followed Dole as head coach there. Another great FHS lineman who later distinguished himself as a college player was Mike Marr. Frank Turner became a close friend of mine after he gave up football for the ministry and went off to Bob Jones University. I went to that school largely because of him, but I quickly became disenchanted and left, while he stayed on and graduated. As for Mike Marr, I cannot remember when I didn't know him. We grew up together. His mother, Mitchell Marr, and my mother were very close friends. During our boyhood years Mike and I played together often, and I knew him as John Michael. As good as Frank and Mike were, they were linemen, and it is the ball carriers who get the glory. It is the likes of Nub Smith, Howard Cheshire, and Leon Dale who are remembered.

I would be remiss if I didn't note that there was football in Fayetteville before Coach Dole. In fact, the Bulldogs had won a state championship in 1921. It's just that Bulldog football had never been as big as it became with Dole's winning back-to-back state championships. And, before there was Nub Smith and Howard Cheshire, there was Don Clayton, who became a Bulldogs' hero in 1942 by returning a kickoff 66 yards against Elizabethtown. Fayetteville won that game 38-0, but Clayton went on to become famous for something besides football, namely, the founding of putt-putt golf and selling franchises for miniature golf courses on a nationwide basis. Putt-putt golf is still alive and well, and it should be a matter of local pride that it began in Fayetteville as the brainchild of a former high school football hero.

More than ever before, Fayetteville became very enthusiastic about its high school football program during and after Dole's short tenure at FHS. Many citizens of the city also became, at about the same time, strong supporters of Fayetteville's professional baseball teams. In 1946 Fayetteville got a new baseball park called Cumberland Memorial Stadium and a farm team from the Chicago Cubs. The stadium was located on Bragg Boulevard at Bonnie Doone. More than 3,000 fans showed up in May when the Fayetteville Cubs opened the season against the Wilson Tobs. The Cubs lost that game 6-2, but two years later, in 1948, the Cubs were champions of the Carolina League. That was the year that Babe Ruth died in August at age fifty-four, and all baseball fans felt a profound loss, especially in Fayetteville, where Ruth had hit his first homerun as a professional.

Less than two years after the Cubs won the Carolina League championship, Mike Boosalis, who owned Cumberland Memorial Stadium, sold it in January 1950 to R. L. Pittman Investments, Inc. Real estate tycoon Dr. R. L. Pittman, president of the corporation, announced that the Philadelphia Athletics would now place a farm team in Fayetteville. As noted earlier, I became a ball boy and finally the batboy for that team—a heady experience that I will never forget. Most of the players that I came to know were wonderful people, and my admiration for them has grown through the years—in spite of the fact that only a few of them made it to the major leagues and not one of them ever became a big star. The only player I know about who played in Fayetteville and achieved stardom in the majors was

Smokey Burgess. He had played catcher earlier for the Cubs and had gone on to become a star catcher with the Chicago Cubs. I saw him play in Fayetteville on several occasions, but I never knew him.

Although sports had high visibility along the Cape Fear in the late 1940s, there were other developments that were more fundamental and lasting as far as Fayetteville's future was concerned. For example, in 1949 the city dumped its longtime form of government, which consisted of a mayor and an eight-member board of aldermen. In May the city elected its first city council. Those elected included J. O. Tally, Jr. who, as the highest vote getter, became mayor, George Herndon, Bob Shaw, Gene Plummer, and Dr. W. P. DeVane. At one time or another I crossed paths with Tally, Herndon, and Plummer, and Jimmy Herndon, George's brother, was a friend of mine. The most significant aspect of the change in government at the time was the election of Dr. DeVane, for he was the first black person elected to a city office in Fayetteville since the days of Reconstruction.

DeVane's election to the city council in 1949 was one of several hopeful signs that Fayetteville and the Cape Fear region would move forward on some civil-rights issues. In 1947 a black physician, Dr. M. L. Perry, was granted a building permit to build a black maternity hospital. That same year the African-American soldiers of the 555th Parachute Infantry Battalion were integrated into a regiment of the postwar 82nd Airborne Division. Never before had blacks and whites been linked in an Army combat unit. This was a harbinger of things to come. Seven years down the road (1954), black citizens, with the help of the United States Supreme Court, would launch the Civil Rights Movement that would eventually make all citizens equal before the law—except women. Women, too, would make gains, but they would see the Equal Rights Amendment, for which they fought, go down to defeat. One glimmer of hope for women along the Cape Fear came in March 1947 when three housewives—Mrs. Arthur Rugheimer, Mrs. Edwin Knarr, and Mrs. Howard Smith—made history as the first women ever to serve on a jury in Cumberland County. They were jurors on a divorce case. This came more than a dozen years before militant feminists vociferously demanded the liberation of women by publicly burning their bras and engaging in other gestures of defiance.

How important or unimportant they were, there were other developments that shared the headlines during the forties. Fayetteville got a new City Hall on Green Street, just down from the Market House, which, itself, got a facelift during the decade. I first remember the Market House as being yellow, but in 1948 the yellow paint was sandblasted away, and the old structure's bricks were restored to their original red color.

A new Baptist church was formed in 1949 to serve the worship needs of Baptists who lived in the western part of town. It was named Snyder Memorial Baptist Church in honor of Dr. Joel Snyder, who had served as the pastor of First Baptist Church from 1912 to 1941.

Also in 1949, the voters had another round of voting alcoholic beverages in or out. In August 1948 Cumberland County had voted beer and wine out, but that was contrary to the vote in the city. The following January, the city held a separate referendum and gave its approval to the sale of beer and wine by a vote of 2,144 to 1,144.

Signs of modern, big-city life came to Fayetteville in July 1949 when Robert Burgess, who owned and operated Burgess Radio Service, brought the first television set to the city. It was a Magnavox with a sixteen-inch screen, and it received the first telecast out of Charlotte on 1 July. Burgess put up a seventy-five-foot antenna for better reception. Reportedly, the reception was pretty good on a clear day. Not until 1950 was I invited to watch someone's TV set. All I remember seeing was snow. That all changed during the next five years. By 1955 we had a television set at our house, and the reception was usually decent—with a very high antenna on top of the house, of course.

It is hard to believe that Fayetteville, given its size and phenomenal growth, did not have a *paid* fire department until June 1947. Gradually the city was getting on the map literally as well as figuratively. In 1945 it had been placed on the route of U.S. Highway 301, dubbed a postwar "super-highway." This was a major artery that ran the length of the eastern seaboard.

Last, but certainly not least, on the medical front there was both good news and bad news for Fayetteville and the rest of the country during the forties. In 1944 penicillin made its appearance as the first antibiotic, and that was good. That news was followed by several outbreaks of polio, news that was truly devastating. I have personal reasons for remembering the appearance of both penicillin and polio.

First, penicillin. Our next-door neighbors on Robeson Street were the Manoses. They were Greeks. Paul, the father, owned and operated a restaurant on Hay Street, practically next door to the building occupied by the *Fayetteville Observer*. Mrs. Manos, whose first name I have forgotten, was a loquacious woman with a loud voice. I can still hear her yelling out for her son Johnny, whom she called "Yanocky"—Greek for Johnny. Christine, whom we all called Becky, was Johnny's older sister. Usually Johnny and I were buddies, but sometimes we would fall out and fight. One day I heard that Johnny was seriously ill and might die. I was disturbed for days, thinking I was about to lose my friend and playmate. Then I heard that he was doing much better and that he was going to make it after all, thanks to a new miracle drug called penicillin. The new antibiotic was introduced to doctors in Fayetteville in May 1944, and Pittman Hospital was named as the depot for civilian use of this wonder drug. All I knew was that it had to be powerful medicine and that it had saved Johnny's life. It would later help me fight a number of infections until I finally became allergic to it.

Second, there was polio. Fayetteville went through two epidemics of this dreaded disease in the forties, the first in 1944 and the second in 1948. People I knew and liked—both children and adults—contracted the disease and went from being healthy and vibrant to being paralyzed and having twisted limbs. Stanley Tew was the brother of Elta Tew, whom I knew and went to school with all of my life. We were close friends of the Tew family, and we were deeply saddened when Stanley, a very young boy, came down with polio. For a long while his survival was in grave doubt, but he lived. One side of his body virtually withered up. His mother, Nita (a distant cousin of ours), would not allow Stanley to feel sorry for himself and pushed him to go on with his life as if he were normal. He did, and he went on to become a productive citizen and a very pleasant and caring person.

In the adult category there was George Matthews, who owned and operated Matthews Pharmacy, which was next door to the Carolina Theater on Hay Street. George, a most congenial man, was about six feet and four inches tall and looked like a candidate for tight end on a professional football team. When polio finished with him his body was twisted up, his chin was drawn down to his chest, and he was a shell of his former self. He took this tragic defeat in stride and, after recovering as much as was possible for him, he went on running his pharmacy in the same cheery manner as he had before his illness. I could not help but pity him, but I admired him more.

Besides Fayetteville's growth and progress during the forties and its bouts with two polio epidemics, there are some accounts of human relationships run amuck, with the result being murder. In 1946 the war was over. At least the world war that had resulted in the death of millions of people and the destruction of several nations was over. Another war, one between a woman and her husband, raged on Pearl Street in Fayetteville. This war would have been comparable to the mighty United States attacking the tiny island of Cuba. For the husband in the case was Wall C. Ewing who tipped the scales at close to 250 pounds, while his wife, Douglas Southerland Ewing, hardly weighed 100 pounds. On 13 March 1946 the hulking Ewing beat his spouse to death.

Ewing was not a Fayetteville native. Born in Mt. Gilead, North Carolina in 1891 and reared in Dillon, South Carolina, Walter Christian ("Wall") Ewing was one of the eight sons of Dr. Joseph Preston Ewing and Sallie Hearne Christian Ewing. Wall attended Donaldson Military School in Fayetteville in 1907 and then the South Carolina Military Academy (later renamed the Citadel) in 1910. Meanwhile, Ewing's father closed his medical practice in Dillon and moved his family to Fayetteville in 1909. He soon became engaged in farming and in the real estate business, but died in 1916.

Dr. Ewing's son Wall was engaged in the wholesale fertilizer business by this time and was already politically active at the young age of 25. In 1920, he married into a prominent Fayetteville family when he took as his wife Miss Douglas Southerland. For many years the couple lived with Douglas's widowed mother, Mrs. R. A. Southerland, and a younger sister, Kate Southerland, at 301 Green Street until they moved to Pearl Street in 1943. Ewing was regarded as a prominent businessman, and he served during most of the 1930s in the North Carolina legislature, first in the House and then in the Senate. He was also chairman of the Cumberland County Democratic Party. Eventually he became manager of the Cumberland Broadcasting Company and its popular local radio station WFNC. Kate Southerland was his office manager.

While there was some question about when Ewing began drinking to excess, it is clear that he was doing it frequently by 1946. And he was reported to have been drinking heavily on the day he beat Douglas Ewing into unconsciousness. Hence, as had usually been the case in previous local murders, John Barleycorn was an accomplice. Fourteen days after Mrs. Ewing died of the brain hemorrhage caused by the beating she had taken, Wall Ewing went to jail and remained there without bond. Indicted on first-degree murder, he went to trial on 27 August 1946.

Presiding over the Ewing trial was Judge R. Hunt Parker. Longtime solicitor Ertyle Carlyle served as prosecutor. W. C. Downing and James

McRae assisted Carlyle. To defend him, Ewing hired a high-powered team of lawyers led by James R. Nance and R. Glenn Cobb of Fayetteville. T. A. McNeill and H. E. Stacy of Lumberton joined Nance and Cobb in the effort. Two of these lawyers I knew—Nance and Cobb. I knew Mr. Nance personally, and I went to school with his daughter Nancy Lou and his son Jimmy, who was several years younger than I was. Nancy Lou and I were in the same grades at Central School. She was a pretty girl and quite sophisticated for her age. As a young man I came to regard Mr. Nance as one of the smartest people I had ever met. Mr. Cobb I knew on sight and spoke to on a number of occasions. Both Nance and Cobb had big reputations as highly successful attorneys. When it came to criminal defense, few lawyers in the whole state of North Carolina were in Jim Nance's league, while Cobb, it was reported, would do just about anything to "get his client off."

The state called many witnesses to the stand, and they bore damning testimony to various acts of violence Ewing had committed against his wife. Several neighbors testified that during the two-and-a-half years the Ewings had lived on Pearl Street, they had heard Wall tell Douglas that he was going to kill her. One of those neighbors was Neal C. McLeod, the father of Billy McLeod, my pal during junior high school days. Mr. McLeod claimed that "not less than fifty times" he had heard Douglas Ewing cry out to her husband that he was killing her. He went on to say that in less than a week after the Ewings moved in he had heard Ewing cursing and Mrs. Ewing screaming. Many times, Mr. McLeod asserted, there were fights and threats to kill and noises like beatings—"sounds of blows and slaps." In all, twelve witnesses testified to the beatings, the curses, and the screams. One witness said he had once seen Ewing going through the yard with a shotgun while calling for his wife. Another witness reported that during one beating, he heard Mrs. Ewing scream out, "Wall, don't do that. Don't hit me anymore. You know I love you. I've loved you since I was thirteen years old."

The state contended that Ewing's motive for constantly beating his wife was to get Douglas out of the way because of a romantic interest he had in her younger sister, Kate Southerland. Two witnesses swore they saw Ewing kissing and hugging Kate. One testified that she had seen Kate sitting in Ewing's lap in the yard of the Ewing home. Another stated that Douglas had confronted Kate and accused her of doing everything she could to take her husband away from her. Another testified that Ewing was together with the sister at 6:30 a.m. at his WFNC office "winter before last." The state was eager to put Kate Southerland on the stand and issued a subpoena for her to appear. After looking everywhere he could within his jurisdiction, Sheriff McGeachy wrote on the back of the subpoena "Not to be found" and returned it to the court.

Another witness testifying for the state was Captain W. G. "Nig" Clark, chief of Fayetteville detectives and later the sheriff of Cumberland County. He said he was at Duke Hospital when the autopsy was done on Mrs. Ewing, and he saw twenty-five or thirty bruises on her. Furthermore, several doctors testified to Mrs. Ewing's many bruises sustained by her before her death.

Naturally the defense attorneys had explanations for all the bruises—Mrs. Ewing was a drunk and a drug addict, they claimed, who fell down time and again. As to the cause of her death, Nance tried to argue that she fell and sustained a blow on her head, and that caused her death. Ewing's brother testified that he had seen his sister-in-law fall a number of times. Not only was Mrs. Ewing prone to fall down frequently, it was alleged, but her husband himself was falling-down drunk at the time of her death—perhaps drunk out of his mind and thus incapable of premeditating a murder, said his attorneys. They called Dr. John Turner, chief neuropsychiatrist at the Veterans Administration Hospital to testify that in his opinion Ewing was insane at the time he was alleged to have killed his wife. Therefore, he did not have the mental capacity to commit a premeditated murder. Moreover, following his wife's death Ewing supposedly began hallucinating. Dr. Turner went on and on testifying about the defendant's hallucinations. Ewing claimed he saw his wife coming to visit him in his cell to tell him that everything was going to be all right. Not only his wife, but also Ewing's dog came to visit him, he told Dr. Turner. On cross-examination Dr. Turner admitted that he was not licensed to practice medicine in North Carolina.

Another witness for the defense was Paul Moyle, a former employee of Ewing's. Moyle testified to his former boss's "prodigious drinking and irrational behavior." He contended that when Ewing was in the "third stage of drunkenness"—whatever that was—he did not know right from wrong.

The defense rested on 5 September. The state rebutted by attempting to discredit the idea that Ewing was insane. Twenty-two citizens testified that Ewing had been and was still mentally competent. Dr. M. T. Foster, the county health officer, testified that he had had a conversation with Ewing some months before and that he seemed perfectly normal. Captain W. G. Clark said he had talked to Ewing on 16 March—three days after Douglas's death—and had found him sane and capable.

In his closing argument lawyer Nance spoke for two-and-a-half hours. He argued that his client was not guilty of any crime. The state, he contended, had failed to prove that Douglas Ewing had been slain, or, if she had, that the defendant did it. He continued to argue that she died of a fall when she was drunk or on drugs.

During his closing argument, Carlyle asserted that Kate Southerland would have made herself available to the court if she were not in league with Wall Ewing. He said, "We tried to get Miss Kate here to testify. Had she not been in sympathy with this defendant she would have been here eager to assist the state in bringing to justice the murderer of her sister."

At the end of closing arguments, Judge Parker charged the jury, telling them that the jurors could find one of four verdicts—murder in the first degree, murder in the second degree, manslaughter, or not guilty. Jury deliberations began on 11 September 1946 and lasted only two hours and thirty-five minutes. The verdict arrived at by the jurors was guilty of manslaughter. Following the announcement of the verdict, Judge Parker denounced Ewing. Dozens of people, he said, had seen Mrs. Ewing knocked down, slapped, thrown out of doors, and bruised by her husband. No one except for members of Wall Ewing's family had ever seen her fall down, the judge remarked sarcastically. Then he proceeded to sentence the defendant to 18 to 20 years at "hard labor" in Central Prison.

Almost before Judge Parker could finish pronouncing sentence, Ewing's attorneys served notice that they would appeal the conviction to the North Carolina Supreme Court. Ewing was released on a $25,200 bond, pending the hearing of his appeal. The judge thanked the jury for their service and ordered double pay for them.

The North Carolina Supreme Court heard Ewing's appeal and upheld his conviction. The justices said that he could thank the able defense put on by his attorneys and the mercy of the jury that "his present plight is no worse." They said further that Ewing had exhibited a "hatred and brutality hardly equaled in the annals of the court." Members of the court practically laughed at the defense's contention that Mrs. Ewing's death could have been caused by a brain injury suffered in a fall.

The state supreme court upheld the conviction in early June 1947, and Ewing gave himself up to Sheriff McGeachy on 16 June. He entered the courthouse at 9:30 that morning, accompanied by his attorney, Jim Nance. Deputy sheriff David McNeill drove Ewing to Raleigh and delivered him to Central Prison. There, Ewing was assigned the number 46644. For five days he stayed in a quarantine cellblock while being processed. After undergoing physical and psychiatric examinations and being fingerprinted, Ewing appeared before the classification board for his work assignment while in prison.

The former state legislator and radio station manager had hardly gotten settled in prison before a variety of people went to work to win his freedom. In December 1948 petitions were sent to Governor Greg Cherry asking the governor to grant Ewing executive clemency. Purportedly, two Fayetteville policemen had signed the petition. Cherry denied the petition, but two years later, paroles commissioner Dr. T. C. Johnson held out "a ray of hope" for Ewing. He said he would take no action at the time. However, he did indicate that the Ewing case merited further investigation, because the prisoner had gained time for good behavior and because every member of the jury that convicted Ewing recommended freeing him. It was reported that the jurors had recommended mercy and expected Ewing to be sentenced to 3 to 5 years and that they would have voted not guilty if they had known Judge Parker was going to be so harsh. One can only wonder what might have happened if there had been any women on that jury. One can only speculate, but it is doubtful that women would have been so sympathetic with a drunken wife beater.

In 1950 Ewing was serving his time at the prison camp in Perquimans County doing clerical work—scarcely the "hard labor" to which he had been sentenced by Judge Parker. By February 1951 he was reported to be undergoing a mental breakdown and was transferred from Perquimans to Central Prison Hospital for a psychiatric examination. The camp officers at Perquimans claimed that he "was about to crack up." There was speculation that Ewing's condition might lead to a parole or clemency, since Fayetteville businessmen had petitioned Governor Kerr Scott to commute his sentence. The request made to the governor was "not allowed."

Fifteen days after entering Central Prison Hospital, Ewing was judged to be of sound mind and remained confined. Petitions on his behalf continued to flood the governor's desk. Hounding Governor Scott ultimately paid off, for on 13 June 1952 the governor signed a parole for the former state legislator—effective 14 June 1952. Ewing, who was now

61 years of age, had served less than seven years of his sentence. And the favors continued to flow to Ewing. As Scott was leaving office the following January, he released Ewing from his parole. Kent Ewing, Wall's brother in California, had gotten Wall a salesman's job that would net him $7,500 to $10,000 per year, if he could arrive in California without strings. He had to be free from parole supervision, or the job would not be waiting for him. The lame-duck governor proved very obliging, and Wall Ewing almost literally disappeared into the western sunset. He died in Los Angeles in November 1971 at age 80. His case demonstrates for us how much the life of a Fayetteville woman was worth in 1946, if she were married to a prominent man. The penalty for beating her to death was a little over six years behind bars.

Wall Ewing's day in court was the first murder case I remember from my childhood years. Though I was only nine years old, I recall hearing my parents discuss the case. I also remember reading headlines about it in the *Fayetteville Observer*. I knew, or came to know later, several of the people who participated in the trial—Jim Nance, Glenn Cobb, Neal McLeod, and Dr. Foster, the county health officer. My connection with all of them except Dr. Foster has already been noted. While I knew Dr. Foster only to speak to him, I knew his son Malcolm quite well. Malcolm and I attended Sunday school together at the First Baptist Church for a number of years, and we graduated together from Fayetteville High School in 1955. Like his father, Malcolm became a doctor. Unfortunately, when I saw my classmate at one of our class reunions, he told me that what he remembered most about our younger days together was my prowess with a cue stick at Brunswick Billiards. Who could have known that six years after Wall Ewing went to prison and about the time he left Fayetteville a free man, I would become a lawbreaker by lying about my age and frequenting Brunswick Billiards and other pool halls?

Wall Ewing was convicted and sentenced in September 1946. His conviction was upheld by the North Carolina Supreme Court in June 1947. In between those dates, Lenward Hair committed his second murder. On 31 January 1947 Hair was charged with stabbing to death a nineteen-year-old soldier on the Lumberton Road. After being released from prison in 1940, Hair had moved with his family to Randleman, North Carolina, where he worked in the cement- or cinder-block business. Upon his return to Fayetteville for a visit in January 1947 he met up with Joe Scoggins and Mrs. Augusta Nichols. Hair took them down the Lumberton Road in his car and ran into a ditch. Three soldiers stopped to help. When the men pushed the car out of the ditch, it wouldn't start. Mrs. Nichols walked away, apparently in disgust. Hair followed her and knocked her out. The soldiers revived her and told Hair to leave her alone. One of the soldiers was Pfc. Lawrence Simmons of Ashville, Alabama. Simmons and Hair got into an argument, and Hair stabbed him with a pocketknife, causing the soldier to bleed to death on the spot. After the fight, everybody but Hair seems to have fled the scene. Police claimed that they found him under his car asleep, while he said that he was checking the gas lines and trying to start his car. He admitted to them that he had drunk a little beer and whiskey.

On 12 February a coroner's jury recommended that Hair be charged with second-degree murder and held without bond. That recommendation was not honored. After conferring with Judge Q. K. Nimocks, Coroner Joe Pinkston set bond at $10,000, and the bond was signed by Dr. L. G. Hair. The coroner's jury, meanwhile, had failed to write the cause of death or the person responsible and had to be reconvened in order to do it.

Hair's trial for murdering Pfc. Simmons got under way on 6 March 1947. Jim Nance, assisted by H. E. Stacy of Lumberton, defended Hair, while Ertyle Carlyle led the prosecution. The case was tried in the court of Judge W. H. S. Burgwyn.

Called to the stand by the prosecution, Private Orval Dillon said that Hair had struck the first blow and knocked Simmons down. When he, Dillon, saw blood on Simmons's clothes, he got a beer bottle and hit Hair in the head, he said. Then he ran from the scene and did not see what Private Clarence Fine, the third solider, did.

Testifying for the defense, Joe Scoggins, who had been in the car with Hair, said that he didn't know who hit first. He saw no weapons, he claimed, except a brick in Private Fine's hand and a beer bottle in Dillon's.

Called to the stand in his own defense, Hair said, "All three of the soldiers had jumped on me and I had been knocked down. One of them was kicking me, and I had been cut. I got my knife out and cut him on the leg. I didn't want to kill him. I wanted to make him stop kicking me."

In spite of the fact that Lenward Hair was defended by two of the best criminal defense attorneys in North Carolina, the jury did not buy his claim of self-defense. Instead, it took only three hours to find Hair guilty of manslaughter on 8 March 1947, and Judge Burgwyn sentenced him to seven-to-fifteen years. His lawyers appealed to the North Carolina Supreme Court, and bond was set at $10,000. Apparently the appeal was quickly dropped, for Hair went to Central Prison on 15 March to begin serving his time. Interestingly, his sentence was commuted to three years on 21 December 1948, and on 15 March 1949—two years to the day after he began his confinement, Hair walked out the prison door. Once again, one is left to wonder about the workings of the justice system in North Carolina. For the right people, and perhaps the right amount of money, minimum jail time, even for murder, is obtainable.

Several people have told me that Lenward Hair went on to kill two more people. I have been unable to confirm this. Supposedly he killed someone in Texarkana, Texas, and he did break into a woman's home on Sapona Road, across the Cape Fear from Fayetteville, in April 1963 and hit her in the head with a baseball bat. Whether or not she died, I have been unable to discover. Nor do I have any proof concerning the person he allegedly killed in Texas. I do know that after 1949 he lived in Fayetteville at several different addresses—North Kennedy Street and Glenville Avenue—and then disappeared, following the incident on Sapona Road, from the city directory. I know that in his later years he lived across the Cape Fear on a farm purchased some years earlier by his father and that he died in Highsmith-Rainey Hospital in Fayetteville on 4 June 1995, reportedly of cancer, and that his obituary said he was a "retired farmer," a member of First Baptist Church, and a "past chairman of Vander Voting Precinct." One of the ministers who conducted his graveside service was my mother's pastor for thirty years.

As it turned out the oldest son of "Old Dr. Hair" was not his only worry. In 1950, when various citizens from Fayetteville were working hard to get Wall Ewing released from prison and after Lenward had recently been paroled, Dr. Hair was moving heaven and earth again to get another son out of the penitentiary. This time it was Raymond, the third of his four sons. Just before the Christmas break at Wake Forest College in 1949, Raymond murdered a fellow student named Roy Coble.

On the night of 15 December, Coble, age twenty, was found unconscious in a wrecked car on the campus of the small Baptist college. A bloody, snub-nosed pistol loaded with dum-dum bullets was found under the front seat of the car. Coble had been hit in the head with a bullet fired from that gun, and the wound soon proved fatal. The wrecked vehicle, a 1946 Oldsmobile, belonged to twenty-three-year-old Raymond Hair of Fayetteville. After the car crashed into a wall, the police arrested Hair for drunken driving, not knowing that Coble was slumped over in the car.

When they discovered the fatally wounded student, their attention was diverted, and Hair fled the scene. Police used bloodhounds to trail him to the Durham highway, but there the dogs lost the scent. Hair was soon sought in a three-state manhunt—North Carolina, Georgia, and Pennsylvania—where he was known to have relatives. Rumor had it that he had gone to Raleigh and bought a Greyhound bus ticket to Fayetteville. Eventually the manhunt was extended to the entire nation.

Hair's parents retained a Raleigh attorney, J. William Bunn, to represent Raymond. The attorney promised to notify the police if he or the parents learned of the fugitive's whereabouts.

For twenty-eight days Fayetteville-born Raymond Hair was the object of a coast-to-coast manhunt. Finally, he was caught in Los Angeles, California, where he was living under an alias. Brought back to North Carolina, young Hair went to trial on 5 April 1950 in Raleigh. Judge Clawson Williams of Sanford presided.

There was no eyewitness to the shooting. The only story available was the one Hair had to tell. He was at the mercy of a jury of twelve men, one of them a black school principal. He had to convince them that Coble's death was an accident, not murder. He told how both he and Coble were drinking and got into an argument over a gambling debt. He said that Coble pulled the pistol and that the two fought over it. The pistol finally went off after it had exchanged hands several times. Since the gun ended up in Hair's hand—after the shot was fired, he claimed—he got scared, put the pistol under the seat, and fled as soon as he could get away from the police.

The jury was not convinced, and for good reason. An autopsy had shown no alcohol in Coble's system. Lying about that no doubt tainted the rest of Hair's story, leaving the jury no recourse but to find him guilty. Judge Williams instructed the jurors that they could find Hair guilty of first-degree murder, first-degree murder with mercy (which carried a mandatory life sentence), second-degree murder, manslaughter, or they could find him innocent. The state sought a conviction of murder in the first degree.

On Easter Sunday 1950 Raymond Hair was convicted of second-degree murder and sentenced to 25-to-30 years in prison. As sentenced was pronounced, Raymond sat silent and crestfallen. His mother did not weep, but she was "visibly shaken." My aunt and uncle, Vara and Milton Holmes, lived in Raleigh at the time, and they went to the courthouse that Sunday.

They knew the Hairs and spoke to Dr. and Mrs. Hair as that sad couple left the courtroom.

But all was not lost. The North Carolina justice system had been generous to the Hairs twice already, and it would be again. In June 1952 Governor Kerr Scott was in a particularly generous mood. He granted Wall Ewing a parole and reduced Hair's sentence to 20-to-25 years. Becoming even more generous on the eve of leaving office in January 1953, Scott released Ewing from his parole and further reduced Hair's sentence to 15-to-20 years. This meant that, with time off for good behavior, Raymond Hair would be able to walk out of prison before very long. He did exactly that, being released on parole on 19 December 1955. He had served a little more than five years of a much longer sentence.

In 1939 Lenward Hair had killed Willis Genes and gone to prison briefly for it. Ten years later, Raymond Hair had killed Roy Coble seventy miles from his Fayetteville home and had entered Central Prison in the spring of 1950. Meanwhile, Lenward Hair had killed again and had left Central Prison a year before his younger brother began serving his sentence. Also, Wall Ewing, a very prominent man in Fayetteville, had gone to prison for beating his wife to death. Fayetteville was beginning to look like a town that bred murderers, but there were many positive things about the place, too, as the forties ended. Though having experienced the effects of war, a huge riot by soldiers, a significant increase in prostitution, and the departure of Sheriff N. H. McGeachy from office after forty years—along with murders committed by prominent citizens—Fayetteville came through the forties in good fashion. In fact, those tumultuous years, which featured the biggest war that the world had ever known (the war that made Fort Bragg the nation's most visible Army base), turned Fayetteville into a thriving boomtown. There was much to celebrate when that horribly destructive conflict ended, and there were adjustments to be made because of Fayetteville and Cumberland County's expanding population. The area took steps to capitalize on its new status, as new businesses, new organizations, and new forms of entertainment emerged to meet new needs. For five years there was peace and prosperity, and the Cape Fear area breathed a sigh of relief—in spite of those sensational murder cases that somewhat marred the city's image.

Not yet did the city know to take pride in the arrival of a new citizen in 1948, for it would be twelve more years before that new arrival, a young lawyer, would run for governor of North Carolina and win. The new citizen was Terry Sanford from Laurinburg, and he would go on to become a U.S. senator, and president of Duke University as well as governor of the state. Also, what had always been known as Fayetteville High School would eventually become Terry Sanford High School. No one could have known in 1948 what impact Terry Sanford's arrival in town would have. Nor did anyone know that a little more than two years after he came, the nation would be at war again and that the boom times of the early forties would return with full force. That would happen because, on 25 June 1950, the communist regime in North Korea would invade South Korea for the purpose of uniting the entire Korean peninsula under a communist government. President Harry Truman was determined to prevent that from happening and quickly committed American troops to prop up and save the South Korean government of President Syngman Rhee. It was war again, and in Fayetteville—because of Fort Bragg—the early fifties would seem like a repeat of the early forties.

Part Two

Introduction

Except for 1941–1945, the years 1901 to 1951 along the Cape Fear were definitely quieter than would be the last fifty years of the twentieth century. Fayetteville had been a tranquil little town when the nineteenth century ended. It was surrounded largely by cotton farms until tobacco came into its own a few years later, but it was still decades later before the town would move from a place dependent upon agriculture to one dependent upon the Fort Bragg payroll and finally, to a considerable extent, on manufacturing. The first five decades saw plenty of crime, most of it related to drunkenness and prostitution. Occasionally there were sensational murder cases. The ones that claimed the headlines of the newspapers, however, could be numbered on a person's ten fingers. Less than that number have been examined in detail so far.

There was no Fort Bragg until 1918 and after, and it grew slowly until World War II. That Fayetteville might have remained a small town, growing slowly but steadily—if World War II had not happened—is more than possible. Indeed, it is likely that such would have been the case. World War II provided great impetus to expansion in the Cape Fear region. Then came the Korean Conflict and after that the Vietnam War. In other words, before the area could get over war in the forties, war came again in the early fifties. Then in less than ten years after we extricated ourselves from Korea, we were in Vietnam, and that war went on as long or longer than the other two before it combined. Our country was at war, off and on, for almost thirty-five years. That meant countless soldiers coming and going at Fort Bragg. Many came and stayed, once their tours of duty were up. All of this changed the size of Fayetteville and the culture of the region.

Fayetteville achieved more and more recognition as it expanded, acquiring new hospitals, shopping malls, and even a television station. Some of the most celebrated people in the country, indeed in the world, came to Fayetteville and Fort Bragg—Presidents John F. Kennedy, Lyndon Johnson, and Jimmy Carter, entertainers Elvis Presley, Bob Hope, and Louis "Satchmo" Armstrong, movie stars John Wayne and Audie Murphy, presidential candidate Ronald Reagan, evangelist Billy Graham and many others. Also during the postwar years, industry started moving into Fayetteville—Rohm and Haas, Black & Decker, DuPont, and the biggest of them all was the Kelly-Springfield Tire plant. The city and the county were metamorphosing in the fifties and following from the rural world of yesterday to a modern industrial world. Jobs were coming in and there were people to take them. The growth and expansion did not go on uninterrupted, however. There were economic slowdowns, but the trend was up, and the boom years outnumbered the lean years, as the population continued to explode.

Because there were more people, there had to be more houses, more businesses, more services, and, yes, more crime. Even more murders. And the new murders were far more sensational than the previous ones. Outside of the Cape Fear region, few people ever knew that Marshall Williams shot and killed Deputy Sheriff Al Pate in 1921 until many years later when Williams became famous as the inventor of the M-1 carbine. Even then, thanks to Hollywood distortions, most people thought he had killed a federal agent. As for Lenward Hair's murder of Officer Willis Genes, news of that deed hardly received mention outside Cumberland County. The first murder along the Cape Fear that was heard about around the world was that of Ricky Monsour, following his death at the hands of a former cab driver in December 1954. News about Ricky spread rapidly because of Fort Bragg, for hundreds of soldiers from the base had swilled beer in his bar and had made friends with him. When they heard that Ricky had been killed, these soldier-friends notified other friends who had left Bragg, and those friends in turn notified others until the news had reached all the places on earth where former Bragg soldiers had been transferred.

Yet, no murders along the Cape Fear, before or since, have ever been as publicized as the "MacDonald murders" that occurred in early 1970, the last year of the 1960s decade. On 17 February 1970 the pregnant wife and two young daughters of Green Beret Captain Jeffrey MacDonald were found murdered in the MacDonald home at Fort Bragg. MacDonald, a doctor, received injuries and went to the hospital. He claimed that a group of drugged out Hippies attacked him while murdering his family. MacDonald himself immediately came under suspicion, but he was not charged with the murders at that time. Ultimately, though, he was accused, indicted, tried, and convicted. Legal maneuvering kept his case in the news for more than fifteen years. A best-selling book called *Fatal Vision* was written about it, and the book was turned into a movie for television. Most

Americans who lived through those years, as well as many people around the world, became familiar with the name of Jeffrey MacDonald.

During some of the same years that the MacDonald case regularly made the news, the Velma Barfield case also received an abundance of publicity. In the course of her trial it was revealed that she had poisoned her late husband, a man for whom she was a caretaker, and her mother, but it was for poisoning her fiancé that she was convicted and sentenced to die in December 1978. After a long series of appeals, she was executed in November 1984. MacDonald was high profile because he was military, a Green Beret officer, and a doctor, and he was convicted of murdering his own wife and children. Velma Barfield achieved her notoriety because she, too, murdered her kin and because she was the first woman executed in North Carolina in forty years and the first in the United States in twenty-two years.

Crime climbed to new heights along the Cape Fear at the time MacDonald and Barfield were constantly in the news. In 1972 ten murders were committed in Cumberland County during June and July alone. That was an all-time high for the county. When asked why there were so many killings, Sheriff Nig Clark said that part of the reason was that the U.S. Supreme Court had banned the death penalty. Whether the sheriff was right or not is debatable, but the picture did not soon improve. In November 1975, an FBI crime report ranked Fayetteville fifth nationally in violent crimes during 1974. Ahead of the burgeoning little city on the Cape Fear were New York, Miami, Baltimore, and Detroit. As much as Fayetteville had grown in recent years, it was still just a spot in the road compared to the four cities that were ahead of it in violent crimes. I had left Fayetteville long before 1975, but I was always in and out of town, and I know that many folks constantly muttered something like "It's because of Fort Bragg."

The murders mentioned above are only the most publicized of the acts of violence in Fayetteville and its vicinity. There were other killings, too—especially in the 1980s and 1990s—that were sensational and gruesome. In due course the reader will come to know about Norris Taylor, the Golphin brothers, Mark Edward Thompson, Jeffrey K. Meyer, and Kenneth Junior French—murderers all but not soldiers all.

Chapter 6

More War, More Murder: The 1950s

From the bottom of Haymount Hill to the Market House, Hay Street was alive with thriving businesses in 1951. There were restaurants, theaters, hotels, numerous clothing and department stores (the largest of which was Sears, Roebuck & Company), 5-and-10-cent stores, banks, the offices of the *Fayetteville Observer*, a few beer joints, several pool halls, and a host of other establishments. No one could have guessed that during the fifties downtown Fayetteville would peak and begin a gradual slide toward decadence. As suburbs sprang up like wild onions around town, businesses moved away from the main drag into shopping centers that were built near the new suburbs. Eutaw Village Shopping Center, the first of many such places, emerged in 1955. Located on Bragg Boulevard near Greenwood Homes, it opened with twelve stores. Soon there was another shopping center, and then another. By the 1980s, only a few of the old businesses remained on Hay Street, as empty buildings and topless bars replaced the earlier establishments, many of which had folded, while others had moved to one of the numerous shopping centers. Some of the later ones made Eutaw look small by comparison. Finally, the sprawling Cross Creek Mall, off the Highway 401 bypass, overshadowed all of them.

In Fayetteville and at Fort Bragg during the early fifties it was a little like World War II all over again. This time, however, no war was declared by the U.S. Congress. President Harry Truman sent troops into South and North Korea and never asked for a declaration of war. Hence, we became mired in the mud and ice of Korea in what became known as the "Korean Conflict," which some people designated a "police action." Whatever it was called, it had the same effect—albeit on a smaller scale—on Fayetteville and Fort Bragg that the huge war just before it had had. Once again, soldiers from across the nation passed through Fort Bragg, and in the wake of the human tide that inundated Cumberland County there was tremendous expansion in population and commerce along the banks of the Cape Fear. At the end of the decade, in 1960, Fayetteville, according to the Federal Census, had 46,743 residents. Since 1940, after two wars, Cumberland

County had registered a population growth of 52.7 percent, making it the fastest growing county in North Carolina.

Just as the 1950s was a defining decade for Fayetteville and vicinity, it was for me, too. I began the decade as a teenager. By the time it was over, I had graduated from Fayetteville High School and Baylor University, had married my high school sweetheart, and had become a father, all in the span of ten years. The fifties marked the end of my intimate relationship with Fayetteville, for when I moved away in 1959, I was to return no more, except to visit. Still, because my parents and other family members continued to live there and because my wife's parents remained, I visited frequently and continued to be interested in what was happening in my hometown. When it came to the latest murders, I was quickly told all about them by family members, who abhorred the continuing evil influence of Fort Bragg. The murder case featured in this chapter, though, concerns Ricky Monsour, who was shot and beaten to death in his own house, not by a soldier but by an unemployed cab driver. Ricky met his unfortunate end in 1954, my senior year in high school.

Those first four years of the 1950s were among the most memorable of my life. In 1951 I became an usher at the Colony Theater and worked at that job for two years before taking a job at the Commercial and Industrial Bank, just next door to the theater. As I neared my sixteenth birthday, I tried to pass for eighteen so I could enter the pool hall known as Brunswick Billiards, which was operated by a man named George Green. I never knew for sure what George's country of origin was, but it was plain that he was a foreigner. He spoke with a heavy accent. A number of people said he was a Greek. George didn't seem to care if I hung out in the poolroom as long as the police gave him no trouble about it. Whenever a policeman started in the front door, somebody would announce it. In a flash all of us "illegals" were out the back door.

As I continued to hang out and shoot more pool, I became a pretty good "stick," as the saying went, shooting what some considered a mean game of pool. A number of people thought I was the best in high school, but that wasn't true. Reese Bullard, who was a year or two older than I was, was a better player. Not in Reese's class, but probably in mine, was Jerry Richardson, one of our high school football heroes and later owner of the pro-football team known as the Carolina Panthers. I heard that Jerry got rich by means of his interest in a chain of hamburger restaurants after a heralded career in college and pro football. Except for catching a glimpse of him on television occasionally, I have not seen Jerry in almost fifty years.

Besides us wannabe pool hustlers, Fayetteville drew a goodly number of pool "sharks" from out of town. They always came to town at the end of the month, around payday at Fort Bragg. Everybody knew they were there to lure soldiers into shooting pool for money. I came to know a few of these out-of-town sharks. Two that I remember vividly were "Goldsboro Jack" and the "Fairmont Kid." "Goldsboro," as everyone called him, was a big, friendly man with a noticeable harelip. Although good with the cue stick, he was not in "Fairmont's" class. But, then, nobody else was either. The kid from Fairmont was in his early twenties. He had a round face and wore his hair in a crew cut and usually had an unlit cigar butt stuck in the corner of his mouth. Few of the guys who knew him dared take him on at any game of billiards. Those who did always wished they hadn't. The story was that the "Kid's" father owned a country store in or near Fairmont, a small town on the North Carolina/South Carolina border about forty-five miles south of Fayetteville. As a small boy, the "Kid"—I never heard anybody use his real name and have no idea what it was—had started shooting pool on the pool table in his father's store. Not only was he a natural, he never missed a day chalking up his cue stick and either practicing or playing. Simply put, he was the best I ever saw play. That is saying a lot, because I saw some excellent players, some of whom I thought could have held their own with the likes of Minnesota Fats and Willie Mosconi.

The Fayetteville poolrooms were not without their own local hotshots either. Two of the best were Billy Morris, who hung out at Brunswick Billiards, and L. D. Godwin, who usually played at Wellons Pool Hall. All of these people, the local sharks as well as the out-of-towners, were always on the lookout for "suckers," and soldiers from Fort Bragg were the most likely to fit that category. Occasionally there was a soldier from Fort Bragg who could hold his own with the hustlers, but there weren't many. During the Korean conflict, quite a few of the soldiers who passed through Fort Bragg lost some of their money in Fayetteville pool halls.

I met a lot of characters at Brunswick Billiards. I became friends with the two "rack boys," Herb and LeRoy. I can't recall their last names. Both were black, one dark and one light of skin. I also came to know many of the customers who hung out or passed through the place. I recall talking to one fellow many times. I knew him as Glen, but have no recollection of his last name. He was young—mid-to-late twenties—and handsome with his crew cut and perfect athletic build. I can still see him sitting on the bench near the front of the poolroom, drinking beer and pretending to be a tough guy. A graduate of Georgia Tech, he was an engineer who was working on a building project at Fort Bragg. He had me believing that he would fight anybody in the place, if anybody gave him any trouble. It was a big surprise to me when I found out he was a homosexual, a term no one used then. To everybody I knew, homosexuals were "queers." The way I found out about Glen's sexual orientation was a bit unusual. One of my best friends at that time was Corbett McMillan. Corbett gave Glen a ride one night, and Glen propositioned him. Furious, Corbett threw him out of the car after Glen begged him not to tell me about the incident. Glen was almost desperate, Corbett said, to keep me from finding out that he was a homosexual. Corbett promised he wouldn't tell and meant to keep the promise, but one night it slipped out that he had encountered a "queer." Hounding him about it, I wore Corbett down until he gave me a hint. The hint was enough to enable me to guess who the "queer" was and I really had a hard time believing that this guy whose build and swagger could have enabled him to play Tarzan in the movies was one of those presumed "sissified" men about whom I had only heard. To my knowledge, Glen was the first homosexual with whom I had ever carried on a conversation. In those days, such people usually stayed in the closet and only cautiously revealed their orientation to straights that might be receptive to their advances.

All sorts of men and no women came and went at Brunswick Billiards. Frequently in and out of the place was Ricky Monsour, but I never saw him shoot pool. I did see him bet on others who were shooting, and I heard that he was a big-time gambler. Just a few doors from the poolroom, he ran an establishment known as Ricky's Food Store. Actually, he sold more beer and wine than anything else, and he ultimately converted his business into Rick's Bar, just about a year before he was murdered. I have previously described Ricky as reminding me of Groucho Marx.

Ricky was not the only Monsour in town. I was told that the Monsours were Syrians, and they certainly looked Middle Eastern with their coal-black hair and swarthy complexions. Apparently a whole group of Monsours moved into Fayetteville around 1924, hoping to cash in on the flush times of the Roaring Twenties. Listed in the 1924 city directory were Faris S., Isaac, Joseph S., Samuel, and Solomon Monsour. All resided at 718 Lumberton Road, and all were listed as grocers. In 1946 there was an Eli Monsour who owned Monsour's Bar at 473 Hay Street, but two years later the place was called the Horseshoe Bar & Grill, and Faris Monsour was listed as the owner. This establishment was immediately next door to Ricky's Food Store. Eventually, Ricky established another such place called "Chrisy's Food Store" at 131 Maxwell Street. Run by his wife Evelyn, Chrisy's, like Ricky's, was more of a wine and beer store than a food store. Chrisy's was the place where Evelyn Monsour met a man named Robert Williams and came to know him too well. Her alleged involvement with Williams would lead to Ricky's death.

Even though the Korean conflict had raged and exciting things had happened in Fayetteville in the four years leading up to Ricky's murder, there were few events as sensational as his untimely demise. There was a long list of normal, though unspectacular, developments. For instance, Horace Sisk, the longtime racist city superintendent of schools, retired in 1951. Then, too, women joined the police force for the first time that same year, and the police began using a device called the "whammy" to catch speeders. I well remember the two wires that were laid about ten yards apart across streets and highways. People quickly knew to be on the lookout for them and to slam on brakes when seeing them. Usually, the operator of the electrical device called the "whammy" was hidden somewhere near the road, looking at a box that registered one's speed when he or she ran over the wires. In January 1952 the first speeder was convicted in Fayetteville with evidence recorded by the "whammy."

The year 1952 was notable for several other developments and events. The Hamont Theater burned down in March, ironically just after 213 moviegoers had been watching the movie called *The Flame of Araby*. In April the city sponsored Babe Ruth Day, and Ruth's widow unveiled a marker on Gillespie Street at the spot where the King of Swat had hit his first homerun as a professional player. Baseball luminaries Connie Mack, Johnnie Allen, and Bill Dickey were on hand for the occasion. April 1952 was a month to remember, for it was also the month that "Carbine" Williams Day was held, featuring the world premiere of the movie about the firearms inventor's life.

Excitement of a different kind came in the summer when three luminous disks, believed to be UFOs, were reportedly seen over the city. This was widely discussed, but no satisfactory explanation was ever given—at least none that satisfied all Fayettevillians. There were those who actually believed UFOs were spacecraft from outer space. Most, however, thought that those who professed to have sighted the objects were perhaps inebriated or a bit "touched in the head." Apparently very few citizens believed that an attack by visitors from outer space was imminent.

November 1952 saw Fayetteville make some political news when local attorney Terry Sanford won a seat in the North Carolina senate. Probably no one suspected at the time that Sanford would later be elected governor of the state and go on to national prominence. Sanford remains the most noteworthy political figure to come out of Fayetteville in the twentieth century.

Religion caused a bit of a stir along the Cape Fear in the early fifties. In 1952 a new version of the Bible, the Revised Standard Version, provoked a strong reaction from conservative ministers and others who had long been devoted to the King James Version. Ministers at three Fayetteville churches gave their unqualified endorsement to the new RSV after being asked about a Rocky Mount pastor's plan to burn a copy of that version because it changed the word "virgin" to "young woman" in a controversial passage in the book of Isaiah. The verse in Isaiah was generally interpreted as a prediction of the coming Messiah, who, according to the King James Version, would be born of a "virgin." To conservatives, changing the term to "young woman" in the new version was an attempt to deny the virgin birth of the coming Messiah. This controversy would go on for years, as Fundamentalists strapped on their ideological armor to combat what they perceived to be an attack on Christian orthodoxy by the forces of "Modernism" and "Neoorthodoxy." Eventually this struggle would bring about divisions in several denominations.

Nearly two years after the quarrel over the RSV, in September 1954, a delegation of twenty-five Baptist ministers, urged local authorities to close drive-in movies during Sunday church hours. They contended that "Sunday movies are immoral influences on young people." Although Fayetteville appeared to be falling more and more under secular influences, it was obvious that the forces of religion were not altogether intimidated and were quite willing to raise their voices in protest. A variety of Fundamentalist-oriented ministers would make plenty of noise in the next few years, as they loudly lamented the "worldliness" that was trying to take over the Cape Fear region.

Meanwhile, the Korean conflict began winding down in 1952 and 1953, coinciding with the ascendancy of Dwight David Eisenhower to the presidency of the United States. In May 1953 an American prisoner of war arrived in Fayetteville, where he was reunited with his parents. He was

Corporal William W. Smith, who had been held prisoner by the North Korean communists since November 1950. He was the first POW from the Korean conflict to arrive in Fayetteville following the cessation of hostilities. That the fighting was over and soldiers and POWs were coming home was cause for celebration.

Yet, as this another foreign conflict ended, the groundwork was being laid for a deep internal conflict that had been building up pressure in the bowels of American society for decades. The famous *Brown v. the Board of Education of Topeka* decision was handed down in May 1954 by the liberal U.S. Supreme Court presided over by controversial Chief Justice Earl Warren. In a nutshell, the decision declared racial segregation in the public schools of the nation to be unconstitutional, and it set off a social revolution committed to establishing civil rights for black Americans. Ironically, the Fayetteville City School Board had only recently decided to build two new high schools—one for white students and another for black ones. Population growth had made the old schools inadequate, but in laying out the plans for new schools the authorities demonstrated no awareness— despite the fact that President Truman had integrated the armed forces— that segregation was already coming under increasing attack by organizations like the NAACP. In June 1953 the city broke ground for a new white high school—Fayetteville High School—on the Fort Bragg Road. In August, on Seabrook Road, the city broke ground for the new E. E. Smith High School for black students. The two new schools were indicative of the racially divided dual school system—recognized as legal since 1896—that the U.S. Supreme Court would declare unconstitutional less than a year later.

Segregation was not limited just to the schools in Fayetteville. Many businesses were conspicuous for the absence of black faces. At seventeen I was employed at the Commercial and Industrial Bank, when, in April 1954, most of the male employees grew beards and most of the women wore old-fashioned dresses to participate in the celebration of Cumberland County's bicentennial. All of the bank's employees posed for a commemorative picture, which later appeared in the *Fayetteville Observer*. Of the twenty-four of us in that picture, none had a black face. My young face stands out, but almost undetectable in it are my youthfully thin sideburns and moustache, which I had tried so hard to grow. The point, however, is not the appearance of those who are in the picture. It is the fact that the Fayetteville workplace, at least in most banks and other prestigious establishments, was lily-white. There were plenty of black people in the area, of course, and their numbers—as did those of the whites—continued to climb. It would not be long before those black citizens insisted on their rights. A burgeoning city could not long expect to avoid the winds of change, especially after the *Brown* decision by the Supreme Court in May 1954.

Not only was Fayetteville outgrowing its old school buildings, it was outgrowing its old hospitals, too. In October 1953 ground was broken for the new Cape Fear Valley Hospital on Owen Drive. From a relatively small facility (yet much bigger than Pittman and Highsmith Hospitals), Cape Fear Valley Hospital would grow into a huge medical center before the century's end. At one point, I believe in the late sixties, its administrator was a Fayetteville man, Carl Strayhorn, who had been a close friend of mine in high school. Carl and I spent quite a few hours together studying Spanish as students in Miss Lee's Spanish I and II classes.

Not only Fayetteville, but Fort Bragg as well, was in need of more hospital facilities in the early fifties. In December 1954 Army officials announced the construction of Womack Army Hospital. This was to be an impressive new facility featuring 500 beds. It was in that hospital that Jeffrey MacDonald, sixteen years later, would spend nine days following the murders of his wife and daughters.

The year 1954 was memorable for another reason than the announcement about Womack Hospital. Mother Nature again hammered the Cape Fear region. In October, Hurricane Hazel slammed into the coasts of North and South Carolina and then moved inland. Cumberland County suffered extensive damage as winds gusted up to 125 miles per hour and 4.5 inches of rain fell. Fortunately, no residents of the county died, but some were injured. Hundreds of trees were pushed over and uprooted by the fierce winds. I recall going hunting along the Cape Fear River some weeks after the storm and seeing big trees with huge root systems fallen in all directions. I stood beside root systems measuring eight and ten feet in height, turned skyward from the ground by the mighty winds of Hazel. I remember standing in awe, as I looked and thought about how forceful those winds had been.

Two months and two days after Hazel moved up the Cape Fear River from the coast and roared through Fayetteville, Ricky Monsour, the forty-one-year-old owner of Rick's Bar, was beaten and shot to death in his own home at 207 Hillcrest Avenue. Shortly before midnight on Friday, 17 December Evelyn Monsour was awakened, she claimed, by a commotion downstairs in her home. Her story was that she rushed downstairs and saw a man on top of her husband. When her children, Ricky, nine, and Christine, seven, followed her downstairs and witnessed the fierce struggle between their father and a man they did not know, Evelyn took them back up, presumably for their safety. She did this at least twice. On her third trip down, she heard three shots ring out. Supposedly, she hit the "unidentified man" with a chair at this point, and he fled from the house. Evelyn then ran into the backyard and screamed for help. No one came. She returned to the house and tried to call the police, but she was too nervous to dial the telephone. Mortally wounded, Ricky told her to call 2-411. When she asked what number that was, he answered, "Police."

When the police arrived, Ricky, struggling to hold on to life, could not speak. He was asked to nod, if he knew who shot him. He nodded. Rushed to Highsmith Hospital, Frederick Solomon Monsour was pronounced dead by Dr. H. W. Miller.

Exactly what happened at 207 Hillcrest Avenue that night and why it happened will never be known. Two stories emerged. One was told by Evelyn Monsour, while another one, which was entirely different, was told by Robert Williams, the man ultimately caught and charged with Ricky's murder. Part of Mrs. Monsour's story is noted above, but there is more, much more.

First, however, consider the results of the police investigation. It was discovered that Ricky had left his bar on Friday night around 11:30 and had driven an employee home to Cross Creek Court. He then drove himself home and parked his car in the back of his house. Once inside the house he was shot at close range three times. One bullet struck him in the right side, while the other two hit him in the chest on the left side. Coroner Joe Pinkston said there were "dense" powder burns on Ricky's shirt. In addition to the bullet wounds, the body had several cuts. It was taken to North Carolina Memorial Hospital in Chapel Hill for an autopsy. After an intensive search for the murder weapon, the police found it—"a hefty six-inch-barreled Smith and Wesson revolver." Robert Williams had thrown it away at some point during his flight from the scene and had caught a taxi home. He was arrested on 18 December at his residence on Cool Spring Street, and little Christine Monsour, Ricky's seven-year-old daughter, positively identified Williams as the man she had seen on top of her father the night before. Why Monsour was killed was "shrouded in mystery," according to Police Chief L. F. Worrell, since there was no sign of a break-in and Ricky had $612 in his pocket. Robbery as a motive was obviously ruled out. Beyond these few facts, the police had to rely on the conflicting stories of Evelyn Monsour and Robert Williams.

Both Williams and Monsour changed their stories several times. Williams was a twenty-eight-year-old former cab driver and the father of two children. He was divorced from two wives. Several months before his arrest on 18 December, he was convicted of aiding and abetting prostitution. On 21 December, three days after his arrest, Williams confessed to the killing. He said that Monsour picked him up on Hay Street between 11:30 and 11:45 p.m. and took him to the Monsour residence. Once there, Ricky accused Williams of having an affair with his wife Evelyn. An argument ensued and Ricky brandished a blackjack and a gun. Williams grabbed the gun and, during a struggle for it, it went off. Then Williams took it away from Ricky and fired two bullets into him. At this juncture Williams emphatically denied any "intimacies" with Mrs. Monsour, but he soon altered his story on that and other points.

Williams insisted on making all his admissions in the presence of Mrs. Monsour, her brother Al Bahouth, Coroner Joe Pinkston, Chief L. F. Worrell, several detectives, and Judge Seavy Carroll, who had fined Williams $300 in the recent prostitution case. He admitted to having known Mrs. Monsour for some time, ever since she had operated the wine, beer, and grocery store at the corners of Maxwell and Franklin Streets, but he still steadfastly denied "being familiar" with her at anytime. Only later would he admit to having an affair, and Mrs. Monsour remained adamant in denying a relationship of any kind with Williams. At first the former cabbie claimed that he was in the Monsour home moving some furniture at Ricky's request on the afternoon before the murder. When Evelyn denied this, Williams retracted his statement. She claimed that he came that night trying to borrow money, but she had refused to lend him any. Since she claimed to have hit Williams with a chair during the fight and knew him well, one had to wonder why she was unable to identify him—especially in view of the fact that her seven-year-old daughter had no trouble making a positive identification. Williams said that he didn't believe she got close enough to get a good look at him. When Evelyn finally did admit that she had recognized Williams, she claimed she refused to identify him because she was afraid that, if she did, he might return and hurt her children.

After being charged with murder, Williams waived a preliminary hearing and was transferred to the county jail to await indictment by the grand jury. The state asked for an indictment of first-degree murder and got it from the grand jury on 17 January 1955. A special venire resulted in jurors from Robeson County being brought in to help insure a fair trial. Judge Henry L. Stevens, Jr. presided over the case, while Malcolm Seawell, assisted by heralded local attorney Jim Nance, served as prosecutor. Williams's defense attorney was Lacy Hair.

The Williams trial did not last long, but some confusing tales were told and much conflicting testimony was heard from the witness stand during the proceedings. During their respective testimonies, Evelyn Monsour and Robert Williams contradicted each other at every turn. Williams had changed his story considerably with regard to his and Mrs. Monsour's relationship. Indeed, they had been lovers, he asserted. In fact, he insisted, he had made love to her many times. He said, "I love her. I'd do anything in my power to save her from embarrassment." He went further, "I worship the very ground she walks on. I am not trying to smear her. I tried to plead guilty to manslaughter so I wouldn't have to come here and bring Mrs. Monsour into it." Suggesting a motive for Mrs. Monsour's alleged infidelity, Williams said that she complained to him that Ricky lost too much money "on the races and numbers racket." On the other hand, Williams claimed to have gotten money from Mrs. Monsour totaling between $600 and $900. He said he had "never seen a woman yet that wouldn't give me money when I wanted it."

Through it all Williams stuck to the story that Ricky picked him up on Hay Street close to midnight on 17 December, took him home with him, and confronted him about the affair with his wife. When Ricky began brandishing a blackjack and a pistol, he said that he was taking Williams upstairs and that the two of them and Evelyn were going to have it out. Williams claimed he tried to leave, and the fight broke out.

Mrs. Monsour denied everything, again insisting that she did not immediately identify Williams out of fear that he might harm her children. She emphatically denied a love affair with Williams, but admitted that he hounded her for money and that he was at the house on the night of the murder for that purpose. This Williams denied. Little Christine Monsour said that she had never seen Williams at her house before the night that he killed her father.

The prosecuting attorneys scoffed at Williams's story, and Jim Nance said he showed a "reckless disregard for womanhood." Judge Stevens, indicating some skepticism of both stories, declared, "No one will ever know exactly what happened, but I believe he [Williams] was there at 9:30 and overstayed his time when old man Monsour came home. It adds up to a dead man killed by a wife robber. Your sins have overcome you."

On the second day of the trial, 19 January 1955, Williams's attorney, Lacy Hair, entered a plea of guilty to murder in the second degree on his client's behalf. The plea was accepted by the state, and Judge Stevens promptly sentenced Williams to thirty years in prison. Thus ended a "he-said-she-said" murder case, and the truth of it will remain forever shrouded in mystery. After the trial ended, Evelyn Monsour's name could not be found in the city directory. Presumably, she left town.

Ricky Monsour was the first person I knew personally who became a murder victim. He and I were certainly not friends or even familiar acquaintances. We saw each other fairly often at Brunswick Billiards, and we spoke when we saw each other. I also saw his wife Evelyn a number of times, but not nearly as often as I saw Ricky. Evelyn was a veritable beauty, a woman who would turn the heads of most men. I remember her as appearing aloof, not the friendly sort. Of course, I can think of no reason why she should have been friendly with a teenage boy who admired her looks and thought Ricky was pretty lucky to be going to bed with that woman every night.

I didn't go to the trial; I just read about it in the *Fayetteville Observer*. As in the case of some other murders, I knew people who were involved. I have already noted that I knew Jim Nance personally, and Seavy Carroll, who fined Robert Williams when he was convicted of aiding and abetting prostitution, was a cherished friend of mine for many years. During Seavy's first political race, a boy named Billy Guy and I had handed out campaign literature for Mr. Carroll. It was many years later before I addressed him by his first name. He was elected to a judgeship on several different occasions. More than once he helped me land a job during holidays and summers when I was in college. He was as good a man as I ever knew, but I was surprised when he married relatively late in life, began a family, and went off with his wife Virginia and their children to Rhodesia, where they served for several years as Methodist missionaries. After he came back, Seavy was once more elected judge. On a number of occasions when I returned to Fayetteville, I visited with his family, and his children and mine played together. I was deeply saddened by his death, which occurred well short of his seventieth year. The coroner, Joe Pinkston, was also a friend of mine. His oldest son, also named Joe, was a classmate of mine in high school.

When I first met Mr. Pinkston, he ran a paint and wallpaper store on Hay Street. Occasionally I dropped in at the store and said hello, since I walked by it almost everyday and since he had once helped me get an invitation to attend a luncheon at which University of North Carolina football hero Charlie "Choo Choo" Justice was the speaker.

None of the other people connected with Ricky's murder and trial were friends of mine, but I knew Malcolm Seawell on sight, and everybody knew Police Chief Worrell on sight. He was police chief for many years, and his picture was constantly in the newspaper. Although I didn't know him, I vaguely remember seeing Al Bahouth, Evelyn Monsour's brother, a few times. Why Williams insisted on having him present when he confessed to the murder and told his "first" story is a mystery to me.

Less than a month after the trial that resulted in Robert Williams going to prison for murdering Ricky, my family moved from Robeson Street to Catawba Street. My maternal grandmother had died in September 1954, and she had left her house on Mechanic Street (the one built by my great-grandfather in 1890) to my mother, who, it was understood, would look after my grandfather. My mother sold the house, and we bought a house in the new section of Fayetteville called Greenwood Homes, just a few blocks off Bragg Boulevard and behind where Eutaw Village Shopping Center would soon be built. For the first time in my life, my mother, father, sister, and I lived in a brick house. For the next nine years—until his death in 1963—my grandfather would live in it with my mother and father. I would soon be in and out, while my sister would marry and leave home in 1958. A few months after we made the move to 1917 Catawba, I graduated from Fayetteville High School. In the fall of 1955 I went away to college. At the time I did, I fully intended to become a flaming evangelist—the next Billy Graham. But education changed my perspective enormously, causing me to land in the college classroom as a history professor.

So many things of interest happened in Fayetteville in the last few years of that decade. On 29 August 1955 the city got its own television station when WFLB-TV went on the air. The station was on Bragg Boulevard and its programs were seen on channel 18, a UHF (Ultra High Frequency) band. Among those who managed the station were Bill Belche and Bill Bailey. I knew Belche and talked to him many times, and Bill Bailey was my next-door neighbor on Catawba Street. Besides locally produced programs, the station aired such network shows as "Arthur Godfrey's Talent Scouts" and "The Howdy Doody Show." Unable to compete with the VHF (Very High Frequency) stations, WFLB-TV went off the air after three years, but it continued operating as a radio station.

The year 1955 also witnessed the first Salk vaccine polio shots being given to Cumberland County children by local physicians. First and second graders were the first to receive them. Along with this significant medical advance, came demands for a similar advance in race relations. The NAACP petitioned both the city and county school boards, demanding integration of the public schools. The demand was made just a few months after the two new high schools, E. E. Smith for black students and Fayetteville High School for white students, had been dedicated. My class was the first to be graduated from the new Fayetteville High School. There was not a black face in our graduating class. The Fayetteville school board apparently had no intention of integrating the city schools until forced to do so.

The new high schools were indicative of the vast growth that Fayetteville had already experienced and would continue to experience during the next five years. The city had attempted in vain to persuade a new Presbyterian college, St. Andrews, to locate there, but instead the school was built in Laurinburg, about forty or so miles southwest of Fayetteville. Despite the disappointment of failing to land St. Andrews, the city fathers persisted in their efforts to bring another college to town and ultimately brought in Methodist College, which opened its doors to students on the Raleigh Road in September 1960. Terry Sanford was chairman of the new college's board of trustees, and Dr. L. Stacy Weaver was the school's first president. In the mind of Dr. R. L. Pittman, one of Fayetteville biggest real estate developers, the coming of Methodist College was "the greatest thing that has happened in Fayetteville in our time." The city had long had the black school known as Fayetteville State Teachers College on the Murchison Road and another small educational institution known as Worth Business College, which had quite a reputation for teaching Speedwriting shorthand. In 1959 the small business school moved from its location on Gillespie Street, where it had been for thirty-five years, to 724 Hay Street, just across the street from Highsmith Hospital. Thus, by the end of the decade, when Methodist College opened its doors in 1960, Fayetteville was on the educational map, at least in North Carolina.

Along with the new educational institution and the long-established ones, the area also benefited from new medical facilities when Cape Fear Valley Hospital was dedicated in June 1956, and Womack Hospital at Fort

Bragg opened in August 1958. Womack was named in honor of a North Carolina soldier, Pfc. Bryant H. Womack of Rutherford County. Pfc. Womack, an army medic and Medal of Honor winner for his heroism in Korea, was killed during the conflict while serving on a night patrol. His parents, Mr. and Mrs. George Womack, were on hand to see the hospital dedicated.

There were just so many signs of growth and of Fayetteville's becoming a place of many attractions and a city on the move. During the single month of January 1957 the 82nd Airborne Memorial War Museum opened at Fort Bragg, the Fayetteville Symphony Orchestra was formed, and the *Fayetteville Observer* published its first Sunday edition. Two months later Fayetteville became the headquarters for the North Carolina Natural Gas Company. In June, Beth Israel Synagogue broke ground for its new synagogue building on Morganton Road. At the end of the year, in December, Fayetteville annexed Massey Hill, a suburb where the area's several mills were located.

Along with all of these signs of growth and development came additional shopping centers. The Eutaw Village Shopping Center proved very successful commercially, and in 1959 announcements were made that two new shopping centers would soon make their appearance. One was Tallywood on the Raeford Road, and the other was Bordeaux, located very near the Cape Fear Valley Hospital.

On the sports scene not much happened in Fayetteville during the fifties. There were a couple of notable exceptions, however. The Fayetteville Bulldogs won the AAA Eastern football championship in 1956. They ended up as co-state champions when they played Greensboro to a 7-7 tie in the state championship game. Then, in 1958, Fayetteville native Ray Floyd, at age fifteen, won the Fayetteville Junior Golf Tournament. Floyd went on to become a famous golfer on the national professional tour. Two years after Ray Floyd distinguished himself as an up-and-coming golfer, Don Clayton, Fayetteville football hero of yesteryear, launched his company to manufacture the materials and equipment for the construction of putt-putt golf courses.

Although sports seemed to be in a lull during the fifties, there was plenty of entertainment news. In 1957 the Highland Players organized and staged their first production, a melodrama entitled *Dirty Work at the Crossroads*. A year later Andy Griffith, a North Carolinian who had launched a career as a comedian and an actor a few years earlier, arrived in

Fayetteville. He appeared at the Colony Theater to promote his new movie called *No Time for Sergeants*. Griffith would later achieve wider fame as a television actor for his portrayal of Sheriff Andy Taylor on "The Andy Griffith Show." The Mount Airy native and former member of the Carolina Playmakers at the University of North Carolina was the first movie star to make a personal appearance in Fayetteville since Audie Murphy had come to town in 1954. Murphy, a Texan, was the most decorated soldier of World War II, having won, among many other medals, the Congressional Medal of Honor. He rode his military fame into Hollywood and became famous for his role in the movie *The Red Badge of Courage*. He showed up in Fayetteville as part of a Southern tour promoting another of his movies, *Ride Clear of Diabolo*. I met Murphy in 1954. Knowing that he had gone to radio station WFLB for a radio interview, I went with some family members to the station and waited outside. When he came out, I spoke to him. He came over to our car and graciously greeted us. We told him that we were among his admirers. He thanked us and humbly told us that we were very kind. Murphy was never a super star in the movies, but he probably could qualify as second level, as did Wendell Cory whom I met in 1952 at the world premiere showing of *The Carbine Williams Story*. The only other movie star (besides these two) I ever met was Penny Edwards, who appeared in only a few movies in minor roles. All three came to Fayetteville during the fifties.

In the midst of the good times of Fayetteville's growth and development there was tragedy, too. In June 1957 a truck carrying a load of migrant farm workers was struck at the "Nine Mile Post" north of town on Highway 301 by a tractor-trailer truck. Twenty-one of those workers died in the crash, while seventeen were injured. It was probably the worst single vehicle accident in the entire history of the area. In 1958 death struck again, taking out a beloved Fayetteville citizen. He was the well-known attorney, John A. Oates, who was also the author of *The Story of Fayetteville*, the first true history of Fayetteville. Oates was not a professional historian, of course, but his study is one of some value. As previously noted, I knew Mr. Oates from the time I was a small child until he died at age eighty-seven. Indeed, most of the people in town knew him or knew about him. One story about this very interesting gentleman was that his first marriage was for money—to a woman forty years his senior. The second was for love—to a woman forty years his junior.

A constant in Fayetteville's life was religious fervor. Besides the usual Protestant churches, the city had its Catholic church and its Jewish synagogue. And, as earlier noted, Pentecostalism was big in the area. From time to time, the nation's most fervent evangelists came to town or, sometimes, to Fort Bragg. In October 1958 America's foremost evangelist, Billy Graham, spoke to a crowd estimated at 9,000 in Towle Stadium at Fort Bragg. Around 525 people responded to Graham's invitation to come forward and claim Christ as their savior. Less than a year later, in May 1959, Oral Roberts, a faith healer as well as a revivalist, spoke to about 9,000 people in a canvas tabernacle on the Raeford Road. One of my uncles who viewed Roberts as a "phony" said that when the faith healer pulled out. of town there was not enough money left in the Pentecostal community to "buy a Pepsi Cola," because Roberts was well known for taking up numerous offerings at all of his services.

Attendance at such meetings and attitudes among local officials indicated that religious influences were strong along the Cape Fear. As regards the latter, in 1957 Sheriff Leon Guy, backed by a committee of thirty-six citizens, labeled forty magazines as unfit and asked magazine dealers in the Fayetteville and Cumberland County to remove them from their stands. This, of course, was not the first time that puritanism and censorship had reared their ugly heads along the Cape Fear. It happened again in September 1959 when the Fayetteville city council refused to allow grocery stores to open on Sunday. In so many ways Fayetteville was marching toward the future during the fifties, but it couldn't seem to break away completely from the antiquated restraints of the "old-time religion."

The last year of the fifties, 1960, turned out to be a crucial year for Fayetteville. It was a year of conflict in two critical areas—politics and race relations. Six years had passed since the U.S. Supreme Court had ordered an end to segregation in the public schools, but it had not ended in Fayetteville. Tensions ran high between blacks and whites, as blacks began pushing for their right of access to all public facilities as well as integrated public schools. Early 1960 saw black college students wage "sit-ins" at local lunch counters where they were refused service. Two Hay Street variety stores, F. W. Woolworth and McCrory's, had lunch counters. In February 1960, when black students attempted to eat at those places, the managers removed the stool seats and said that flowers would replace the stools. However, the counters reopened the next day and served white customers only. Students continued their protest by carrying signs and marching up and down in front of the stores. Demonstrations of this kind and other kinds would become commonplace over the next few years and would eventually lead the federal government to pass civil rights legislation making it illegal for the owners of public businesses to discriminate against blacks while providing their services. Civil rights was a dynamite-laden political issue in 1960 and during the next few years.

In the midst of this turbulent time, Fayetteville attorney and state senator Terry Sanford chose to run for governor of North Carolina. In order to win he had to overcome two controversial positions that he courageously took. First, he refused to disavow the Supreme Court's order to integrate the public schools, and second he enthusiastically endorsed John F. Kennedy for president at the 1960 Democratic National Convention.

Sanford's insistence that the Supreme Court decision in the Brown case was the law of the land and had to be obeyed caused him considerable trouble in his quest for votes in the state Democratic primary. Segregationist sentiment in the state was strong enough to force Sanford into a second primary against an outspoken proponent of segregation, Dr. I. Beverly Lake, a Wake Forest University Law School professor. The second primary was hard fought and bitter, but Sanford prevailed. Then he had to take on the Republican candidate, Robert Gavin, in the general election. Gavin castigated Sanford for endorsing a Catholic for president. Southerners, predominantly Protestant, had voted against Catholic presidential candidate Al Smith in 1928, and many were determined to vote against Kennedy on the ground that he would receive the cues for his decisions from the Vatican. On the national scene Kennedy managed to overcome concerns about his religion and won by a very narrow margin. Sanford, too, faced a stiff challenge from his Republican opponent because of Kennedy's religion and was forced to take Gavin quite seriously, something North Carolina Democratic gubernatorial candidates of the past had not been compelled to do. It was a bitter race, but the Fayetteville attorney won, and Fayetteville showed up on the state political map bigger than ever before.

After serving a controversial term as the governor who caused the state sales tax to be extended to food, Sanford would go on to become the president of Duke University and then U.S. senator. At one point he made a half-hearted attempt to seek the Democratic nomination for president of the United States, and I offered to support him. Although I never met Sanford, we corresponded about his presidential candidacy until he gave it up as hopeless. Still, after all these years, he remains the most important political figure ever to come from Fayetteville.

As 1960 moved toward its end, Fayetteville and the nation stood on the brink of the tumultuous decade of the sixties. Just ahead lay an expanding conflict in Vietnam that would profoundly affect the Cape Fear area and the country at large, as soldiers would pass through Fort Bragg again in large numbers, this time on their way to Southeast Asia. Fayetteville was on the verge of being tagged with a new nickname—"Fayettenam"—while simultaneously enjoying greater expansion and gaining considerable prominence on the state and national level. The murder of Ricky Monsour in 1954 would eventually be overshadowed and largely forgotten in the wake of the enormous publicity surrounding the MacDonald murders at Fort Bragg in the final year of the next decade.

Chapter 7

Industrial Strides, Racial Strife, Vietnam, and Jeffrey MacDonald: The 1960s

When the decade of the sixties began, few people along the Cape Fear—or anywhere for that matter—could have suspected that it would be so turbulent. After all, on 20 January 1961 a young, idealistic American President, John F. Kennedy, was sworn in to replace the outgoing conservative, but revered, Dwight David Eisenhower. Although Ike's two administrations had had their foreign policy successes, the Cold War still appeared ever ready to become a hot war, and the nation's economy had been sluggish for quite some time. Kennedy promised to change all of that with a program he called the New Frontier. The country needed to get moving and become aggressive, he claimed, in order to enhance America's position as a super power and to restore economic prosperity. His strong rhetoric, delivered with a thick Massachusetts accent that added Rs to words that had no Rs and left Rs out of words that did have them, inspired confidence in many, but his apparent commitment to racial equality angered white people in the South and in some other parts of the country too. The struggle for racial equality would reach its zenith during the sixties, accompanied by unprecedented racial strife that would lead finally to such breakthrough legislation as the Civil Rights Act of 1964 and the Voting Rights Act of 1965. Thus, the groundwork was laid for equality for black Americans.

Not only could the people along the Cape Fear take hope in a dynamic, young American President, they could also rejoice that one of Fayetteville's own, Terry Sanford, had been sworn in as the new governor of North Carolina over two weeks before Kennedy became President. Many of Sanford's hometown friends and supporters went to Raleigh for the inauguration and listened with appreciation when the former attorney and 82nd Airborne paratrooper declared that North Carolina was in for a "new day." Many opponents of integration feared that the "new day" meant that black and white students would be attending school together. Still, to most rational people, Sanford offered a progressive outlook for the state, just as President Kennedy did for the nation. As already noted, Sanford had previously provoked some criticism and lost some supporters by endorsing Kennedy, instead of Lyndon Johnson, for president in 1960.

In spite of—or perhaps because of—men like Kennedy and Sanford, the sixties were filled, it seemed, with one crisis after another. The tumultuous aspects of the sixties—for both the nation and the Cape Fear region—obscured the many positive strides forward during the decade. New businesses, significant ones, had come to Fayetteville during the fifties, but it was during the sixties that Fayetteville once and for all ceased to be a rural, agrarian town and became an urban, industrial one. The groundwork for turning Fayetteville and vicinity into an industrial area was laid in January 1964 when a "Committee of 100" was formed to lure industry to Fayetteville. Before the year was out, Fasco Industries, Inc. moved its electronic division operations to town, leaving Rochester, New York behind. The Cape Fear area reeled in a big fish in October 1966, when Black & Decker Manufacturing Company of Towson, Maryland—the nation's leading producer of power tools—announced plans for building a five-million-dollar plant on Highway 301, three miles south of Fayetteville. Up and running the following year, Black & Decker was followed by Rohm and Haas, a manufacturer of polyester fabric. That firm built a plant in 1967, locating it across the Cape Fear from Fayetteville. The Rohm and Haas plant soon had more than two thousand employees. In 1968 came Purolator Company, which made auto filters. And, before the decade ended, Fayetteville landed a whale when, in 1969, Kelly-Springfield Tire Company built an enormous plant a few miles north of Fayetteville and became Cumberland County's largest industrial employer. To cap off this impressive industrial expansion of the 1960s, DuPont, Inc., in 1970, selected a site on the Cape Fear for its "Fayetteville plant." Actually the plant, which manufactured plastic articles used by the automotive industry, was about fifteen miles south of Fayetteville and was just across the Bladen County line. Still, it had a noticeable economic impact on Fayetteville and Cumberland County as well as Bladen. Although Fayetteville and Fort Bragg remained inextricably bound together, the city was gradually becoming at least a little less dependent on the huge military installation.

As always, more industry and a mushrooming population (53,000 in Fayetteville by 1963) called for the expansion of many services and the improvement especially of transportation and communication facilities. The Cumberland County legislative delegation was disappointed in 1967 when the State Highway Commission announced that Interstate 95 would bypass

Fayetteville east of the Cape Fear. Apparently Fayetteville's city fathers had hoped the Interstate would come right through town, but there was no need for worry, since the highway was not that far away for those who wanted to exit and drive into town. Actually, the highway's slight distance from the city provided the best of both transportation worlds: on the one hand it was near enough, while on the other it was far enough away to spare Fayetteville an enormous amount of excess traffic. In truth, Fayetteville was more accessible to automotive traffic than it had ever been. And air travel improved as well. In 1969 a new terminal building was dedicated at the Fayetteville Municipal Airport as part of a $2.5 million expansion and modernization project. Much earlier in the sixties telephone communications had been enhanced when, in January of 1963, it was announced that Fayetteville telephone subscribers would soon have direct, long distance dialing, thus enabling them to dial their own station-to-station, person-to-person, collect, and credit-card calls to anywhere in the nation. Mail services were also expanded. The stately old Post Office Building on Hay Street lacked the capacity to handle the mountains of mail now pouring into Fayetteville. So, in January 1966, the post office moved into the huge new Federal Building on Green Street, the site where once had stood the house of Wall Ewing's in-laws and where he and his wife Douglas had lived with her mother and sister before moving to Pearl Street.

Not only transportation and communication facilities but also the major institutions in Fayetteville were required to expand to meet the needs of this burgeoning urban area. Cape Fear Valley Hospital grew steadily into an enormous medical center. The old Highsmith Memorial Hospital, in 1963, took the new name of Highsmith-Rainey Memorial Hospital in recognition of Dr. W. T. Rainey's forty-eight years of dedicated service to the hospital and to his patients prior to his death in 1961. A county authority was to run both hospitals. The two hospitals reported in July 1966, just after the federal Medicare program went into effect, that they were serving 42 patients under the new program. Four years earlier, when President Kennedy had proposed Medicare, the Cumberland County Medical Society had gone on record as opposing it. Once the program was put into place, however, area physicians, reluctantly but necessarily, fell into line.

Just as the hospitals expanded to meet new demands, the schools had to do likewise. Crash building programs in the late 1950s and throughout the 1960s were scarcely sufficient to keep pace with the increasing number of students. In 1963 alone the number of new students in Cumberland

County and Fayetteville amounted to ten percent of the new students for the entire state of North Carolina. Only Mecklenburg County and Charlotte, the most populous area in the state, had more new students that year. As part of the expansion program, a new high school named for city superintendent of schools C. Reid Ross opened on the Raleigh Road in 1967, and, while naming the new school, the city school board changed the name of Fayetteville High School on Fort Bragg Road to Fayetteville/Terry Sanford High School. Because control of the city and county schools was clearly in the hands of conservatives, the schools were more or less directed to defy the U.S. Supreme Court in 1962, after the Court ruled that mandatory school prayer was unconstitutional. The Cumberland County Board of Commissioners declared that the county schools would, as in the past, begin every school day with a devotional. School authorities had shown similar defiance regarding the Court's orders to integrate the schools, and they continued to do so for a long time.

The growth in educational institutions was not limited to the public schools. In February 1962 the Fayetteville Area Industrial Education Center was dedicated, and the occasion was important enough to lure Governor Sanford to participate as the main speaker. Soon the new institution would evolve into the highly respected Fayetteville Technical Community College, or Fayetteville Tech for short.

Clearly Fayetteville and Cumberland County were coming up in the world. Terry Sanford's election as governor and the dramatic increase in population gave the area increased political clout. In April 1961 a bill increasing the county's representation in the state's House of Representatives from two members to three was passed. Because of its increasing importance in state and national affairs, Fayetteville and Fort Bragg, too, were visited by more and more celebrities. President Kennedy visited Fort Bragg in October 1961. His brother, Attorney General Robert Kennedy, appeared twice during the decade, first in 1965 and then again in 1968, and Vice President Hubert Humphrey was briefed at Fort Bragg in 1965. Republican presidential candidate Barry Goldwater brought his campaign to Fayetteville in 1964. Rod Serling, host of the popular television program called "Twilight Zone," showed up at Fort Bragg in April 1964 to make a parachute jump with eleven of his army buddies who had jumped with him during World War II. World-famous boxer Muhammad Ali made an unexpected stop in town after a bus accident and drew a huge crowd in April 1965. Then, in April 1966, movie star John Wayne visited the John

F. Kennedy Center for Special Warfare as part of his preparation for a movie about the Green Berets. The great entertainer Louis "Satchmo" Armstrong followed in November 1967, when he performed at Lee Field House in Fort Bragg. In February 1968 none other than President Lyndon Johnson appeared at Fort Bragg to bid a personal farewell to some of the soldiers he was sending to Vietnam. He claimed that it was not easy for him to send men to war, but quickly added that "the duties of freedom are not easy." Not all of the celebrities who came received a warm welcome. This was clear in May 1970 when Jane Fonda showed up in town as a Vietnam War protester. She led demonstrators to Fort Bragg to hand out antiwar leaflets and was escorted, along with her fellow demonstrators, off the base by Criminal Investigation Division agents. The antiwar demonstration then moved to Fayetteville, where about 2,000 gathered at Rowan Street Park for a peaceful protest.

By the end of the sixties, controversy over the Vietnam War was seriously dividing the nation. At about that same time the country was getting through the worst of the racial tension that had rocked America throughout most of the decade. The Cape Fear region had experienced its share of that turbulence. As noted in the previous chapter, students from Fayetteville State Teachers College staged sit-ins at the F. W. Woolworth and McCrory's lunch counters on 10 February 1960. Those students were part of the vanguard of what we now call the Civil Rights Movement. More actions and reactions and many inflamed feelings quickly followed the sit-ins. Racial issues constantly plagued school officials and local businessmen as local blacks persistently contended for their rights. Trying to ease some of the tension, the Fayetteville Board of Education assigned four black students in July 1962 to three of the city's previously all white schools— one each to Ramsey Street Elementary and Alexander Graham Junior High and two to Haymount Elementary. This token gesture did not satisfy the more ardent advocates of black rights. In the spring of 1963 students from Fayetteville State once again demonstrated at downtown stores, restaurants, and theaters, demanding equal rights. In spite of these protests, the Fayetteville Area Restaurant Association voted to leave the matter of serving blacks or not up to individual restaurant owners. This resulted in more demonstrations, as well as Fayetteville policemen arresting black students and charging them with trespassing. In July, black students and servicemen from Fort Bragg—both black and white—staged a large-scale demonstration for civil rights on Hay Street in downtown Fayetteville.

Following this demonstration, the Mayor's Biracial Committee met with local NAACP officials, who persuaded the students to stop their downtown demonstrations. During the following month the trustees at Cape Fear Valley Hospital voted to remove all racial barriers at the facility. Progress was being made, as integration crept forward inch by inch. When school opened in 1963, Mary R. Pohlman, the wife of a Fort Bragg soldier, enrolled at Fayetteville State. She became the first white student in its history to enroll in the institution. By demonstrating for their rights, blacks won a great victory when, in the summer of 1964, President Lyndon Johnson signed into law the epoch-making Civil Rights Act. Following that momentous development, the Fayetteville Area Restaurant Association announced a new policy, simply saying that "the law must be obeyed." Blacks were now free to eat in public eating places just as whites were— thanks to federal law.

Even though progress was being made, the strife was not yet over. Down in Alabama, less than a year after the Civil Rights Act became law, one of the struggle's most dramatic incidents occurred. In March 1965 Dr. Martin Luther King, Jr. led demonstrators on a five-day march from Montgomery to Selma. Blood was shed when the demonstrators crossed the Edmund Pettus Bridge into Selma. During those five, tension-filled days Fayetteville State students marched, sent wires, and voiced their support for what King was doing. A little more than three years later these same people and many others had occasion to mourn for King, who was assassinated on 4 April 1968 in Memphis, Tennessee. Three days after King was struck down by a bullet fired, presumably from a rifle wielded by James Earl Ray, two hundred people marched around the Market House, silently mourning the death of the slain civil rights leader. Some of the group marched on to the Cumberland County courthouse to protest the fact that the nation's flag had not been lowered to half-staff in King's honor. They arrived to find that the flag had been lowered. Pleased by this, the marchers applauded, sang a hymn, and went their respective ways.

King's work and his death were not in vain. Little by little, in response to civil rights activism, the barriers of segregation were being removed. In August 1967 the Fort Bragg post commander, Lt. Gen. Robert H. York, informed a group of real estate, business, and civic leaders in Fayetteville that the Army would no longer tolerate segregation in housing rentals for soldiers and their families. The following March saw the taverns and go-go clubs on Hay Street integrated without incident. However, fearing that there would be trouble, Fayetteville policemen and Fort Bragg MPs kept a watchful eye on the downtown area. Progress toward integrating the schools was also being made. The city's school system offered a new desegregation plan in July 1969, and it was approved by federal civil rights officials. Many white parents, though, were not on board with the plan. They formed the Concerned Parents Association in protest and called for boycotting the public schools. The boycott failed to materialize, but the association started a freedom-of-choice movement, and the Cumberland County Republican Party went on record as favoring the neighborhood school concept and opposing the bussing of students to achieve integration.

Obviously, many whites along the Cape Fear were going to resist integration as long as possible. One reaction against federally forced integration was the establishment of private schools where, presumably, whites only could afford the tuition. Fayetteville's first such school, Fayetteville Academy, opened in September 1970. The new school, located on Cliffdale Road, began operating with 105 students. It was one of the many "schools that fear built" in the wake of federally mandated school integration.

Although the struggle to desegregate the public schools lasted through the decade of the sixties, there were signs here and there that racial barriers were crumbling and that the courts in Fayetteville were going to uphold the law. In September 1962 Sylvia Allen, the first black woman to graduate from the University of North Carolina Law School, was given the right to practice law in Cumberland County, being sworn in at a ceremony in the county's Superior Court. Passage of the Civil Rights Act in 1964 pushed aside other barriers and forced white officials to yield to the inevitable. Faculty integration of the Cumberland County schools was approved by the county's Board of Education in April 1965. That same month Judge Hamilton H. Hobgood dismissed charges against seventy-five people who had been arrested during civil rights demonstrations in Fayetteville two years earlier. Like the walls of Jericho, those of segregation were collapsing under the trumpet blasts of civil rights demonstrators throughout the Cape Fear region and the rest of the nation.

As if racial strife were not enough to deal with, Fayetteville—again because of Fort Bragg—was forced to wrestle with fallout problems associated with a variety of world crises, especially the Vietnam War. The Cold War was still very much on, and in September 1961 President Kennedy ordered troops from the 1st Logistical Command at Fort Bragg to go to

Berlin as part of the 40,000 soldiers deployed during the crisis over the erection of the Berlin Wall. A little more than two years later, in November 1963, Fayetteville joined the nation in mourning Kennedy, who was shot in Dallas, Texas, by Lee Harvey Oswald. Fort Bragg soldiers gathered in silence and listened to the official announcement that their commander in chief was dead. In Fayetteville, flags were lowered to half-staff, and businesses closed for much of the day of the slain president's funeral.

While it was President Johnson, Kennedy's successor, who was most responsible for our expanded involvement in Vietnam, many forget that it was Kennedy who took the first steps in that direction. His support for an unpopular regime in South Vietnam ultimately embarrassed Kennedy, and it was rumored that he gave his approval for a coup against President Ngo Dinh Diem, a military coup that resulted in Diem's assassination. It is ironic that Kennedy himself was assassinated not long afterward. His death put Lyndon Johnson in the White House, and, after being elected in his own right in 1964, Johnson, a thoroughgoing Cold Warrior, made a decision to defeat North Vietnam. He clung stubbornly to that decision, as a divided America and a determined North Vietnamese government and Viet Cong guerrillas made an American victory virtually impossible.

Fayetteville's close connection to Fort Bragg meant that the city would be directly affected as long as the war lasted. During the forties and fifties thousands of soldiers from across the nation had passed through Fort Bragg and Fayetteville. Seeking to capitalize on their presence, some Fayetteville business people opened up new entertainment establishments on Hay Street, some of which were not exactly wholesome. In the 1960s more beer and go-go joints than the city had ever seen were to be found up and down the main drag and side streets. Fayetteville rocked to drinking, lewd dancing, and dope in many forms. The go-go scene was dealt something of a setback in April 1967 when two of the most notorious clubs—the Elite Lounge and the Starlight Club—burned down. Wild times were certainly not new in town, but the decadence reached unprecedented levels in the sixties. Drug abuse, in particular, became a huge problem of the times. In 1969 it was estimated that 25,000 people, or eleven percent of Cumberland County's 225,000 residents, were drug offenders. A thousand of those were hooked on heroin. Another thousand heroin addicts lived among the numerous drug users on the Fort Bragg reservation. The drugs flowed in from New York, Miami, and directly from the Far East. Several soldiers stationed at Fort Bragg died in drug-related incidents in 1969. Meanwhile, soldiers were leaving for and returning from Vietnam. In November 1965 seventeen hundred Fort Bragg troops received their orders for Southeast Asia, and this was just the beginning. The numbers climbed precipitously over the next few years, as Fort Bragg was designated an Army training center for soldiers taking their eight-week basic training course in preparation for going to Vietnam. Not a few who went to that theater and made it back returned as drug addicts.

Not all Fort Bragg soldiers went to Vietnam, however. Occasionally some had to be used to stem violence at home, for there were constant demonstrations everywhere in the country against the war. In October 1967 troops from Fort Bragg went to Washington, D.C. to hold in check antiwar demonstrators who threatened to ignore government restrictions and lay siege to the Pentagon with acts of civil disobedience. It was just four months later when President Johnson appeared at Fort Bragg to say goodbye to the 1,300 troops that he was sending to Vietnam. And not all Fort Bragg soldiers were eager to go to Vietnam. There was a group at Fort Bragg known as GIs United Against the Vietnam War, and its members published a newspaper called "Bragg Briefs." The group held several antiwar parades and rallies in Fayetteville in September 1969. A month later the first Vietnam Moratorium Day was held. It was the largest antiwar protest in American history, and thirty-two North Carolina colleges observed it with prayer vigils, candlelight processions, and mass meetings. The colleges in Fayetteville were among them.

With public opposition of this magnitude, Lyndon Johnson could hope for neither victory in Vietnam nor reelection to the presidency. Realizing this, he withdrew himself from contention for the Democratic nomination in 1968, determined to leave the quagmire in Southeast Asia, into which he had led the nation, to his successor. Fayetteville continued to be affected directly by events in Vietnam for another five years.

Fayetteville muddled through the sixties, dealing with growing pains and the tensions of race and war as best it could. Not all the news was bad. The city was certainly taking great strides forward economically, and the lighter side of life was never completely overshadowed by the tragedies of racial animosity and military conflict. In fact, Fayetteville and Cumberland County produced some heroes during the decade. One of them was Rusty Clark, who was destined to become Fayetteville's all-time great basketball player. In January 1964 this lad, who stood nearly seven-feet tall, scored 33 points in a game that pitted the Fayetteville Bulldogs against the Asheboro

Blue Comets. The following year Clark led his team to the state 4-A championship, beating Durham in the finals. Fayetteville's record that year was 24-1. From Fayetteville, Clark went to the University of North Carolina, where he played center for the heralded Tar Heels under legendary coach Dean Smith. He distinguished himself there as one of the Carolina greats, and in April 1969, when he was in Fayetteville playing with an all-star team, Clark was honored by having Mayor Monroe Evans proclaim "Rusty Clark Day." After four years at UNC, Clark went to medical school and then returned to Fayetteville to practice medicine and launch a number of business enterprises.

Another Fayetteville hero who emerged in the sixties was golfer Raymond Floyd who had won the National Jaycee tournament in 1960. In May 1961 he announced that he was turning professional. He did well on the pro circuit. In 1969 he earned more than $100,000 in prize money and was named golfer of the year by the Carolinas' Golf Writers Association. More than forty years after becoming a pro, Floyd, in 2003, was still active in golf as a member of the elite senior circuit.

Two Fayetteville area sports figures that were not as highly publicized as Clark and Floyd were Luther "Nick" Jeralds and Cal Koonce. Both had their admirers along the Cape Fear. Jeralds, a football player, signed a professional contract with the Minnesota Vikings in June 1961, while Koonce, a baseball player, pitched for several major league teams. He played for the Chicago Cubs and later with the champion New York Mets, who traded him to the Boston Red Sox in 1970.

Along with sports, the arts made some advances in the area during the 1960s. The Fayetteville Little Theatre was founded late in 1962. That same year it was noted that the jukebox industry had made giant strides in the county over the past ten years. Right after World War II there had been only one distributor of coin-operated phonographs, but by the summer of 1962 there were five distributors servicing more than 500 jukeboxes in the county. Music lovers in the area could select their favorite songs and hear them played for only ten cents. Not everyone was thrilled with some of the new "culture" that made its way to Cumberland County. By early 1962 the dance known as the Twist, made famous by entertainer Chubby Checker, had made its way to Fayetteville, and local doctors warned teenagers that the dance was dangerous. Among the casualties of the Twist, according to the doctors, were twisted knees and back strains. In 1964 Beatlemania hit town, when a high school senior named Shikery Fadel, sporting a Beatles-style haircut, was used by Tallywood Shopping Center owners to promote Beatles records. The Beatles and their music skyrocketed to number one on the music charts.

Along with the innovative music came new fashions, including the miniskirt. Local—and prudish—Judge Joe Dupree was deeply offended when a woman wearing a short skirt appeared in his courtroom. He issued orders to his bailiff to lock up the next woman to appear in his courtroom similarly dressed.

The fast-food culture also arrived in Fayetteville in the sixties. Hardee's, one of several fast-food hamburger restaurants, opened on Bragg Boulevard in January 1962. To promote their opening, Hardee's offered a hamburger, french fries, and a Pepsi Cola for a quarter. The most famous of such establishments, McDonald's, opened their first restaurant in Fayetteville five months later. The rest of the world was invading the bustling city along the Cape Fear on a scale never before seen in the area.

There were so many huge stories connected with Fayetteville during the sixties, stories that spread the city's fame far and wide. The most powerful people in the world showed up there at various times. Famous entertainers and sports figures performed or played there, and several of the sports figures were natives of the area. Great American industries located there. So many stories, but the biggest of all concerned a gargantuan tragedy—the murder of Colette MacDonald and her two daughters, Kimberly and Kristen.

The MacDonald murders was the most publicized crime ever committed along the Cape Fear. Newspapers covered the story in rivers of ink for more than fifteen years. Books were written. Movies were made. The entire nation knew. Indeed, the whole world knew about the gruesome butchery that took place at 544 Castle Drive at Fort Bragg on 16-17 February 1970, the final year of the sixties.

The story begins with a telephone call taken by Fayetteville operator Carolyn Landen at 3:33 a.m. on 17 February. From the other end of the line the words came with difficulty: "My name is Captain MacDonald . . . stabbings . . . need a doctor . . . MP's and an ambulance at 544 Castle Drive." When Landen asked if MacDonald were calling from the post, he replied, "Damn it, lady . . . my family . . . it's on post." The operator put the call through to the MPs, and MacDonald told the desk sergeant, "Thank God . . . we've been stabbed . . . people are dying . . . I may be dying . . . we need a doctor and ambulance . . . 544 Castle Drive."

When the MPs arrived at the house, they found blood everywhere. The two little MacDonald girls had been murdered. Colette, also dead, was sprawled out on the floor, all bloody, with Jeffrey MacDonald by her side. Both were twenty-six years of age. Jeffrey struggled to speak and said, "Four of them. . . . She kept saying 'Acid is groovy. . . . Kill the pigs. . . . ' " He continued: "Why did they do this to me? I can't breathe . . . I need a chest tube." Upon looking at his wife, the captain blurted out, "Jesus Christ. Look at my wife." Then he mumbled, "I'm gonna kill those goddamned acid heads. I don't know why in the hell I fuck with them. I'm not gonna help them anymore." He described the "acid heads" in question as two white men, one black man, and a white woman with long blond hair, a floppy hat, high boots, and holding a candle.

Colette had been stabbed sixteen times with a knife in the neck and chest and twenty-one times in the chest with an ice pick. Her skull was fractured by a blow from a club. Both of her arms were broken. Kimberly and Kristen had been clubbed and repeatedly stabbed—all done by drug-crazed hippies, according to Captain MacDonald. One of the investigating officers—John Hodges, who was second on the scene—said that he never bought MacDonald's story and noted, "People just refused to believe what was there. They couldn't bring into their minds that someone of his caliber did this. It's easier to believe crazed hippies did this. And still people believe this, to this day."

Hodges spoke those words in the year 2000, thirty years after the horrible crime. At that time, Dr. Jeffrey MacDonald sat in a federal prison, having been incarcerated most of the time since 1979, but his lawyers insisted that DNA testing results, for which they were waiting, would clear their notorious client. Three years later, as these words are being written, MacDonald remains in prison, serving three life sentences for murdering his family.

How did the MacDonalds come to be at Fort Bragg? Where had they come from? Both Jeffrey and Colette grew up on Long Island, New York. After graduating from Patchogue High School, where he was named "most popular" and "most likely to succeed," young MacDonald matriculated at Princeton University as a premedical student. Some personal developments intervened to slow him down a bit in his quest for the M.D. degree. During his second year at Princeton, he was running back and forth between Princeton and Saratoga, New York, where Colette was a freshman at Skidmore College. The two Long Islanders were lovers by 1963, and that summer Colette got pregnant. She dropped out of Skidmore, married Jeffrey, and moved with him to Princeton. Over the next few years, two daughters, Kimberly and then Kristen, were born to the couple, but MacDonald, in spite of his family responsibilities, managed to work his way through medical school at Northwestern University School of Medicine. After being awarded his medical degree, Jeffrey enlisted in the Army, and was inducted on 1 July 1969. He took paratrooper training at Fort Benning, Georgia and volunteered for the Green Berets. In September 1969 he was assigned to duty as a medical officer at Green Beret headquarters at Fort Bragg. Colette was soon pregnant again and was expecting a son in July 1970. That male fetus turned out to be the fourth victim on that infamous February night, five months before his expected birth.

MacDonald himself sustained several stab wounds in the chest on the night in question. Whether or not they were life threatening, or perhaps self-inflicted, became a matter of serious controversy in the years that followed. The Criminal Investigation Division (CID) of the Army suspected MacDonald of the horrendous murders at the outset. The lead investigator on the morning of 17 February was a twenty-six-year-old agent named William Ivey, a high-school dropout turned career soldier. His military rank was Specialist E-7. Ivey quickly concluded that MacDonald had committed the murders and then "staged the scene" to convince investigators that intruders had done it. Worth noting is the fact that this was Ivey's first murder investigation. MacDonald, who spent ten days in Womack Hospital and underwent two surgical procedures for a collapsed lung, was not informed that he was a suspect. Nor were Alfred ("Freddie") and Mildred Kassab, Colette's stepfather and mother respectively, told of the CID's suspicions. During March, MacDonald and his in-laws hounded the CID for progress reports concerning the investigation.   Meanwhile, Colonel Robert J. Kriwanek, commander of the CID unit at Fort Bragg, told the FBI to "butt out" of the investigation. The colonel insisted that this was a "cut-and-dried-case" of a family dispute that ended in murders and a botched suicide attempt. Finally, in early April, MacDonald was told by the CID that he was the leading suspect in the case. He was flabbergasted, and the Kassabs vigorously defended their son-in-law. On 6 April the young Green Beret doctor was put under house arrest, and on 1 May he was formally charged with the murders. On 6 July the Army opened an Article 32 hearing to determine whether or not MacDonald would be held for a full court-martial. The accused had two civilian defense attorneys—Bernard

Segal and Dennis Eisman—and two Army attorneys—James Douthat and Michael Malley. Segal was a highly acclaimed attorney from Philadelphia, while Malley had been a Princeton classmate of MacDonald's. Conducting the hearing was Colonel Warren V. Rock, commander of the 4th Psychological Operations Battalion at Fort Bragg.

In their revisionist book, *Fatal Justice: Reinvestigating the MacDonald Murders*, published in 1997, Jerry Allen Potter and Fred Bost assert that "At the army Article 32 hearing the army prosecutors and CID agents presented their claims against MacDonald as if they had encountered nothing, either at the murder scene or out of it, to support his story." The coauthors note that the accusers failed to mention a great deal of physical evidence found in the house and kept quiet about MP Kenneth Mica's seeing a woman wearing a blond wig and a floppy hat standing on a corner, not far from the MacDonald residence. Since the woman fit the description MacDonald gave of one of the intruders and since a woman standing on a street corner at approximately 3:55 a.m. was more than passing strange, to ignore this fact looked very much like the CID agents were out to get MacDonald anyway they could. Eventually, a woman who was a drug addict and a "snitch" for the Fayetteville Police Department, was investigated, and she might very well have been the person Mica saw. Her name was Helena Stoeckley. A Fayetteville man named William Posey, who lived near Stoeckley, told Colonel Rock that he had seen Stoeckley and several of her friends wheel into her driveway between 3:45 and 4:30 the morning of the murders. She, according to Posey, had hinted that she might have been at the murder scene, but that she was so wasted on drugs that night that she could not be sure.

After hearing all the charges and the evidence, Colonel Rock released his report recommending that all charges against MacDonald be dismissed, because they were "not true." Rock urged that Helena Stoeckley and her friends be investigated immediately. General Edward Flanagan, commander of the post, was surprised by the "Rock Report," for the CID had assured him that MacDonald was guilty. Rock, however, assured the general that there was no case against the Green Beret doctor. "It isn't there," he said. Flanagan did not clear MacDonald but dropped the charges because of "insufficient evidence," leaving the door open to prosecution further down the road. MacDonald was discharged from the Army following the hearing.

From Fort Bragg the young doctor went to work for a short time in New York City. Then he moved to Long Beach, California, where he worked in the emergency department of St. Mary's Hospital. Over the next nine years MacDonald became something of a celebrity in southern California as a result of his lavish lifestyle and community involvement, but after much legal maneuvering during that time, the doctor was eventually brought to trial in 1979 on three counts of murder. On the eve of the trial a writer named Joe McGinniss was accepted by MacDonald as the person to tell the story of the trial and the now world-famous murders. It was tacitly understood that McGinniss believed MacDonald to be innocent. When the writer first met his famous subject in 1979 he looked upon a five-foot-eleven, muscular, tanned, affable, thirty-five-year-old man with blond hair that was turning gray. At that time MacDonald was living in a condo at Huntington Beach and was director of Emergency Medicine at St. Mary's Hospital in Long Beach. He headed a group of fourteen doctors, taught at UCLA on the side, and was writing a medical textbook. MacDonald had acquired the means to own a thirty-four-foot yacht, which he called "Recovery Room."

This ER physician, who was involved in numerous worthy causes, was obviously well thought of by his California friends. To help with his defense fund, they sponsored a going-away "raffle party" for him at $100 per person or $500 for those wishing to sit at MacDonald's table. McGinnis took note of the fact that all of these admirers praised MacDonald and that he charmed them all.

The question arises: How could this former Green Beret doctor go from being exonerated by the Rock Report in 1970 to going on trial for murder in federal court in 1979? Was this not a clear case of double jeopardy? MacDonald's lawyers insisted that it was, but the federal courts concluded that it was not. Many unusual developments led step by step to the high drama that unfolded in Raleigh, North Carolina in 1979. Following the Article 32 hearing, Freddie Kassab became convinced that MacDonald was indeed guilty, and he importuned everybody he knew in Washington, D.C. and many people he did not know to put pressure on the Justice Department to indict and try his son-in-law for murdering his family. Just as convinced of MacDonald's guilt was Warren Coolidge, U.S. attorney for the Eastern Division of North Carolina. Coolidge and others who were sure MacDonald was getting away with murder went to work, collected the evidence gathered in 1970, and took the case to a grand jury in Raleigh during late 1974 and early 1975. The Justice Department named Victor Woerheide to prosecute the case. MacDonald appeared at the grand jury hearing on 21

January 1975. Three days later—on the 24th—he was indicted on three counts of murder. Bernard Segal fought the indictment with an appeal based on "speedy trial" issues. He won in 1976, then lost in 1978, when the government appealed to the U.S. Supreme Court. Segal argued that the indictment of his client constituted double jeopardy, but the court ruled that the Army hearing in 1970 was not a true judicial hearing and that double jeopardy consequently did not apply in MacDonald's case.

MacDonald's attitude at the grand jury hearing in 1975 clearly revealed an arrogant man and, apparently, in the minds of the grand jurors, a guilty man. Federal attorney Victor Woerheide asked MacDonald if he knew Laura Talbot. The doctor answered that he did not recall her. When asked if he remembered working at Atlantic Construction, Inc. in 1964, MacDonald said that he did, but that he did not remember the year. He then remembered Laura Talbot, a secretary who worked there. When asked by Woerheide what had happened between them, MacDonald flippantly replied, "I balled the girl. Big deal, she was a secretary." The remark clearly suggested that MacDonald held women in low esteem and used them at will. It got worse. In his final comments, he told the grand jurors, "I didn't kill Colette. And I didn't kill Kimmy and I didn't kill Kristy and I didn't move Colette and I didn't move Kimmy and I didn't move Kristy and I gave them mouth-to-mouth breathing and I loved them then and I love them now and you can shove all your fucking evidence right up your ass." The obvious contempt MacDonald had for the proceedings of the grand jury boomeranged on him and brought about his indictment.

The legal maneuvering after the grand jury indictment—appeals and counterappeals—finally ended in 1978, and MacDonald's trial began in Raleigh on 19 July 1979. The case was tried before Judge Franklin T. Dupree, Jr. of Fuqua-Varina, North Carolina, a small town a few miles south of Raleigh. Assistant U.S. Attorney James Blackburn, assisted by Brian Murtagh of the Justice Department and other government attorneys, led the prosecution. Bernard Segal was still MacDonald's lead attorney. Michael Malley, who had assisted during the Article 32 hearing, assisted once more, and Wade Smith, a North Carolina football hero and a prominent defense attorney, also assisted.

Blackburn's opening argument was that the case against MacDonald was based on a crime scene that had been well controlled and evidence that had been flawlessly preserved. This was far from true, as Jerry Potter and Fred Bost would demonstrate a few years later. Their investigation, made possible by the 1983 Freedom of Information Act, enabled them to uncover a great deal of evidence that the prosecution had denied to the defense. But the truth is that the evidence presented at the trial was rather compelling—enough so as to persuade Joe McGinniss, who was almost regarded as a member of the defense team, that MacDonald was guilty. The case could be made either way. McGinniss made it his way; Potter and Bost later made it another way. Whether or not MacDonald received a fair trial and, especially, whether or not Judge Dupree was biased against MacDonald from the start will always be open to debate.

To begin with, Judge Dupree refused to allow psychiatric testimony to be admitted into evidence. Segal had psychiatrists ready to say that in their opinion MacDonald was an unlikely person to perpetrate such a heinous crime. Their opinions were not heard, since Dupree did not want the case to be bogged down by pitting "shrink versus shrink." On the issue of MacDonald's mental state, it was probably just as well for Segal that Dupree ruled as he did, for potentially damning evidence existed. After the trial, Joe McGinniss found a document that Segal had kept from him. It was the report of the prosecution's psychiatric team. That report, signed by Hirsch Lazaar Silverman of South Orange, New Jersey, was highly negative and would have removed any and all doubt of MacDonald's possible innocence, if the jury had seen it and believed it. Silverman contended that MacDonald had little capacity for accepting guilt and that he was not capable of "emotionally close or mutually cooperative relationships with women." Moreover, said Silverman's report, MacDonald was amnesic about what he did not want to remember and that his credibility was suspect. Surely Segal could not have expected psychiatric evidence to be admitted without the jury being made aware of this damning report. Perhaps he thought his psychiatrists would be more believable than those of the prosecution.

What Segal certainly did not want presented was a photograph of the crime scene, which the government placed into evidence at the beginning. The defense attorney from Philadelphia argued that the photograph showed the scene *after* things were moved, including the victim's bodies. He claimed, "It is not right to introduce a photograph when it does not represent the crime scene as it was found. They simply want to skip how they found it." Dupree denied Segal's objections, and the gruesome details of the murders were visually implanted in the minds of the jurors. Step-by-step, the prosecutors explained the physical evidence, developing a scenario that was difficult to refute. And Brian Murtagh stated emphatically that nobody had offered any evidence that anybody was inside the MacDonald house during the night of the murders except the MacDonalds. He conceded that others, even Helena Stoeckley, might have been in the area, but there was no evidence that they were in the MacDonald home.

Blackburn and Murtagh made a strong case, but the person who was probably the most instrumental in convicting MacDonald was MacDonald himself—indirectly and directly. Part of the prosecution's evidence was a tape recording of MacDonald's interview with the CID on 6 April 1970. Several jurors were convinced after hearing the recording that the accused was indeed guilty. One juror said, "He just didn't sound like a man telling the truth." Another said, "There was a cockiness. Arrogance when there should not have been arrogance. . . . It just started me wondering what kind of man he really was." Even more damaging was MacDonald's testimony in his own behalf. Before he took the stand, Segal begged his client to avoid coming across as arrogant when it came time for the prosecutors to cross-examine him. This was apparently beyond MacDonald's powers, for he regarded James Blackburn as "a chicken shit" and Brian Murtagh as a "turd." He told Segal he hated Murtagh. His animosity toward the prosecutors was obvious on cross-examination, and this helped sink him. He took the stand on 23 August 1979.

All along MacDonald and his lawyers thought that if they could just get Helena Stoeckley into court and put her on the stand, it would come out that she and some of her friends were the intruders whom MacDonald had described and that they had committed the horrible murders. This was wishful thinking. Stoeckley came to court, all right, but, if anything, her testimony did exactly the opposite of what the defendant and his lead attorney had hoped for. Segal confronted her before she testified and tried to browbeat her into admitting she was at the MacDonald house on the night in question. She refused, telling Segal, "I can't help you." She said she remembered none of what happened that night. Earlier she had confessed to being there to a number of people, but Judge Dupree would not admit their testimony, because it was hearsay. On the stand, Helena turned out to be a star witness for the prosecution. She denied everything and said she could not remember where she was that night.

Out of court Stoeckley kept changing stories, telling people she was there and then denying it. The people she identified as being there with her were investigated by the FBI and the CID and cleared. Her boyfriend, Greg

Mitchell, was cleared in 1971. In June 1982 he died of liver cancer. All of the others Helena implicated denied any knowledge of the murders, and one of them called her story "totally insane, the craziest thing I've ever heard." One person named by Stoeckley as being with her that night had been in jail between 28 January and 10 March 1970 and could not possibly have been there. Still, Helena gave indications that she had been at MacDonald's at the time of the murders. She told her friend Prince Beasley, a Fayetteville narcotics officer, that she wouldn't stick her neck out for MacDonald, because her friends might hurt or kill her.

At the time of the trial Stoeckley was twenty-seven years old and living in Seneca, South Carolina. Her involvement with the case would go on for four more years until her death in 1983. She remained a mysterious figure in this dramatic case, for a woman matching her description had indeed been seen by MP Kenneth Mica near MacDonald's house around 3:55 a.m. on 17 February 1970. Also, she had told people, many people, that she thought she might have been there when the murders were committed. Moreover, MacDonald's Article 32 hearing resulted in a recommendation by Colonel Rock that she and her friends be thoroughly investigated. They were, but how thoroughly, remains a debatable question.

A decade and a half after the trial, Potter and Bost would find that there was plenty of physical evidence indicating that Helena Stoeckley and friends, or at least some other intruders, *might* have been inside the MacDonald house. Evidence found by the investigators, but kept from the defense, included a bloody syringe, blond wig fibers, a burnt match, candle wax, and several bloody gloves. None of this was mentioned at trial, simply because the defense had no knowledge of it at the time, and the prosecution remained silent about it. There was other evidence that Stoeckley *might* have been at the murder scene. MacDonald described one of the intruders as a black man wearing a field jacket, and Stoeckley was seen with such a man at Dunkin' Donuts on Bragg Boulevard an hour or so after the murders. Helena's name just kept coming up.

In spite of the knowledge that Stoeckley was a drug addict who somehow might have been present at the murders, she turned out to be of no use to the defense. That, coupled with the fact that the jury did not see any physical evidence that intruders were in the house, plus MacDonald's arrogance on the witness stand resulted in the doctor's conviction. The jury deliberated only six hours before finding him guilty of second-degree murder in the cases of his wife and older daughter and of first-degree murder in the death of Kristen. A stunned MacDonald said, "I'm not guilty. I don't think the court has heard all the evidence." On 29 August 1979 Judge Dupree sentenced the convicted doctor to three consecutive terms of life imprisonment.

When MacDonald appealed the conviction and asked for a new trial, Dupree denied the appeal. Next MacDonald, in July 1980, took his case to the 4th Circuit Court of Appeals, where three justices overturned the conviction because the defendant had been denied a "speedy trial," but the court did not deal with the question of guilt or innocence. The following month the Justice Department appealed the ruling to the U.S. Supreme Court, and MacDonald was released after posting a $100,000 bond. He remained free until March 1982, when the U.S. Supreme Court reinstated his conviction, ruling that his right to a speedy trial had not been violated. MacDonald went back to prison.

Meanwhile, Helena Stoeckley continued her now-familiar pattern of confession followed by denial. In South Carolina she had married a man named Ernie Davis, and after the trial in 1979 she told him that she had been present at the murder scene. He came to believe that she was in fact there but had not participated in the brutal killings. Helena also confessed to Fred Bost and to a retired FBI agent named Ted Gunderson, whom MacDonald hired to investigate the crime. However, two months after the Supreme Court's decision had sent MacDonald back to prison—in May 1982—Stoeckley again retracted her confession to being a witness to the murders. On 10 January 1983, without comment, the Supreme Court refused to hear MacDonald's request to review the 4th Circuit Court's rejection of his claim that he had not received a fair trial. A few days after the high court's refusal to intervene further, Helena Stoeckley Davis was found dead in her apartment at Seneca, South Carolina of cirrhosis of the liver and pneumonia. She had been dead for several days, and her body was decomposing. MacDonald called Helena's death "highly suspicious." Her demise, plus the Supreme Court's slamming its doors in the face of MacDonald's appeal, appeared to close the books on the MacDonald case. But not so.

If anything, more about the MacDonald case was heard after the Supreme Court's decision of January 1983 than before it. Joe McGinniss finished his book, which he had planned to call *Acid and Rain*. Instead, it was called *Fatal Vision*, and it did anything but portray MacDonald as innocent. Indeed, McGinniss did more than the prosecution by explaining why MacDonald had murdered his family. The prosecuting attorneys had focused little on the doctor's motive, sticking to their theory of what had happened and how it had happened. What was the motive? That was a question McGinniss answered by devising a rather imaginative scenario. There had been no signs—outward ones, at least—of a troubled marriage. Most people who knew the MacDonalds thought that Jeffrey and Colette were happy with each other. And Jeffrey had bought his daughters a pony for Christmas in 1969. So, what could have triggered the murders? According to McGinniss the triggers were drugs and suppressed psychological problems. Specifically, the writer claimed that MacDonald was taking "Eskatrol Spansules," which combined with his "narcissistic personality disorder" to precipitate "an amphetamine psychosis."

Also, since childhood, Jeffrey MacDonald had repressed a "boundless rage" which psychological maladjustment had caused him to feel toward "child or woman, wife or mother . . . the female sex." MacDonald was particularly upset when Colette balked about her husband's supposed trip to Russia with the Army boxing team, and then he presumably went berserk because one of his daughters could not seem to be broken from bed-wetting. The Green Beret doctor was also cheating on Colette. In a word, his family was an impediment to his running to and fro freely—ostensibly on Army business. The problem was that he apparently made up some of the stories about why he had to be away, for there is some doubt that he was actually invited to travel with the boxing team. Thus, a man who was overworked, taking drugs, and suffering from latent psychological problems and who always had to have everything his way, felt hemmed in by his family and snapped over a bed-wetting incident in the wee hours of 17 February 1970.

McGinnis finished his book with the prediction that appeals and claims of innocence would go on for years, and he was right. In his words:

> As long as there is money to pay them, of course, the lawyers and private investigators will be able to keep busy for years. There will always be "new witnesses," "new leads." And, no doubt, there will be money; no small amount of it supplied by that remaining hard core of true believers— those who accept Jeffrey MacDonald at face value; those who did not attend the trial in its entirety (or at all) and who have never taken the time and trouble to read the record; those who are still so mesmerized by the glittery surface of MacDonald's personality . . . that their allegiance remains unpolluted by fact.

In August 1983, seven months after the U.S. Supreme Court turned down MacDonald's appeal on the fair-trial issue, McGinniss's book, *Fatal Vision*, was released, and of course its main conclusion was that Jeffrey MacDonald had indeed killed his family. Utterly incensed by the book, MacDonald accused McGinniss of violating an agreement to "fairly portray" the events of the 1979 trial. In April 1984 MacDonald's attorneys moved for a new trial, claiming that there was new evidence. Much of the world already knew about the tragic MacDonald murders by the spring of 1984, and most of the rest of it learned about it via television in November 1984, when the movie version of *Fatal Vision* aired on NBC. MacDonald called it "garbage," and he ended up suing McGinnis for fraud. The writer offered to settle out of court for $200,000, but MacDonald refused, and the suit went forward. For six weeks the trial went on in the summer of 1987. The jury hung—five for MacDonald and one for McGinniss. Lucille Dillon, allegedly enamored with McGinniss, claimed that the writer would be denied his First Amendment right of free speech if the jury decided for the plaintiff. After thus losing the case, the convicted doctor vowed to go to court again, but on the advice of his attorney he settled out of court for $325,000. A new trial would not commence for a year, and MacDonald needed money. So, he took McGinniss's offer.

MacDonald would have preferred vindication instead of the money he received, but money enabled him to hire new lawyers and keep his appeals going. Among his new attorneys were two high-profile barristers named Harvey Silverglate and Alan Dershowitz. Among other appeals, MacDonald sought an "evidentiary hearing" for the consideration of new evidence before the 4th Circuit Court of Appeals, but on 2 June 1992 that appeal was denied because of "procedural default." The appeals continued, but to no avail. By the end of the nineties, MacDonald, languishing in prison at the Sheridan Federal Correctional Institution at Sheridan, Oregon had appealed to the U.S. Supreme Court again, but he despaired of receiving any relief. He had concluded that only an act of Congress could help him. Yet, in 2000, he and his lawyers were hopeful that DNA tests might somehow lead to his exoneration. In fact, MacDonald expressed frustration over delays in the testing, and said he was "worn out" with the press. He predicted that the testing of hair samples would soon be completed, and "Then I'll be back in court winning vindication." Of course, to date, none of this has happened.

About all MacDonald could ever take real comfort in was that his suit against Joe McGinniss had shown that writer, at least to some extent, to be a practitioner of shoddy journalism. Potter and Bost concluded that McGinniss was far worse than a shoddy journalist. To them he was an out-and-out fabricator, a man who manufactured evidence when he needed it and couldn't find it legitimately. They claimed that Sterling Lord, McGinniss's literary agent, boasted of "saving the book," meaning *Fatal Vision*, by persuading the author to junk the original title and the presumed premise that drugged-out hippies had committed the murders and to argue that MacDonald turned out to be guilty after all. Lord and the publisher allegedly decided that the story of a murdering doctor-husband would sell far more books than a tale of murdering hippies wasted on drugs. And so, according to Potter and Bost, McGinniss concocted a theory to explain why MacDonald was guilty. Nor, as they point out, was this McGinniss's only case of fabricating stories. In 1993 he wrote a book called *The Last Brother*, which purported to be a biography of Ted Kennedy. When critics accused him of making up entire conversations between the Kennedy family, McGinniss defended his work as an "interpretive biography." Should such a writer, a man who made things up to suit his purpose, be believed? Not according to Potter and Bost.

In addition to arguing that McGinniss is a fabricator, the two writers, who believe MacDonald to be innocent, assert that they are not alone in concluding that MacDonald was wrongfully convicted. They list some very impressive people who believe as they do. Among those who became convinced of MacDonald's innocence are Ted L. Gunderson, former chief of the FBI's Los Angeles Bureau; Raymond Shedlick, Jr., a retired New York City detective; Dr. Ronald Wright, Broward County (Florida) medical examiner; Dr. Thomas Noguchi, a former Los Angeles County coroner; Dr. David Raskin, a leading polygraph expert; and Dr. Emmanuel Tanay, an expert on the psychiatric aspects of homicide. Equally convinced is Alan Dershowitz, who claims that the so-called "mass of evidence" offered by the government against MacDonald was "an absolute myth" and "a product of prosecutorial chicanery at its worst." And, of course, MacDonald has steadfastly proclaimed his innocence for the past twenty-four years. In 1997, he declared:

> Joe McGinnis convinced the world that I'm not only guilty, but I'm nuts, like some hideous monster. I loved my wife and children. I did not kill them. But the power of the printed word, in the form of *Fatal Vision*, appears to legitimize my conviction, and in so doing, I believe, legitimizes the court's refusal to allow an evidentiary hearing. I find it horribly humor-

ous, macabre in fact, that the only way Joe could convince the world that I was guilty, even with the conviction, was to convince them that I was on drugs and committed the mayhem and overkill that only a drug-wasted mind could have committed. He totally ignored Stoeckley, Colonel Rock's request to investigate her, and all her murderous friends. Then, to convince the readers that I was on drugs, he went to ridiculous lengths, made up doctors' opinions, misquoted medical books, and, in short, invented a theory that he finally admitted, under oath mind you, that he didn't even believe himself. Kafka would have had a field day with this.

It is interesting to note that some of the people who were hell-bent on convicting MacDonald ultimately ran afoul of the law themselves. Warren Coolidge proved to be an embezzler and was disbarred. Jay Stroud, who assisted Victor Woerheide in the grand jury proceedings, bribed a key witness in a high-profile case, causing a reversal of the conviction when the verdict was appealed. James Blackburn, lead prosecutor at MacDonald's trial, turned out to be both an embezzler and a forger. He went to prison for a short time. In a sense, it is neither here nor there that these prosecutors had feet of clay, but it does lend some credence to the contention that the government, a government represented by less than admirable people, was out to get MacDonald by any means possible.

So, what are we to believe about the guilt or innocence of Jeffrey MacDonald? This, of course, is almost tantamount to asking what we are to believe about ultimate questions. Only the individual can decide for herself or himself. There will always be those who believe MacDonald is guilty and got what he deserved, while others will maintain his innocence. Some may think he is probably guilty and committed the murders for some of the reasons set forth by Joe McGinniss who, after all, knew MacDonald very well and sat through the whole trial and heard all of the evidence. It is clear that MacDonald has a narcissistic personality and that he is contemptuous of women, regarding them as objects to be used. He is also a liar. When Freddie Kassab kept hounding him about finding the killers, MacDonald told Kassab in a telephone conversation that one of the murderers had been tracked down and killed by the doctor and some of his Green Beret friends. This was an outright lie. It is quite possible that MacDonald saw Helena and some of her drug-addict friends outside his window on the night of the murders and saw his opportunity to kill his family, blame it on the hippies, and gain his domestic freedom. Clearly, Helena Stoeckley or someone who resembled her was near MacDonald's residence at just before 4:00 a.m. on 17 February 1970. Also, it is known that MacDonald was cheating on Colette and using trips on Army business as his cover for doing it. When she began to balk at his taking such trips, he felt trapped and flipped out, as noted earlier, for some of the reasons given by Joe McGinnis. If, indeed, he saw Stoeckley and her hippie friends outside his windows, he might well have decided to seize the moment.

On the other hand, if MacDonald's trial were held today, it would seem that top-notch lawyers like Alan Dershowitz and Harvey Silverglate (or even Bernie Segal with what is now known) could create reasonable doubt in the minds of most jurors. No one will ever know for sure if Helena Stoeckley and her friends were in the neighborhood that night or, more to the point, if they were inside the MacDonald residence, but Mica's sighting of her, or someone who looked like her, certainly makes that a possibility. Also to be considered is the Rock Report in which Colonel Rock expressed strong suspicion that Helena Stoeckley was involved. And there is the considerable physical evidence that was found in the MacDonald house by the prosecution and hidden from the defense attorneys. Obviously, the CID officers who investigated the murders, the federal attorneys who prosecuted the case, and Judge Dupree who presided over the trial, all believed so strongly in MacDonald's guilt that they didn't want any questions raised. All of them, at least to some degree, contributed to concealing evidence. Jerry Potter and Fred Bost have demonstrated this conclusively. How the federal courts could steadfastly refuse to allow an evidentiary hearing in view of the pertinent information that came to light following the passage of the Freedom of Information Act in 1983 remains a mystery.

MacDonald was found guilty and sits in prison twenty-four years after being sentenced, because the authorities made sure that he would be found guilty and that there would be no reasonable doubt about it. The irony is that plenty of evidence existed to prove reasonable doubt, but a man who was probably guilty failed to get the benefit of it and went to prison for life. Given the evidence that has been brought to light since 1983, it is entirely likely that a jury today would find reasonable doubt and that Jeffrey MacDonald would be a free man instead of fretting behind bars.

In 1970, the final year of the sixties, Fayetteville was suffering from a bad reputation because the Vietnam War had brought a new dimension to hell-raising in the area—an unprecedented flow of drugs and an increasing number of drug addicts. The MacDonald murders made for additional notoriety. Almost lost to the world, because of the steady flow of negative news about "Fayettenam," was the fact that Fayetteville was experiencing, throughout the sixties, unprecedented growth and progress. Little by little it was even lowering the barriers to racial equality, and that was attributable in large measure to pressure from Fort Bragg, which, to many Fayette-villians, was the source of all the area's manifestations of evil. The worst excesses of the Vietnam era gradually faded from memory along the Cape Fear, but the horror of the MacDonald murders was kept before the American public for years. And, during the decade of the seventies, the case of Velma Barfield joined that of Jeffrey MacDonald to keep Fayette-ville continually in the national spotlight. A good town in so many ways, Fayetteville could, seemingly, never get away from being identified with sensational murder cases.

Chapter 8

Velma Barfield Moves into the Spotlight with Jeffrey MacDonald: The 1970s

When I first met Velma Barfield, she was Velma Burke, a young mother in her early twenties. She was holding a baby in her arms. My recollection is that it was a newborn child, and so it would have been Kim, since Ronnie was at least two years old by that time. I was introduced to this young woman with blond hair, blue eyes, engaging smile, and friendly disposition, although she was shy and bordered on being obsequious. She seemed eager to make a good impression on me, and she did. The introduction took place in the home of Ed and Annabel Burke, the parents of Velma's husband, Thomas Burke. I was there on a date with Mary Frances Burke, the younger of Thomas's two sisters. The Burke residence was on a country road south of Fayetteville, perhaps fourteen miles south of the city and just a mile or two from the little town of Parkton. I made many trips to that house and saw all the Burkes numerous times. On one of the trips I took my cousin, Charles Cox, to meet Mary Frances's older sister Doris. Both girls had jet-black hair and gorgeous blue eyes. Charles soon married Doris, but, unfortunately, the marriage lasted only a few years. Mary Frances and I dated for only a few months, and she later married a young man who lived in the Parkton area. Most of this happened between 1953 and 1955.

The Burkes were good people, and, as far as I could tell, so was Velma. No one could have ever made me believe that twenty-three or twenty-four years later this young mother would be arrested for murdering one man and then subsequently admit to poisoning three other people, including her own mother. Not sweet, flattering, obsequious Velma! To me she seemed to be a good, caring, harmless soul. I would have thought it inconceivable that she could ever commit a single murder, much less four murders. And even four might not tell the whole story, because Thomas, her first husband, died in a house fire that some family members thought Velma set. Some others thought that, even if she didn't set the blaze, she walked away from it and left Thomas to burn to death. If she did either, she never admitted to it, but she did confess to the other murders during the investigation that led to her indictment and trial.

By the end of the seventies the Barfield murders were as highly publicized along the Cape Fear as were the MacDonald murders, although they never received as much national and international notice as did those connected with the Green Beret doctor who managed to dodge going to trial until 1979. Velma's day in court came much quicker. Arrested in March 1978, she was convicted on 2 December of the same year. The Bladen County jury that found her guilty recommended that she be given the death sentence. For the next few months the state and national spotlight was on her until Jeffrey MacDonald went to trial in Raleigh on 19 July 1979. Then, for the next few years, both of them were constantly in the news. More of Velma's gruesome story will follow, after we examine some of the developments that shaped Fayetteville and the surrounding area during the seventies.

Throughout that decade Fayetteville and the Cape Fear region continued to grow apace. The war in Vietnam began to wind down early in the decade, and "Fayettenam" promised to become a normal town again, at least as normal as a town situated next to the world's largest army base can be. The decade opened on a highly positive note, when the long-awaited Kelly-Springfield Tire Company plant opened in April 1971 on Highway 401 just north of town. The forty-million-dollar plant was the biggest industry Fayetteville had ever had. Eventually it was expected to employ 1,700 people and have a payroll of about $10.5 million per year. The company's officials were sure the plant would make Fayetteville one of the manufacturing capitals of the world.

A month after the momentous opening of Kelly-Springfield came another plant opening, that of DuPont. One of the premier chemical companies in the world, DuPont opened its new plant in May between the Cape Fear River and Highway 87, a few miles south of Fayetteville, just across the Bladen County line.

The good economic news continued to roll in for the Cape Fear region when, in November 1972, Kelly-Springfield announced plans for a multimillion-dollar expansion that would add 250,000 square feet to the plant and increase the number of its employees by ten percent. Fayetteville seemed poised to shake off its image of an army town dependent on the Fort Bragg payroll and to acquire the new image of industrial giant—at least by North Carolina standards.

Almost before Fayettevillians could finish congratulating themselves on these encouraging economic signs, events beyond their control conspired to dampen their optimism. In May 1973 OPEC (the Organization of Petroleum Exporting Companies) declared an oil embargo to drive up the price of oil. Along with other Americans, the people along the Cape Fear were soon waiting in long lines at gas pumps for the little gasoline that was available. Many service stations, with no gasoline to sell, closed their doors. The nation, indeed the whole world, faced an energy crisis that carried into 1974. Waiting in long lines for gasoline continued, and service stations closed on Sundays. The government cut speed limits on major highways to 55 miles per hour and urged heads of households to turn their thermostats down to 68 degrees during the winter months. Some businesses felt compelled to cut back on their operating hours. Not until March 1974 did OPEC call off the oil embargo.

The energy crisis was followed by an economic downturn that brought a recession to the Cape Fear region. Fayetteville manufacturing plants laid off workers and/or cut back production. The number of unemployed citizens took a huge jump. In February 1975 Black & Decker laid off 900 workers. Three months later Burlington Apparel Fabrics announced the closing of the Fayetteville Fabrics weaving plant on Southern Avenue. The following year, in November, the Rohm and Haas polyester fabric plant closed its doors and hung out a for-sale sign. The last of the recession's victims fell in February 1977 when Tolar, Hart, and Holt Mills closed its doors, putting 150 people out of work. Imported yarns being dumped on the American market from foreign countries undercut American producers by twenty-five percent, making it impossible for the Fayetteville mill to compete.

Eventually, the nation and the Cape Fear region with it pulled out of the economic doldrums. An early sign that good times would return sooner or later came at the nadir of the recession when Western Publishing Company of Racine, Wisconsin revealed plans to build a $10 million plant near Highway 301 four miles south of Fayetteville. The next sign of an upturn came just as Rohm and Haas announced that it was closing. In the same month—November 1976—Kelly-Springfield announced that it was planning to add 500 people to its work force over the next year. Rohm and Haas was replaced by Monsanto, which bought the closed Rohm and Haas plant. Moreover, in April 1979 Black & Decker followed the earlier lead of Kelly-Springfield by announcing plans for an expansion that would increase its work force by 500. The next month Westinghouse Electric revealed that it would establish a plant near the airport that would ultimately hire 200 workers. Then, in 1980, the final year of the decade, M. J. Soffe, a manufacturer of casual apparel and sportswear, declared its intentions to build a $1.25 million plant on Middle Road. The gloomy clouds of recession that had hung over the Cape Fear during the mid-seventies seemed to be evaporating.

The opening and expanding of manufacturing plants was certainly the biggest economic news of the seventies in Fayetteville, but there were other economic stimuli at work, too. Some of the most impressive building projects ever seen along the Cape Fear took place during that decade. Word spread in September 1972 that a new shopping mall was on the drawing board. By this time, Fayetteville was the home of several malls, but the ones already standing were expected to be dwarfed by the new Cross Creek Mall, a sprawling complex designed to give Fayetteville the largest shopping center in eastern North Carolina. Located on the Highway 401 bypass, the huge shopping center opened on 25 February 1975 and immediately became the heart of Fayetteville's shopping district.

Downtown Fayetteville, already in decline, began to show signs of becoming a ghost town. Most of its landmark stores moved westward to the new mall—Sears, Roebuck & Company, J. C. Penney Company, and Belk's Department Store. Fleishman's Big Store remained, but had to close its doors near the end of 1979. Seven months earlier, in May 1979, S. H. Kress's store closed, ending the five-and-dime era in the city. This was the first store in Fayetteville that I remember hearing about as a child. Called "Kressie's" or the "dime store," by most Fayetteville natives, it was a genuine landmark for me, and so was the Capitol, which managed to hang on until 1990 before it folded. Cross Creek Mall mushroomed as downtown dwindled to almost nothing. An attempt to revitalize the old business district, which was launched in 1979, proved only partially successful. More will be said it about this later.

Another economic stimulus to the area was the Owen Drive Freeway, later renamed the All-American Freeway. State highway funds to purchase the right-of-way were allocated in October 1972, but construction did not begin until May 1974. This 8.2 mile freeway, practically the equivalent of an interstate highway, was a sizeable undertaking that cost millions of dollars. It ran from Owen Drive, near Cape Fear Valley Hospital, all the way to Womack Army Hospital at Fort Bragg. Not until September 1978 did it officially open for traffic. The cost and manpower to build it had a huge impact on the local economy during the recession, presumably helping the area out of its economic funk.

The same was true of the bypass section of Interstate 95, which was being built a few miles east of Fayetteville at approximately the same time. The state highway commission earmarked the funds to buy the right-of-way for the bypass in July 1972. Merchants along Highway 301, which for years had been the main road taking traffic north and south through town, fought hard to prevent Interstate 95 from bypassing the city. They were not successful, and the seventeen-mile stretch of road opened in December 1980, just as the decade of the seventies reached its end. Affected merchants made plans, as best they could, to minimize the loss of business they feared the bypass would cause. In the meantime the enormous outlay of funds to build the superhighway had benefited the local economy a great deal.

Several other building projects provided similar beneficial results. One was the new Wachovia Building, which was finished in 1973. This eleven-story structure replaced the ten-story First Citizens Bank Building as the tallest structure in town. The impressive building featured the Plaza Cafeteria and the Pent House Club, but the major occupant was Wachovia Bank. The skyline of downtown Fayetteville was slightly altered by this tall, new building, making it more eye-catching, just before numerous merchants abandoned the area and headed to Cross Creek Mall to open new businesses there.

Finally, as the seventies drew to a close, the Cumberland County Commission ended years of controversy by approving, in November 1980, the construction of a new private hospital on Robeson Street, right on the site where my old high school had stood. The new facility would replace the old Highsmith-Rainey Memorial Hospital on Hay Street a few blocks up Haymount Hill. It was to be a 150-bed facility and was to cost $11 million to build. When constructed it, like its predecessor up the hill, would be known as the Highsmith-Rainey Memorial Hospital—not an enormous building and by no means comparable to Cape Fear Valley Hospital, but a fine facility by any standard. And, as in the case of the Wachovia Building, it would benefit the local economy and add some luster to the city's skyline.

The seventies had plenty of problems left over from the sixties, including controversy over the Vietnam War and ubiquitous racial tension, particularly regarding the integration of the public schools. Jane Fonda had already visited Fayetteville and Fort Bragg once, protesting American involvement in Vietnam. She had not been well received the first time, and that was doubly true when she returned in March 1971 with black comedian Dick Gregory and fellow actor Donald Sutherland. "Hanoi Jane," as she was ultimately called, found few supporters in town, as she and her entourage performed an antiwar play at the Haymarket Square Coffee House. She called her theater group F.T.A., which stood for "Free the Army." Responsible for inviting her was a local group called GI's United. A year after her second appearance in Fayetteville, Fonda posed for photos on an antiaircraft battery in North Vietnam. More than a few people living in the area were convinced that she was clearly a traitor to her country.

Even though Jane Fonda was despised by many for essentially giving aid and comfort to the enemy, the Vietnam War was obviously the most unpopular war in the history of the nation. Millions of Americans, regardless of the attitude in and around Fort Bragg, had a problem seeing that it was in our national interest to be in Vietnam. Lyndon Johnson had seen this in 1968. He sensed that if he ran again for President, the war issue would bring about his defeat, and so he declined to run. His successor, Richard Nixon, seeing no honorable way to withdraw from the quagmire in Southeast Asia, decided to go all out to win the war by, among other actions, invading Cambodia. When his tactics failed miserably, he agreed to negotiate with the North Vietnamese, and the negotiations seemed to go on endlessly in Paris during 1971 and 1972. Nixon finally reached a peace agreement with North Vietnam in January 1973.

Meanwhile, Nixon had pulled off a daring diplomatic stroke by visiting Communist China in 1972 and opening diplomatic relations with a regime that our government had regarded heretofore as illegitimate. Opening "Red China" to diplomatic intercourse and ending the Vietnam War were impressive achievements, and, one would think, they would insure Nixon's future political aspirations of success. Such was not the case, for the bold president became engulfed in the famous Watergate scandal and was forced to resign his office in August 1974. Designed to make sure of Nixon's reelection in 1972, the break-in at Watergate, which housed the national headquarters of the Democratic Party, caused him to be driven from office. In all of American history, he remains the only man who has resigned the presidency. Even so, he must be credited with finally seeing that the Vietnam War was a lost cause and bringing it to an end.

Tensions over our involvement in Vietnam ended relatively early in the decade of the seventies, but tensions over racial issues held on. In June 1971 the U.S. Department of Health, Education, and Welfare decreed that the Fayetteville school system had to desegregate further. Two months later, in August, the Fayetteville Board of Education signed a contract with Wheatley Motors, Inc. to bus about 3,000 school children to school for the purpose of achieving integration. Still, the federal courts were not satisfied, for a federal judge in September gave the city school system thirty days to desegregate its elementary schools. Almost a year later, in August 1972, the federal courts and the city school board were still not in agreement. The board appealed Judge Algernon Butler's decision to implement a plan that included the busing of junior and senior high school students. Six more years passed before the federal courts were convinced that the Fayetteville school system had complied with the U.S. Supreme Court's order to desegregate.

Finally, in September 1978, the U.S. District Court for Eastern North Carolina lifted the court-ordered integration of the system by declaring that the "matter had reached a satisfactory conclusion." Along with the racial barriers that were coming down in the Fayetteville school system were some old school buildings, including Central School where I attended grades three through six. The building where I spent four very good years had long since been abandoned. In 1973 it gave way to a parking lot that sits across the street from the Cumberland County Public Library. Thus, in a number of different ways, the Fayetteville school system was changing during the seventies.

Discrimination in education was one thing. In the workplace it was another, and both blacks and women began demanding fair and equal treatment in their search for employment. In 1972 women vastly outnumbered men as teachers in the school classrooms, but they were poorly represented in administrative positions. There were forty-six principals in the county schools, and only three were women. In the city schools women held only seven of thirty-one administrative positions. This gender discrimination received more and more attention, as women insisted on their right to fair employment. Controversy over the issue of "affirmative action" in the work place went on for years until, little by little, governments and institutions fell into compliance. For instance, in June 1979 the Fayetteville City Council adopted a five-year affirmative action plan for the purpose of hiring more women and minorities. Even before this action was taken, Fayetteville had taken several steps toward the new world of gender equality. In February 1973 Pauline G. Owen was hired as the city's first policewoman, and in November 1975 city councilwoman Beth Finch became the city's first woman mayor. Another indication that the city was moving toward gender equality appeared in May 1980 when Judy Gardner became the first woman police officer in Fayetteville to complete the course at the Police Department's training academy. She placed in the top five of her graduating class. While the area seemed to be moving ahead on the question of gender equality, there is little evidence that much progress was being made toward racial equality in the work place, even though Fayetteville had long since had black members on the city council.

Still Fayetteville had been making impressive strides toward becoming a truly modern city, and its importance steadily increased throughout the twentieth century—especially following World War II. Nothing demonstrated this quite as much as what happened on the political scene in the seventies. By then Fayetteville had acquired some political recognition and enjoyed some real clout. After all, the likes of Franklin D. Roosevelt and John F. Kennedy had paid visits to the city, and more than a few candidates for the presidency had made Fayetteville a campaign stop in their bids for the White House. Terry Sanford had already served as North Carolina's governor during the early sixties, and in 1972 he announced his candidacy for president. Unfortunately—in the eyes of many, at least—his campaign proved to be abortive, but Sanford would try unsuccessfully again. When he made his second attempt in 1976, I supported him for the short time his campaign lasted. Even so, Sanford would eventually wind up in the U.S. Senate for a brief time.

On several occasions Fayetteville had sent men to Washington to serve, notably J. Bayard Clark for twenty years in the House of Representatives. Regrettably Clark, though a distinguished man in the eyes of Fayette-villians, never made much of a mark in Congress. In 1972, however, a Fayetteville man, Charles G. Rose, III was elected to the seat in the House of Representatives that Clark had once occupied. Rose was a go-getter and did leave his imprint to some degree during his multiple terms in Congress. When he ran in 1972, Rose was something of a political novice, but he carried every county in North Carolina's Seventh Congressional District. His opponent was none other than state Senator N. Hector McGeachy, the son of Sheriff N. H. McGeachy, who had enjoyed a forty-year tenure as the sheriff of Cumberland County.

I knew Charlie Rose when he was a small boy, and I went through some of my school years with him. He was two grades behind me. I also knew—at least to speak to him—his father, Charles G. Rose, Jr., who served a term as mayor of Fayetteville. I can't say that I was friends with either the father or the son, for we didn't travel in the same circles. Yet, I can say that I had great respect for Mayor Rose, and I don't remember anything about young Charlie that I found disagreeable. From what I know about his work in Congress, he was a fine congressman, and I will always be grateful to him for helping my mother when Medicare and Blue Cross couldn't agree on who her primary health insurance carrier was. In typical bureaucratic fashion, each one of them tried to make the other my mother's primary carrier. Only after she wrote to Charlie Rose was the matter finally settled. In my mother's eyes, he was "all right," and that is good enough for me. When visiting Fayetteville through the years, I heard of this accomplishment and that being attributed to the congressman, and it always appeared to me that he was representing his district very effectively. And so, I echo my mother's sentiments: "Charlie Rose is all right."

There was other important political news associated with Fayetteville during the seventies, as presidents and presidential hopefuls passed through. In April 1975 former Georgia governor Jimmy Carter brought his campaign for the Democratic nomination for president to the city. After a luncheon at the Highland Country Club, Governor Carter held a press conference. Even before his appearance in Fayetteville, he already had at least a few supporters, since his sister, Ruth Stapleton, was a resident. Later, after becoming president, Carter would return to Fayetteville. The occasion was the wedding of his nephew, Scott Stapleton, the son of the president's sister Ruth and her husband Dr. Robert Stapleton. Carter's family was with him on 22 December 1977 when Scott Stapleton and his bride, Carol Lee Gainey, said their wedding vows at the Highland Presbyterian Church. Quite a few Fayetteville residents tried to catch a glimpse of the first family and also of the president's infamous brother, Billy Carter. While on hand for the wedding, Billy took the occasion afterward to promote the product known as Billy Beer, which was named for him. At the Bordeaux Inn, Billy posed for a picture with Charles Priest, the local distributor of Billy Beer. When comparing the Carter brothers—the president and his somewhat goofy brother—people could only shake their heads and wonder.

In his quest for the Democratic nomination for president, Carter had visited Fayetteville in 1975, well over a year before the Democratic national convention would nominate its candidate for 1976. Seeking to be the Republican nominee in that same election was former Governor Ronald Reagan from California. Reagan spoke to local supporters on a campaign stop at the Fayetteville Municipal Airport during his unsuccessful campaign in 1976. Helping him to draw a crowd was the beloved actor Jimmy Stewart, who had endorsed the former governor for the Republican nomination. Although Reagan's bid for nomination and election failed that year, it succeeded four years later, and the so-called "Great Communicator" went on to serve eight years in the White House as one of the nation's most popular presidents in the last half of the twentieth century.

Not only people of political prominence but premier entertainers made their way to Fayetteville during the seventies. Fayetteville was a burgeoning city, and it was now deemed worthy of appearances by the elite from the entertainment world. John Carradine, though perhaps not the Frederick March of his day, was certainly a well-established actor who appeared at the Fort Bragg Playhouse in October of 1974. The production was *Inherit the Wind*, and Carradine played the role of Henry Drummond, the fictional Clarence Darrow, of the story about the famous Scopes Monkey Trial of 1925. Carradine's appearance was said to be an experiment in bringing in top actors to work with local actors.

A few months after Carradine's performance at Fort Bragg, jazz-great Dizzy Gillespie performed to the delight of Fayetteville State University students in Seabrook Auditorium. Gillespie, of course, had long been one of the top black performers in the music world, but neither his nor Carradine's appearance compared to the coming, the following year, of the "king of rock and roll," Elvis Presley. The famed rock-and-roll artist performed in August 1976 before wildly cheering fans at the Cumberland County Arena in three sold-out shows. Elvis was scheduled to return on 25 August 1977 for another appearance, but he died nine days before that date. His Fayetteville fans and many who were not his fans were stunned, reacting in disbelief that the king was dead, presumably from overdosing himself on drugs.

Creating about the same excitement over entertainment as the personal appearance of movie stars and musicians was the *Star Wars* mania that hit Fayetteville along with the rest of the world in the summer of 1977. This George Lucas science-fiction movie opened in Fayetteville on 16 June and ran for a couple of months. By August, 46,000 people had been captivated by its special effects, as Luke Skywalker and friends fought it out with Darth Vader and his evil empire. The book on which the movie was based was also in great demand, and copies of it vanished from bookstore shelves quickly after being placed there. Record bars soon found that the official soundtrack and a disco version were hot items, too. T-shirts with *Star Wars* designs sold like lemonade on a hot July day. People along the Cape Fear, like others all over the nation, were made dizzy by the *Star Wars* fever in the summer of '77.

Besides stars from the entertainment world and the excitement generated by *Stars Wars*, the most popular movie ever to be shown up to that time, Fayetteville had visits from at least two of the nation's best-known evangelists during the seventies. The North Carolina Baptist Convention was held in Fayetteville in November 1976, and the most prominent speaker to address convention members was Billy Graham, a native son of North Carolina and the foremost evangelist in America, or even the world. At his Fayetteville appearance he spoke to 5,000 people at the Cumberland Memorial Auditorium. Since the late 1940s Graham had commanded the nation's attention with his dynamic preaching of the gospel. All of his sermons ended with an invitation to come forward and make a decision accepting Christ as savior. Graham's ministry would continue through the twentieth century and into the twenty-first. Although he was eighty-three years of age and noticeably diminished by Parkinson's disease at the time of this writing, he was still preaching the same message that he had proclaimed as a young evangelist. He had served as spiritual adviser to a half-dozen or more U.S. presidents and was truly an American icon.

In contrast to Graham, there was Jimmy Swaggart, the television evangelist who hit town in January 1979 and launched the Jimmy Swaggart Crusade at Cumberland County Memorial Arena. His initial audience numbered about 4,500. This television evangelist was emotional and dynamic and as authoritative as a Marine drill sergeant. For years he cajoled his television listeners into sending him millions of dollars. Eventually, however, Swaggart's true colors came out. He was a phony, and that became evident when he was found cavorting with prostitutes. Unfortunately, he fooled countless numbers of people for years, and even after he was caught in a compromising situation he begged God's forgiveness on his television program. Tears streamed down his face as he admitted, "I have sinned." He certainly had, and everybody in the country knew it. Still, he had the temerity to continue his television ministry. Although the contributions fell off precipitously, enough continued coming in to keep him going on a much smaller scale than before his fall.

A religious leader of a different sort visited Fayetteville in February 1977. He was the Reverend Martin Luther King, Sr., father of the great civil rights leader who had been slain a decade before. It was national Black History Month, and Chapel Baptist Church on Raeford Road was celebrating the occasion. The Reverend Mr. King was the featured speaker. Of course, his appearance generated nothing like the excitement Billy Graham's had a few months earlier, or even as much as Jimmy Swaggart's would nearly two years later.

In addition to having arrived as an important city in the economic, political, and religious arenas, Fayetteville continued to make news because of its sports figures and achievements. Since the sixties Fayetteville/Terry Sanford High School had been a basketball power, but the predominantly black high school, E. E. Smith, came on strong in 1971, when the Golden Bulls of that school defeated the Bulldogs of Terry Sanford 57-45 to win the Eastern 4-A Division I championship. A sports accolade came Fayetteville's way in December 1973 when John Daskal, the football coach at C. Reid Ross High School, was named Mid-South 4-A, Division IV coach of the year. Athletics at Terry Sanford made the news again in 1978 when sisters Lisa and Margit Monaco, who were students there, won the North Carolina High School Athletic Association's girls' doubles championship in tennis for the second straight year.

Beyond high school athletics, Ray Floyd, the city's highly publicized professional golfer, was in for some local competition, it seemed, when young Chip Beck won several golf tournaments in the mid-seventies and showed promise as a future professional. Beck certainly had potential, but Floyd showed that he was still the golfer from Fayetteville with whom to reckon, when he shot a seventeen-under-par for a total of 271 to win the Masters golf championship at Augusta in 1976. Floyd was still "the Man."

There was golf, and then there was track, and the area produced a champion in that field, too. Kathy McMillan was a black woman athlete from Raeford—not Fayetteville. Even so, she was claimed by the entire Sand Hills area when she set a record in the long jump at the Pan American Games in 1975. Her jump of twenty-one feet, two and three-quarters inches broke the old record by one and a half inches. At the Montreal Olympics the following year McMillan won the silver medal in the women's long jump in track and field. Fort Bragg also came in for some recognition at Montreal when Charles Mooney, an Army sergeant stationed at Bragg, won the silver medal in the bantamweight boxing final.

Fayetteville would remember the seventies, too, for a number of other developments that can be lumped into the category of miscellaneous. In January 1971, because of a U.S. Supreme Court ruling the previous month, twenty people in Cumberland County under the age of twenty-one registered to vote. The new minimum age for voting had been set by the court at eighteen. The first county resident to register was a young man named Tommy Pleasant.

Times were changing, as younger people, women, and blacks were gaining additional rights. The old world that had been dominated by white males age twenty-one and over was in jeopardy of fading away. This no doubt upset some people, but there was more to worry about than unsettling Supreme Court decisions. There was also Mother Nature. In February 1971 two people were killed and sixty-seven injured when a tornado tore a path through Fayetteville and northeast Cumberland County. The area sustained damages estimated at $5 million. The weather buffeted the area again in February 1973 when the worst snowstorm Fayetteville had seen in years dumped eight inches of snow on the city. Hundreds of travelers became stranded on Interstate 95 east of town. Another snowstorm in February 1979 blanketed the city briefly, but on that occasion the storm produced little to worry about, as the snow soon melted.

Several Fayetteville institutions were accorded recognition during the seventies. Fayetteville State University celebrated its one-hundredth birthday in April 1977. To mark the occasion Carl T. Rowan, a renowned black journalist, was invited to deliver the keynote address. The school had come a long way, from Fayetteville Normal School, to Fayetteville State Teachers College, to Fayetteville State University (since 1972), and it had made worthwhile contributions to culture and education in the area. In November 1974 recognition went to the city's most visible building, namely, the Market House, which had served as the unofficial symbol of Fayetteville for almost 140 years. The National Parks Service certified the old structure as a National Historic Landmark and presented a bronze plaque to so designate it. Another institution that made the news in Fayetteville during this period was the newspaper that reported the news. The *Fayetteville Observer* had the distinction of being the oldest newspaper in the state that was still printing the news, dating all the way back to 1816. Ramon L. Yarborough, president of Fayetteville Publishing Company, announced in February 1973 that his company would soon publish a morning paper as well as the afternoon *Observer*. The morning paper was to be called the *Fayetteville Times*. Publishing two newspapers at its relatively small facility on Hay Street was a strain, and so, in January 1978, the Fayetteville Publishing Company abandoned its inadequate quarters downtown and moved out to a large plant on Whitfield Road in Massey Hill. More than twenty-five years later, it continues operations in this fine, modern facility.

Not all old institutions in Fayetteville were flourishing. Some were in serious decline, including the Colony Theater. The withering of downtown brought an end to downtown entertainment centers, except the bars and strip joints that catered to the wilder crowd. In April 1976 the Colony, where I had worked for two years as an usher, where I had seen the world premiere of *The Carbine Williams Story*, where I had taken the ticket of the great General George C. Marshall, and where I had awakened quite a few slightly inebriated soldiers after the last show, closed it doors forever. The last film it showed was *Jaws*. How fitting, for the Colony, like so many downtown establishments, was the victim of a monster—the outlying malls to which the vast majority of citizens fled, spurning a once vital and relatively attractive downtown area.

Throughout the seventies, there was plenty of news to report as Fayetteville continued to change rather drastically. The local newspapers reported news of a far graver nature after 7 November 1979. That was the date on which sixty-three Americans were taken hostage in Teheran, Iran, and Americans at home listened to and read about the news coming out of Iran with great concern. Ten of the original hostages were soon released, but fifty-three remained in Teheran. Irate Americans wanted all of their fellow citizens released so that they could return home. About a month after the hostages were taken, downtown church bells tolled, as did the Market House bell, at an appointed time, as Fayettevillians showed their support for getting the hostages out of Iran. Armbands symbolizing support for those being held captive were worn by local citizens, just as they were being worn by other Americans across the nation.

Because of Fort Bragg, Fayetteville felt the crisis more keenly than did other parts of the country, when President Jimmy Carter sent members of the base's "Delta Team," or "Charlie's Angels" to rescue the hostages. The

Delta Team, headquartered at Fort Bragg, was an elite squad whose purpose was that of combating terrorists. Colonel Charles Beckwith, popularly known as "Chargin' Charlie" because of his heroics in the Vietnam War, led the Delta force. In April 1980 he and about ninety of his men were flown into Iran to bring out the hostages. The mission was unsuccessful, primarily because mechanical failures put out of commission three of the eight helicopters that were to be used to extricate the hostages. Concluding that five helicopters were not sufficient to carry the fifty-three hostages out, Beckwith recommended that the mission be aborted. On 24 April, as the rescue aircraft prepared to leave Iran, a C-130 Hercules collided with one of the helicopters, and eight servicemen died in the fiery crash. Fire and exploding ammunition prevented the rest of the rescue force from retrieving the bodies of the eight men who were killed. Beckwith, who said that he sat down and cried over the loss of the eight men, was obviously shaken by the experience. Less than a year later he retired from the Army and established an antiterrorist consulting business in Texas. He also wrote a book on the hostage rescue attempt that had ended in tragedy.

Held for 444 days, the hostages were finally released by the Iranians in January 1981, just as President Carter was turning over the presidency to Ronald Reagan, who had defeated him in the 1980 election. Presumably Carter's handling of the Iran hostage crisis was a factor in his loss of popular support and, consequently, his ouster from office.

On a far-less-serious note—perhaps even a whimsical one—the "streaking" craze that hit the nation in 1974, primarily on college campuses, affected Fayetteville. In May of that year two Fort Bragg soldiers "streaked" down Hay Street in their combat boots—nothing but their combat boots! That is what "streaking" meant. One ran along with almost nothing on. Some "streakers" wore ski masks, while some wore nothing at all. It is interesting that the two soldiers chose to run in their combat boots, but district judge Joe Dupree was not amused. He had already shown himself to be a bit sensitive about people showing off their body parts by threatening to fine or jail women who showed up in his courtroom wearing mini skirts. He levied heavy fines on the two soldiers and warned that the same would be imposed on any more "streakers" who might be brought into his courtroom.

The crime of "streaking" caused some to shake their heads in disbelief and others to chuckle, but there was a crime much older and far more serious than "streaking" that was being committed along the Cape Fear with increasing frequency, it seemed. That crime was murder, and, largely because of Jeffrey MacDonald and Velma Barfield, it made the news in Fayetteville and Cumberland County during the seventies as never before. While these two people got most of the ink in the press and were the most talked about on radio and television, they were not by any means the only murderers of the decade. In the summer of 1972 ten murders were committed in Cumberland County, setting a new record, and, as noted earlier, crime statistics reported by the FBI in 1975 (for 1974) ranked Fayetteville fifth in the nation in violent crimes.

One of the violent crimes that made headlines in the early and mid-seventies had been committed back in 1969. It was the shooting death of a twenty-five-year-old black farmworker named Wilbert Signal at Linden, a few miles up the Cape Fear from Fayetteville. The man accused of the killing was Linden farmer Haywood Honeycutt, who was tried four times for the crime. Two of the juries that sat on the case could not reach a verdict. Then, in 1973, Honeycutt was convicted of the lesser charge of voluntary manslaughter. The verdict was appealed, and the North Carolina Court of Appeals overturned the jury's decision and ordered a new trial. District Attorney Ed Grannis prosecuted the case at the fourth trial, which produced an astonishing result. Judge James H. Pou Bailey dismissed the charges on legal technicalities, in spite of the fact that the state's chief witness, Chester DeBerry (who was then in federal prison), testified that Honeycutt shot Signal without provocation.

Shockingly, Judge Bailey brought the trial to an abrupt end. Dismissing the charges, he explained his decision by reviewing the history of the case. He noted that twice juries had failed to reach a verdict on the charge of murder. The third trial had produced a verdict of voluntary manslaughter, but that verdict had been overturned for errors in the admissibility of evidence. The U.S. Supreme Court, according to Bailey, had ruled in two cases that a person granted a new trial for errors could not be subjected to a future penalty that would be more than could have been imposed for the original verdict. Judge Bailey explained that the jury at the third trial had in effect found Honeycutt innocent of anything but manslaughter. Yet, the state's case clearly indicated first- or second-degree murder, but the Supreme Court rulings prevented him from being retried on those greater charges. Moreover, the state was able to offer no evidence to support the charge of manslaughter (because murder was indicated), and hence there was "only one logical ruling and that is nonsuit." Underneath all of the legal reasoning and terms, Judge Bailey's decision was that a murderer had to be set free. This controversial ruling, which was handed down in late June 1975, provoked many comments along the Cape Fear about the flaws in the legal system that allowed people to literally get away with murder.

Not all murderers beat the system, however, as the cases of Jeffrey MacDonald and Velma Barfield would prove. But they were not the only ones who were "weighed in the balance and found wanting." There was also Norris Carlton Taylor, who, at least for a brief moment, was in the spotlight with them. Taylor, an African American who was a vicious man by any standards, terrorized Fayetteville in the summer of 1978. On 1 September he killed Mildred Murchison, a thirty-year-old mother of two sons. Mrs. Murchison, also black, was pregnant at the time Taylor shot her twice in the back as she tried to run from him. He was trying to steal her car from the parking lot of the Social Security building on Lamon Street, where Murchison worked. He simply gunned her down and sped away in a car he had stolen previously. Ten hours later he was captured in Northampton County near the Virginia line. Taylor soon confessed to the Murchison shooting and twenty-two other felonies, including a total of five murders.

Actually what Taylor did in the summer of 1978 was the tail end of a crime spree that started much earlier in the year. On 2 January he had shot and killed a New York model named Kathileen Ann Mansullo at a motel north of Fayetteville in Johnston County. A Johnston County all-white jury in Smithfield found him guilty, and he received a life sentence. However, on 11 July he broke out of the Johnston County Jail and proceeded, over the next six weeks, to commit rape, murder, and kidnapping, among other offenses. On 28 August he abducted Jewel Kaye Taylor (no relation) from the Wachovia Bank Building parking lot in downtown Fayetteville and raped her. He then stole the car of Malcolm Biles, a Fayetteville resident who lived at 1934 N. Pearl Street. Taylor forced Biles to drive him to Virginia, but along the way he shot the Fayetteville man in the face and left him for dead. Biles somehow managed to survive. On 30 August Taylor kidnapped another woman in Hampton, Virginia and headed south for Fayetteville. Somehow the young woman managed to escape. Two days later, back in Fayetteville, Taylor shot Mildred Murchison, kidnapped a teenager named Patty Bazemore, and headed north again toward Virginia. Before being apprehended in Northampton County, Taylor released Ms. Bazemore. The police had assumed her murder and had already begun dragging the Cape Fear River to find her body. Fortunately, she was found safe and unharmed. It was reported that Taylor was driving Malcolm Biles's car at the time of his capture.

Until the city authorities knew that Taylor was in custody on 1 September, women were urged not to even walk from their places of employment to their cars without an escort. Fortunately, Taylor was on the loose for only a few hours before being captured on his way back to Virginia.

The thirty-four-year-old African-American killer was a native of Hampton, Virginia. Full of rage, this evil man inflicted his wrath on just about anyone who got in his way or simply crossed his path. In July 1979 he went on trial for his life. District Attorney Ed Grannis demanded the death penalty throughout the two-week trial in New Hanover County, where the case was heard in the interest of giving Taylor a fair trial. Everybody in Fayetteville knew about Taylor, and there was no chance of seating an impartial jury there. Several times during the trial he complained of headaches and refused to enter the courtroom. After Taylor made obscene remarks to the jury, the trial continued without his presence, as Judge Robert Gavin placed him in a holding cell near the courtroom. The surly defendant was convicted of kidnapping and armed robbery for which he was sentenced to eighty years in prison. He was given twenty more years on an assault charge. On the murder charge, the New Hanover jury of seven women and five men deliberated less than three hours before recommending the death penalty. Judge Gavin obliged the jury and ordered Taylor executed by asphyxiation on 28 September 1979. Gavin later stayed the execution pending automatic appeal of the case to the North Carolina Supreme Court. Taylor was placed on Death Row in Central Prison. He was still there in 2002.

The Taylor case momentarily diverted the public's attention from the spectacular media coverage of the MacDonald and Barfield murders. MacDonald's case had already been in the news for almost a decade, dating back to early 1970, and coverage of it gained momentum following the Green Beret doctor's indictment by a federal grand jury in Raleigh in late January 1975. That was big news, and it was destined to grow bigger. MacDonald appealed, and the next year the appellate court freed him because he had been denied a speedy trial. More big news. In 1978 the U.S. Supreme Court overturned the ruling of the appellate court. Again, big news. In 1979 MacDonald went on trial (the same month as Taylor), was convicted for three murders, and was given three consecutive life sentences. In December 1978, approximately nine months before MacDonald was convicted, Velma Barfield was found guilty of murdering her boyfriend (or fiancé, according to her), Stuart Taylor, and sentenced to death. For the next few years, Barfield and MacDonald would share the news, as MacDonald sought in vain through numerous appeals to get a new trial, and as Barfield, also through countless appeals, sought to avoid being executed. Taylor's vicious crimes, probably because they were committed in broad open daylight in downtown Fayetteville, had snatched the city's attention away from MacDonald and Barfield; but only briefly.

As indicated above, the coverage of MacDonald's case went on for years after he had been sent to prison for life and that of Barfield's continued until she was executed in 1984 at Central Prison in Raleigh. Why was Barfield, a mother and a grandmother, sentenced to death? Why not to life in prison like the sentence MacDonald received? One reason the sentences came down the way they did was that MacDonald was tried in a federal court, while Barfield's trial was held in a state court. The state of North Carolina can impose the death penalty for murder, but in federal court the death penalty applies only in the case of treason against the United States. Hence, MacDonald never faced the possibility of paying the ultimate price for his crimes, while Barfield confronted that dismal prospect from the day she was indicted. Velma's journey from her troubled, drug-plagued existence to her execution at Central Prison by lethal injection on 2 November 1984 began on 13 March 1978 when she surrendered herself to authorities at the Robeson County sheriff's office and signed a confession admitting to killing her fiancé Stuart Taylor, her mother, and two other people. Fifteen days later, on 28 March, the Robeson County grand jury indicted her for first-degree murder in the death of Taylor. Justice in the form of a conviction and a death sentence came swiftly on 2 December of the same year, but a series of appeals kept the Barfield case before the public for another six years.

What sort of person would poison her own mother? How did Velma change from the shy, flattering, sweet-seeming young mother I had known in the mid-fifties to a calculated murderer? Velma's story began on 29 October 1932, when she was born as Margie Velma Bullard to Murphy and Lillie Bullard of Wade, North Carolina, a small town on the Cape Fear just north of Fayetteville. Velma, as she was always called, was the second of nine children, her brother Olive being the oldest. People who didn't know farmer Murphy Bullard well thought highly of him, considering him to be a person who would help others any way that he could. If a fellow farmer needed help getting his crop in due to illness, Murphy was the first on the scene to offer a hand. Velma saw a far different side of her father, however. According to her, he was a violent man who blew up over nothing, threw chairs across the room, and pulled drawers out of chests. When drinking, he was even more mean-tempered. He treated Velma badly and her older brother Olive even worse. Velma could not understand why Lillie stayed with him. She hated and feared her father as much as she loved him and obviously resented her mother for not standing up for the children. Every time Murphy took the strap to Velma for "smart mouthin'," the embittered daughter felt as much anger toward her mother as she did her father. This no doubt helps to explain Lillie's demise from poisoning at the hand of her first daughter.

At an early age Velma began looking for a way to escape from the father she despised and the docile mother who let her tyrannical husband beat his children without raising a single objection. In 1949, when Velma was in the eleventh grade, she began dating Thomas Burke. By this time the Bullard family had moved to Parkton. At first Murphy would only let Thomas take his daughter to church and school events, and he usually insisted that they double date. Eventually, though, Thomas began showing up in his father's car, and he and Velma would go to Fayetteville to the drive-in movies. Her curfew, rigidly enforced by Murphy, was 10:00 p.m. On those occasions when Velma was a few minutes late, her father took to the road looking for her. When she arrived home, she was subjected to a tirade from him. Murphy didn't like Thomas and finally told him to stay away from Velma. The embittered daughter became so disenchanted with life in Murphy's house that she left for school one day determined to find a way to make it on her own. She had run away, but not far enough, and Murphy and Lillie found her and took her back home. On Velma's seventeenth birthday, Murphy finally allowed Thomas to come back and date his daughter. One night Thomas proposed that he and Velma get married. Velma said that Murphy would not allow it.

Thomas was determined to marry Velma and insisted that they run away to South Carolina, where there was no waiting period and where no parental consent was required. For a time, Velma, fearing what her father might do, resisted. Finally, she decided to do as Thomas wished. On 1 December 1949 Velma pretended to leave for a school function. Instead, with the help of a friend, she rendezvoused with Thomas. The couple drove to Dillon, just across the North Carolina line, and got married. Velma was scared and refused to let Thomas go in and tell Murphy what the two of them had done. Her new husband abided by her wishes and took Velma home in time to meet her curfew.

The marriage took place on Thursday night. Velma told her mother the next day, but not Murphy. She had hoped that Lillie would do that, but Lillie was as frightened as Velma was over what Murphy might do. When Velma finally blurted out the news to Murphy on Saturday morning, he exploded, saying he would not have it and that Velma must have it annulled immediately. Thomas Burke was no good and he had known it all along, Murphy asserted. He lashed out at Lillie for not telling him and not trying to stop the marriage. He turned over a table and threw a chair across the room. Next he lit into Olive, accusing him of being part of the plot to conceal the marriage from him. Olive denied it, but Murphy refused to believe him. Murphy attempted to hit Olive, but the boy said, "You've hit me the last damn time." Olive ran into the woods, with his father giving chase. After awhile Murphy returned breathless, drove away in his car, and returned later with liquor on his breath. He said he was leaving and ordered Lillie to pack his clothes. She did, but Murphy didn't leave. Instead, he began to cry. Ultimately he regained his composure, went into Olive's room, and fell asleep on Olive's bed. While he slept, Velma packed up and went to the home of Thomas's parents.

Apparently Velma was happy with Thomas and their two children, Ronnie and Kim, for a number of years. She performed the duties of wife and mother very well, always being involved in her children's activities. From the home of Ed and Annabel Burke, Thomas and family first moved to a small house just across the field from the Burkes. Later, after Thomas began to make more money by driving a truck for the Pepsi Cola Bottling Company of Fayetteville, the little family moved into a large white house in Parkton. The family was active in the Parkton Baptist Church, which was very close to their house. These were the happiest years for Velma, Thomas, Ronnie, and Kim.

A turning point came in 1963 when Velma was found to have fibroid tumors in her uterus. A hysterectomy followed, and Velma was never the same again. The surgery adversely affected her hormonal balance, and she went into fits of deep depression. She fretted about her weight and started taking diet pills. Next, she went on spending sprees. In 1964 she began to have back spasms and took more and more pain pills. Eventually she went to work and had a blackout spell while driving to work one morning. Velma was on her way to becoming addicted to pills, a wide variety of them.

If that were not enough, Thomas had an automobile accident and began drinking. On 18 July 1966 Annabel Burke found her husband Ed slumped over the breakfast table. Ed was dead at the relatively young age of 60, and his death profoundly affected his son. Thomas's drinking got worse. He and Velma had violent arguments, for Velma remembered how her father was when he was drinking. The couple fussed and cursed each other, and the fights usually ended with Thomas leaving and coming home later dead drunk. It got worse and worse. Thomas was caught for drunk driving, lost his driver's license, and ended up unemployed. At one point Velma had Thomas committed to Dorothea Dix Hospital, "Dix Hill," North Carolina's hospital for the insane. After being released from that facility, Thomas went to Jacksonville, Florida where he stayed with his sister Doris and my cousin Charles, as he looked for employment there. Finding no work in Jacksonville, Thomas returned home. During much of 1968 he was out of work. He became reclusive and drank more than ever. Velma had a nervous breakdown and became unstable. Soon she was on nearly every kind of joy pill there was—Librium, Valium, and Butisol. These were in addition to her painkillers and sleeping pills. Soon it was obvious that her "medicine" was not curing Velma, but controlling her, just as alcohol was controlling Thomas.

All of this pointed to disaster of some sort, and it came in April 1969 when Thomas apparently set the house on fire while drunk. Velma returned from a laundromat, found the house full of smoke, and presumably went for help. There is some evidence to suggest that she locked the door, hoping that Thomas would burn up or be asphyxiated before she could bring help. After firemen came and broke in the locked kitchen door, Thomas was rushed to Highsmith-Rainey Memorial Hospital in Fayetteville, where he died. His funeral was held at Parkton Baptist Church, one month before his thirty-eighth birthday. He was laid to rest in the town cemetery, his grave only a few feet from that of his father.

On 23 August 1970, at a Baptist Church in Fayetteville, Velma married again. Her second husband, Jennings Barfield, was a widower whose deceased wife Pauline had worked with Velma at Belk's Department Store. Barfield lived in a small house in Fayetteville, near the Purolator plant, and Velma moved in with him and his sixteen-year-old daughter. The second marriage did not curb Velma's drug addiction, which became progressively worse. She overdosed several times and had to be taken to the emergency room each time. Jennings himself was a very sick man, suffering from both diabetes and emphysema, and he found it difficult to cope with his own problems, much less Velma's. Soon he was contemplating divorce, but before he could initiate it, he suddenly died in March 1971. Velma told her son Ronnie that Jennings's weak heart had just given out. Not until seven years later would anyone but Velma know that Jennings had died of arsenic poisoning.

After her second husband died at her hands, Velma went on from one crisis to another as she continuously popped pills. She became romantically involved with Al Smith in 1974. A construction worker, Smith was twenty years Velma's senior. One night in August 1974 he was run over by an automobile while crossing U.S. Highway 301 near Fayetteville. Interestingly, he had made Velma the beneficiary on his insurance policy, and the $5,000 she received from it helped to feed her drug habit. By this time Lillie Bullard, Velma's mother, was suffering from stomach cramps and vomiting. Before the end of the year Lillie was dead following more bouts with vomiting and diarrhea. A few days after Christmas in 1974 Velma and her brother Olive took their mother to Cape Fear Valley Hospital in Fayetteville, and there she died. Velma wept out in the hallway and again beside her mother's grave, when they laid Lillie to rest at LaFayette Memorial Park in Fayetteville. Murphy Bullard had preceded his wife in death by twenty-one months, and now she was beside him, dead by the hand of her oldest daughter.

Velma continued spending all the money she could get her hands on for drugs and was continuously in and out of hospital emergency rooms and sometimes spending days in the mental wards. Nothing deterred her from securing drugs, however. To pay for them she wrote bad checks, and this led to her being sentenced to prison for six months in the spring of 1975. Released on parole after serving three months of the sentence, she was back in the hospital because of an overdose of drugs in less than a week.

The birth of a grandchild caused Velma to straighten up briefly, and she found work as a caretaker. She first looked after an elderly woman who soon was placed in a nursing home, leaving Velma again without work. However, the woman's sister recommended Velma to the family of Montgomery Edwards, a ninety-four-year-old diabetic, who had lost his sight and both legs. His wife Dollie was eighty-four and in poor health herself. Velma seemed to enjoy watching over the Edwardses and chatting with Dollie. It was through her that she met Stuart Taylor, Dollie's nephew, to whom Velma would eventually claim to be engaged. The initial warm feelings between Dollie and Velma soon gave way to criticism and bitterness between the two. Even so, Dollie kept Velma on after Montgomery Edwards died in January 1977. The animosity between them continued to mount, and about a month after Montgomery passed on, Dollie became plagued with vomiting and diarrhea. On 27 February she was so ill that Velma called an ambulance for Dollie and rode with her to the hospital. Placed in an intensive care unit, Dollie lasted two days before expiring. Since she was old and her husband had recently died, no one suspected foul play. Velma had poisoned another woman, and no one suspected a thing. At least no one said anything openly.

Less than two weeks after Dollie was buried, Velma moved in with an eighty-year-old farmer named John Henry Lee and his wife, who had the unusual given name of Record. The Lees lived three miles north of Lumberton in Robeson County. Mrs. Lee, aged seventy-six, had fallen and broken her leg. She was in a cast and navigated with difficulty on crutches. She needed help and offered Velma fifty dollars per week. Velma accepted on condition that she have Sunday mornings and Sunday and Wednesday evenings off to attend church. She also asked for time off on Saturday mornings to attend to personal matters. The Lees agreed to Velma's terms. Velma seemed to do a conscientious job of looking after the Lees, and she kept their house spotless. At meals she always said grace. The Lees were very happy with her. Unknown to them, the feeling was not mutual. Record's constant talking grated on Velma's nerves, as did the couple's bickering with each other. In less than two months John Henry Lee, always the picture of health in spite of his age, suddenly was vomiting and suffering from diarrhea. He spent the last few days of April and the first two of May in the hospital. The doctors were unable to diagnosis his problem. Off and on through the month of May 1977 his symptoms returned. Velma was the epitome of concern and seemed to give him such tender care. Rushed to the hospital on 3 June, John Henry Lee died on 4 June. Velma sent a wreath to the funeral and offered comfort to the family during the ordeal. Apparently, neither Record Lee nor her daughters ever dreamed that Velma had poisoned John Henry, and the Lee caretaker stayed on to look after Record.

Velma's dark, unspeakable secret—murdering three people by poisoning them—was known only to her until she decided to add another victim to the list on 31 January 1978. For a while Velma had been estranged from Stuart Taylor, but a couple of weeks after John Henry Lee was buried (June 1977) Taylor showed up at the Lee house to see Velma. He kept returning every day for several weeks and then stopped. Velma didn't know why, but she soon learned that he had a drinking problem and was on a binge. Soon he showed up again, acting as if nothing had happened. Within a brief period Velma and Stuart were in a relationship and talked of marriage. That September, Record Lee fell ill. She was vomiting and had diarrhea. She, too, had been poisoned, but no one would know it until much later. Record did not die, and Velma never admitted to poisoning her. After Record returned home, Velma quit as her caretaker, perhaps fearing that she could not control her urge to poison people and might be caught if she finished off Record Lee.

After leaving the Lee household, Velma spent a great deal of time with Stuart Taylor and moved into his farmhouse near St. Paul's, just north of Lumberton. They fussed and fought continuously. Stuart found out that Velma had served three months in prison, and this disturbed him. Then she began forging checks on his checking account to pay for drugs. He threatened to have her arrested, and she moved out of his house. Velma moved in with her daughter who thought that her mother and Stuart had broken up for good. But not so. Stuart and Velma got back together again. That was Stuart's last mistake. On 31 January 1978 he promised to take Velma to hear nationally known evangelist Rex Humbard, who was conducting a revival meeting in Fayetteville. Stuart kept his promise, but soon after the service started he began to feel sick at his stomach. He had to go outside. Thinking it was something he had eaten, he told Velma to stay through the service while he went to his truck to lie down. Over the next two days Stuart got worse and looked horrible. He ended up at the emergency room of Southeastern Hospital in Lumberton. Diagnosed as having gastritis, Stuart Taylor died on Friday, 3 February—the day after he entered the hospital. He was only fifty-six years old. Except for his alcoholism, Stuart had always been strong and healthy. The doctors were just as puzzled as were his two children, Alice and Billy. Dr. Richard Jordan recommended an autopsy, and her children agreed—after securing Velma's approval! Velma had poisoned her last victim, for the long arm of the law would soon reach out and bring her to justice. Ironically, she assented to the action that would lead to her undoing.

Two books have been written to tell Velma's story—*Woman on Death Row* and *Death Sentence*. The first, *Woman on Death Row*, was purportedly written by Velma herself, while she was waiting to be executed. Actually the book amounted to her story as told to a ghostwriter. Although Velma admitted the wrongs she had done, her version implied that the real culprit was the drugs that had taken over her life. The second book, *Death Sentence*, was written by award-winning journalist Jerry Bledsoe, long after Velma's execution. Bledsoe got a great deal of material for the book from Ronnie Burke, who cooperated with the writer in telling the story. Although Bledsoe did a great deal of research in addition to talking to Ronnie, Burke's interpretation of the events helps color the story. *Death Sentence* remains the most complete account of the Velma Barfield story, and it is a book well worth reading.

Whether from Velma's point of view in *Woman on Death Row* or Ronnie's in *Death Sentence*, it is a story that is both bizarre and tragic. Sometimes when considering it, one is prone to forget that Velma was a mass murderer and that all of the murders were premeditated, notwithstanding the fact that Velma claimed she only wanted to make her victims sick so that she could nurse them back to health while looking for work to pay them back the money she had stolen from them. Was anyone likely to buy a story like that? There is no question about her being a pathetic figure at all times and a sympathetic figure sometimes. My cousin, who was around her often for a while, is convinced that she was basically a kind person and that the drugs made her do it.

At the end there were countless people who felt that she should be spared execution, many of them because she professed to have become a born-again Christian during her confinement. Her conversion near the end is open to question, since Velma had always been a religious person. She was known to go to church regularly, to follow itinerant evangelists who passed through the area, and to send money to South Carolina evangelist Oliver B. Greene. How many times did Velma need to be converted before it was absolutely genuine? None of this made the least impression on Joe Freemen Britt, the man who prosecuted Velma. Nor did the jury buy the claim that Velma wanted only to make her victims sick so that they would need her.

To resume the story, let's return to what happened after Stuart Taylor's death. I said earlier that no one suspected Velma of the poisonings until Taylor's autopsy revealed arsenic in his body. My statement needs some qualification. No person in authority suspected foul play and no one expressed any suspicion of Velma *openly*. There was someone, perhaps more than one, who did suspect Velma, however. One of Velma's sisters called the Lumberton police and told them that she was sure Velma had poisoned her boyfriend, her mother, and others, but the sister, who would not give her name, admitted that she had no proof. The police waited.

Proof was soon forthcoming. On 6 March, it was revealed by autopsy results that Stuart Taylor had died of arsenic poisoning. This revelation prompted an intensive investigation into the deaths of Velma's other victims, and on March 10 Velma's long trek to the execution chamber in Raleigh's Central Prison began. Her doorbell rang that morning. It was the police. Frightened, she excused herself and took a handful of pills that included tranquilizers, painkillers, and antidepressants. She soon felt a "calming effect." When hauled off to the sheriff's office, she took her "medicine" with her. All of her prescriptions were legal.

At the sheriff's office, Lumberton detective Benson Phillips read Velma her rights and asked if she understood them. She answered, "Yes." Phillips then informed Velma that the medical examiner had found arsenic in Stuart Taylor's body. He went on to tell her that Taylor had died as a result of the poison and that she was guilty of killing him. Velma asked what sort of reasons they had for believing such a thing. Now extremely edgy, she wanted desperately to take another Valium. She denied everything. Three hours after the questioning began, Velma was released to go home, without being charged. A sense of guilt came over her, and it was relieved only by her "medication." That night she went to work, but she took four Valium, twice her normal dose.

The next morning Velma drove to the home of her son Ronnie and told him what had happened the day before. Ronnie was puzzled. Where would she get arsenic? he asked. She ignored the question, admitting nothing. She called an attorney in Fayetteville in case the police returned, and he told her to call him, if she were charged in the case. Although she worked on Saturday and Sunday nights that weekend, she could not find rest, and on Monday she considered killing herself by overdosing on drugs. Before she could do it, Ronnie arrived at her home, took her pills away from her, and drove her to the sheriff's office. Once the police read Velma her rights, they asked if she had poisoned Stuart Taylor. This time she answered, "Yes," but said that she did not mean to kill him—only to make him sick. She admitted to using "ant poison" on Stuart and others. She later recalled that she told the police everything to the extent that her "fuzzy mind would let me."

The man who took control of charging Velma was a detective named Al (or Alf) Parnell, who had been a schoolmate of hers at Parkton. He took her through the fingerprinting and booking procedures and then took her to jail without handcuffing her. While waiting for the court to act on her case, Velma received visits from her brothers and sisters and, of course, her children. Parnell, a longtime family friend, arranged for them to be in a separate room for their visits. There was much weeping and agonizing, no doubt, for committing murder by poisoning in North Carolina automatically meant that it was a capital case.

Velma went before District Court judge Charles McLain on 14 March, represented by her court-appointed attorney, Bob Jacobson, a young Lumberton lawyer in his thirties who had previously been an Air Force attorney in the Judge Advocate General's office at Pope Air Force Base. With little ado Judge McLain declared that he was sending Velma to Dorothea Dix Hospital for a psychiatric evaluation to find out if she were mentally competent to stand trial. The next day she was at Dix Hill, where she would stay for nearly five weeks. During her stay she was weaned off her medicine by receiving smaller and smaller doses. Still, the withdrawal was hard on her physically, as her blood pressure shot up to dangerous levels. When Bob Jacobson visited her there, she didn't remember who he was. In just over a month she was returned to jail to await her trial in November, after she had pled not guilty by reason of insanity on 5 May before Judge Hamilton Hobgood. Bail was denied. Ronnie and Kim visited her regularly. She told them of all the wrongs she had done and expressed a desire to commit suicide.

Meanwhile, District Attorney Joe Freeman Britt had persuaded Superior Court judge Maurice Braswell to sign an order allowing the exhumation of Lillie Bullard, Dollie Edwards, and John Henry Lee, and the newspapers in both Fayetteville and Lumberton were giving front-page coverage to the story. Because of the vast publicity, Velma's lawyer managed to secure a change of venue, and the trial was held in Elizabeth-town, the county seat of Bladen County. As does Fayetteville, Elizabeth-town sits on the banks of the Cape Fear. Thus, it was at a courthouse just a little more than rock-throwing distance from that meandering river that Velma Barfield went on trial for her life. Prosecutor Britt was determined to make her pay with her life for four people—perhaps five—that she had murdered. The trial started on Monday, 27 November 1978 in a courtroom presided over by Judge Henry McKinnon. Even though it was known that she had killed four people, she was on trial for causing the death of Stuart Taylor and him only, for he was the only person she had killed *after* the enactment of a new death penalty law in North Carolina.

Joe Freeman Britt automatically excused any potential juror who said he or she could not impose the death penalty. Britt was the son of a prominent Lumberton attorney, but he never meant to follow in his father's footsteps. After "finding himself," however, Britt did decide on a legal career and ended up the district attorney over North Carolina's Sixteenth Judicial District, which included Robeson County. Ironically, as a college student, Britt had opposed the death penalty, but his experience as a prosecutor in Robeson County had turned him around on that issue. He prosecuted killers who received prison terms and watched them go off to prison vowing to kill again when they got out. He didn't trust life sentences, because too many murderers who received them were back on the street as parolees in a few years. Britt, as head prosecutor in his jurisdiction, eschewed using his assistants to try first-degree murder cases. He insisted on trying every one of them personally, and he always went for the death penalty—a drugged-out grandmother not excepted. His objective in Velma's case, as in all other capital cases, was the seating of "a death-qualified jury," and he achieved it.

Although Bob Jacobson, Velma's attorney, did the very best he could and put on a spirited defense, the outcome was never in doubt. The evidence against Velma was overwhelming. Jacobson felt compelled to put her on the stand to testify in her own defense. She admitted to putting some Terro, an ant poison, in Stuart Taylor's beer on one occasion and his ice tea on another, claiming that it was not to kill him but to make him sick.

Upon cross-examination, Velma was tripped up very badly by Prosecutor Britt. He had her contradicting herself at every turn. Velma became deeply angry and defiant. She showed no remorse. Her irascible demeanor on the stand left the clear impression that Velma Barfield was quite capable of premeditated murder, and her contention that she only wanted to make her victims sick so that she could nurse them back to health while raising money to pay back money that she had stolen from them was bizarre, to say the least. Her lawyer deeply regretted his decision to put her on the stand. In his closing statement all Jacobson could do was impress upon the jury that Velma did not intentionally kill Stuart Taylor and remind the jurors that his client was constantly under the influence of drugs. He spoke for only thirty minutes.

The prosecutor, expecting Jacobson to speak for a longer time, thought he would have a whole night to prepare his closing statement. He was taken by surprise when the defense attorney sat down at 4:30 p.m. This meant he had to give his closing statement immediately, and he promised to speak no longer than Jacobson had. It was a simple matter, Britt claimed. Velma Barfield did intend to kill Stuart Taylor. Otherwise, she would have told the doctors at the hospital what kind of poison she had given him so that they could have administered an antidote that would have saved his life. He asked the jury to find her guilty of murder in the first degree. As promised, he stopped talking at five o'clock, thinking that his closing statement was not one of his finest. However, he didn't worry. There was no doubt Velma would be convicted. Britt's real challenge, that of persuading the jury to execute a woman and one who was a grandmother, would come later.

The jury sat for only an hour and ten minutes before reaching a verdict of murder in the first degree. At the sentencing hearing, Velma's children and a longtime friend who had worked with Velma at Belk's testified as to how she had changed after getting hooked on drugs, implying that the drugs were the true culprit. Britt, though, was determined not to let the jurors sympathize with Velma. He kept hammering away at the victim's rights, and Jerry Bledsoe quotes Britt as saying, "She killed him dead! And sent him to his maker! And he is gone for an eternity because of that act of *this* woman!" And again, "He is gone, my friends. He is gone forever, and it is because of this woman sitting over here at the next table." He called for the ultimate penalty.

That is what he got, in spite of Bob Jacobson's insistence that it all went back to "the dope." He begged the jury to give Velma her life, to no avail. After almost three hours of deliberation the jury returned to the courtroom at 5:50 p.m. on 2 December 1978 and announced the verdict that Joe Freeman Britt had so earnestly requested. Kim, Velma's daughter, burst into tears, while Ronnie sat in stunned despair, and Velma stood in frozen silence. She declined Judge McKinnon's offer to say anything, and he sentenced her to be put to death by asphyxiation on 9 February 1979.

Velma, of course, did not keep that date in the gas chamber at Central Prison. The appeals began, and continued for five years. During that time she professed to have a "true" Christian conversion, claiming that she had always gone to church and been religious but had never given her heart to

Jesus. Meanwhile, Bob Jacobson began to write an appeal to the North Carolina Supreme Court. It took months for him to write it, and it took the court until 6 November 1979 to deny it by upholding both her conviction and her sentence. Jacobson served notice that the family would have to pay him to pursue any further appeals. Not having the kind of money that would be required, the family sought the assistance of the American Civil Liberties Union, which provided them with the services of a young idealistic lawyer named Richard Burr III. Burr appealed Velma's case to the United States Supreme Court, which declined to hear it in June 1980. The court declined to reconsider on 17 September of the same year, and the new execution date of 17 October 1980 was set. Burr was determined now to seek relief for Velma in the North Carolina state courts, but he was not licensed to practice in North Carolina. Consequently, he turned for help to Jimmie Little, a former public defender in Fayetteville. Little was by this time a partner in his own law firm.

On Friday, 3 October 1980, Jimmie Little filed an appeal in the Bladen County Superior Court, asking for a stay of execution and a review of the trial. Judge Maurice Braswell of Fayetteville granted the stay of execution and the hearing for a new trial. The hearing commenced before Judge Braswell on 17 November 1980 and went on until near the end of the month. When all the arguments were offered, Judge Braswell ruled that Velma's trial had been fair and impartial. He set a new execution date of 12 December 1980, which was just a little over two weeks away.

There were more stays and more appeals, as Velma languished in prison in Raleigh. She became something of a minister to her fellow women prisoners, and many of them called her "Mama Margie." Velma's case came up before state court and federal court judges for four more years. Signs of hope were soon followed by jarring setbacks at every turn until finally Governor Jim Hunt was called upon to show clemency and commute Velma's sentence to life in prison. He refused. Velma instructed Jimmie Little to offer no more appeals on her behalf. She was ready to meet her maker.

The North Carolina legislature had passed a law in 1983 allowing a condemned prisoner to choose death by lethal injection. Velma chose that over the death by asphyxiation to which she had been sentenced by Judge McKinnon. In the weeks and months before Velma's execution many prominent people and thousands of ordinary people who opposed the death penalty protested her impending execution. All the protests were to no avail, and Velma became the first woman in North Carolina to be executed by lethal injection and only the third woman put to death by the state in the twentieth century. The other two women were black and had been put to death in 1943 and 1944. On Velma's last day before she was to be wheeled into the execution chamber on a gurney, the media in all forms—television networks, radio networks, newspaper and magazine reporters from all over the nation and, indeed, the world—showed up at Central Prison in Raleigh. Instead of a last meal, Velma wanted a Coca Cola and Cheez Doodles, which she ordered just after 6 p.m. on 1 November. She read her Bible as she drank her Coca Cola. She had less than eight hours to live.

All over North Carolina that night vigils were held for Margie Velma Barfield. Standing outside Central Prison were family members, friends, and many sympathizers. Among them was Wade Holder. I can't say how long I have known Wade Holder, but I would guess about forty years. He married Ruth Lee, Pat and Katie Lee's youngest daughter, all dear friends of mine since my adolescence. Ruth and Wade attended my mother's funeral in 2002. They are cherished friends. As I did, Wade knew Velma when she was Velma Burke. He was Kim's basketball coach. He was like a family member to Velma, like one of her brothers. Wade was overcome with emotion as he waited in despair for Velma to die. He spoke to the crowd and assured them that just after 2:00 a.m. Velma would be in heaven. Then he broke down, as words gave way to tears. He couldn't continue.

Dressed in her own pink pajamas and wearing a mandatory diaper, Velma entered the execution chamber just before 2:00 a.m. Three syringes were attached to each of three intravenous lines. Three volunteers were used in carrying out the execution. One of the intravenous lines was a dummy, leaving each of the volunteers free to think that he might not have been the one who actually administered the lethal injection. Velma was pronounced dead at 2:15 a.m. on 2 November 1984. An ambulance took her body away at 2:25 a.m. Velma was gone, but her trial and execution left her family somewhat in disarray. They have been trying to pick up the pieces of their lives for almost twenty years. Kim tried to disassociate herself from her mother and start a new life, while Ronnie dropped out of sight for a long time, unable to come to grips with all that had happened. For about eight years he and Kim lost touch, and she actually thought he was dead. He finally surfaced in the early nineties and decided to face the past head on. Then, in 1995, he began to work closely with Jerry Bledsoe to give as complete an account of the Velma Barfield story as possible.

Even though Hollywood approached Bledsoe about turning his book into a movie, to date no movie has been made of Velma's story. Such a movie may never be made. While the publicity surrounding her case was never as all encompassing as that surrounding the MacDonald murders, Velma Barfield will most likely remain the most highly publicized murderer to be born and reared in the Fayetteville area. Reflecting on the time when I knew her, I am still somewhat astonished that she killed at least four people. I, as so many others, am inclined to believe that drug addiction caused it, but I must agree, too, with Joe Freeman Britt that being a drug addict is not an excuse for committing premeditated murder.

Because the sensational crimes of Velma Barfield came to light at the end of the seventies and because Jeffrey MacDonald went on trial in 1979, the decade is forever tainted with poison and blood. This is unfortunate, for the booming city along the Cape Fear registered so many positive developments during the same period: the unprecedented growth of industry, political recognition on a state and national scale, some progress toward racial and gender equality, visits by celebrities from many walks of life, new malls, new buildings, new superhighways, new sports heroes, and—not to be overlooked—the end of its "Fayettenam" era. Now that the Vietnam War was over and there were signs that justice would be done in the cases of Barfield and MacDonald, Fayetteville could face the eighties with hope for better times. Any hopes that murder would become a thing of the past, however, would be dashed during the eighties. Progress was destined to continue. So was the violence.

Chapter 9

Trying to Overcome
the "Fayettenam" Image: The 1980s

The Vietnam War was over. Velma Barfield and Norris Taylor were on Death Row in Raleigh. Jeffrey MacDonald had been sentenced to three life terms in federal prison. Fayetteville's city officials could only hope that the killing, the drug trafficking, and the lewd dancing in topless bars on Hay Street—all of which had plagued the city during the sixties and seventies— would now pass from the scene. Maybe there would be no more Jeffrey MacDonalds, no more Velma Barfields, no more Norris Taylors, no more hell-raising by inebriated or stoned soldiers in downtown Fayetteville. All of this was a lot to hope for, and a hope destined to be dashed.

Bill Hurley was a man who believed a redeemed Fayetteville was possible, and he was determined to do what he could to make it happen. He ran for mayor, promising during his campaign that he would clean up the 500 block of Hay Street, the location of numerous dens of iniquity, which had housed adult theaters, bars, drug dealers, and prostitutes—everything but legalized gambling. The notorious block had drawn state and national media attention. Hurley insisted that the unsavory joints had to be destroyed. Apparently most Fayetteville citizens agreed, for Hurley was elected. He made good on his campaign promise when, on 28 July 1983, he and an estimated 800 other spectators gathered to watch as wrecking crews began demolishing some of the places where sin and evil had abounded. From the corner of Robeson Street to the corner of Winslow Street buildings located in the infamous 500 block were razed. This marked the beginning of a city trying to create a new image for itself. Mayor Hurley declared that the demolition of the 500 block "signifies an end of an era and the beginning of another." He was right, but only in part.

The next year Fayetteville was named an All-America city for 1984–1985, and in 1986 a new medical-office building sat on the site where other buildings had once provided wild entertainment for soldiers and others seeking forbidden thrills. Bill Hurley, who initiated the effort to clean up Fayetteville, was soon able to parlay his popularity as a reform mayor into a seat in the North Carolina House of Representatives. Popular city councilman J. L. Dawkins became mayor in 1987, and he was determined to continue the cleanup campaign begun by Hurley.

Local citizens were genuinely and justifiably proud of Fayetteville's designation as an All-America city. Hundreds gathered around the Market House in March 1985 to celebrate the occasion by listening to a speech given by then-councilman Dawkins. Still, the city had to hire a public relations firm in August 1986 to begin a year-long campaign to continue efforts to improve Fayetteville's negative image. Obviously, it would take years for people to forget about "Fayettenam."

In spite of all the efforts made by Hurley, Dawkins, and others, the quest for the city's redemption was clearly not complete, for such places as Rick's Lounge continued to operate in the 400 block of Hay Street. In 1986 Rick's was damaged by fire. When it reopened in August 1987 with topless dancers, city officials were disturbed. Rick's had had topless dancers before zoning changes banned the practice, and so its continuance was grandfathered in as far as that unwholesome establishment was concerned. A new ordinance would have taken away Rick's exemption, if the 1986 fire had destroyed more than fifty percent of the premises, or if the building had not been used for a year. The lounge reopened just ahead of the one-year deadline, but city officials contended that the building's destruction had exceeded fifty percent. Apparently there was no way to prove this, and Rick's once again offered its well-known brand of entertainment to the public.

Meanwhile, something far worse for Fayetteville's image than the reopening of a topless bar had occurred. In May 1985, less than two years after the city's campaign to cleanse itself had begun, a woman and two of her three daughters were murdered in the Summerhill subdivision off Yadkin Road, partway between Fayetteville and Fort Bragg. The third daughter, a toddler, was left alive and unharmed. The woman, Kathryn ("Katie') Eastburn, was the wife of Captain Gary Eastburn, chief of Air Control at Pope Air Force Base. The gruesome Eastburn murders were eerily reminiscent of the MacDonald murders, but this time the husband was never a suspect. He had an ironclad alibi, for he was away at an Air Force training school near Montgomery, Alabama. The police had to look elsewhere for the killer this time.

Almost before the area's citizens could get over the shock of the Eastburn killings, two young soldiers in December 1986 were accused of killing an elderly Cumberland County couple, stabbing them over and over in their chests and backs and slashing their throats. Apparently the two young men were influenced by the role-playing game called "Dungeons and Dragons." Since they were dressed in ninja-style garb when they committed the heinous crime, their evil deed was commonly referred to as the "ninja murders."

Seemingly the violence never stopped. Before the decade ended, a man formerly in the Army at Fort Bragg murdered twenty-nine-year-old Margaret Best Jensen in 1988. Margaret was the daughter of Rudy and Pearl Best, a couple who had rented a room at my house in the late forties, many years before their daughter was brutally murdered. Rudy, who had risen to the rank of chief warrant officer in the Army, and his wife Pearl were almost like members of our family. We knew them long before any of their three children were born. Margaret was the youngest. Some years before Margaret's tragic demise, Rudy had died of leukemia. Pearl was shattered by the tragedy of Margaret's murder and never quite recovered from it. She went on living for more than ten years, but, reportedly, she always seemed depressed.

Not only did murder-most-foul continue along the Cape Fear, but some of the other ugly problems of the past lingered. For instance, in April 1981 a Cumberland County grand jury indicted 132 high school students for selling drugs to undercover drug agents during the year before. Problems continued to crop up in the schools throughout the decade. Some students took weapons to school, prompting the Cumberland County school board in April 1988 to restrict the use of book bags and athletic bags in the junior and senior high schools. This step, it was hoped, would prevent weapons from being brought onto school property in the future.

Another matter of concern in the schools, at least to many parents, was the way sex education was offered. Taught from a practical and scientific viewpoint, students were simply taught about pregnancy, sexually transmitted diseases, and the practical consequences of being sexually active. The schools had avoided approaching the subject from a preachy, moralistic standpoint. Quite a few parents joined an organization called the Coalition for Acceptable Sex Education and pressured the school board into mandating the teaching of sexual abstinence outside of marriage and into requiring teachers to assert that any sexual encounter apart from marriage was morally wrong. The coalition disapproved of male and female students studying some part of the sexual education program together. It would seem that Fayetteville, in spite of its image as a rip-roaring sin city, had retained a Puritan streak that dated back at least to the 1920s. Yet, in spite of all it could do to clean up downtown and improve conditions in the schools, the city seemed unable to curb its crime rate. In August 1989, the next-to-last year of the eighties, violent crimes were up sixty-eight percent in Fayetteville over the year before.

Fayetteville certainly continued to have its share of serious problems, but it would be wrong to say that it did not become a better place in the eighties than it had been in the sixties and seventies, for the city did clean itself up to a certain extent. Still, the violence—the most heinous form of which was murder—obviously did not go away. And, as in the past, much of it was related in one way or another to Fort Bragg, as we will see later when we examine in some detail the murders mentioned above. Before doing that, however, let us examine other developments taking place along the Cape Fear during the decade of the eighties.

Wonderful news marked the beginning of the new decade when, in January 1981, the fifty-three American hostages held by the revolutionary regime of Ayatollah Khomeini in Iran were released and allowed to return home after being held captive for 444 days. Along with the rest of the nation, Fayetteville celebrated, and some citizens gathered at the First Baptist Church in a special service to offer thanks to God.

The good news of the hostages' return was soon followed by some bad news. Many times in the past Mother Nature had punished Fayetteville with floods, hurricanes, and snowstorms. She did it again in the eighties with killer tornadoes and record-breaking subfreezing temperatures. The first tornado hit in February 1981. It killed one person, brought down trees in the Murray Hills area, blew the roof off the auditorium at Seventy-First High School, and damaged the Education Resources Building on Hillsboro Street. Three years later, in March 1984, more tornadoes ravaged the area, killing two people in Cumberland County. Then, in January 1985, the thermometer plunged to a record-breaking three degrees below zero. The old record low—six degrees above zero—had been set in 1943. The winter of 1984/1985 was perhaps the coldest on record for the area, and late freezes in February severely damaged the peach crop in the entire Sandhills area. For the third time in four years, the region's peach crop was virtually wiped out.

Bad weather impacted agricultural production and brought complications to a regional economy that went through peaks and valleys during the eighties. Extremely high interest rates had helped to push the nation into a recession at the end of the seventies. Ronald Reagan was elected president in 1980, promising that he would end the recession without causing inflation. That was a promise he could not keep. As his budgets diverted more and more money to national defense, the nation pulled out of the recession, but inflation descended like a blight upon the land. The economy improved only at a snail's pace. A year after Reagan took the oath of office, the unemployment rate in the Cape Fear region was still at a dismal nine percent level. Soon, however, there were some encouraging signs, but the economic tide continued to rise and fall. The Fayetteville Municipal Airport launched a million-dollar expansion in December 1983 and followed that up with a much larger expansion costing nearly nine million dollars, which was completed in March 1987. Also, in November 1987, DuPont officials announced a thirty-million-dollar expansion at the company's Fayetteville plant south of the city.

Bad news came in the midst of the good, when, in June 1985, Kelly-Springfield laid off 650 of its workers, while Black & Decker shut down for a month, which in effect laid off all 900 of its workers. There was a number of disturbing signs as the economy waffled. Unfortunately, the huge expansion of the municipal airport was followed by a decline in passenger use of that facility over the next few years. It appeared in 1989 that the millions spent to improve the airport had been spent in vain. Another ominous sign was the closing of the Capitol Department Store at Bordeaux Shopping Center in August 1987. Then, in 1990, the downtown Capitol closed after seventy-seven years of doing business on Hay Street. The downtown store's cash registers had rung since 1923. When they went silent in May 1990, Fayetteville had no more downtown department stores, for the Capitol was the last one to close its doors.

Efforts were continuously made to rejuvenate downtown, but they enjoyed little success. Fayetteville businessman M. J. Weeks, as executive director of Fayetteville Progress, Inc., headed such an effort in 1982, and in July 1983 the organization did launch an eight-million-dollar townhouse project on the old Haymount School site, a couple of blocks from the downtown area. While downtown Fayetteville continued to languish, more malls and new stores appeared in the suburban areas. The Marketplace Mall opened across from Cross Creek Mall on Skibo Road in March 1986, and later that year in September T. J. Maxx, a discount apparel store, became the first store to open at the new Cross Pointe Shopping Center.

Helping to promote business during the up-and-down economy of the eighties was a change in the local blue laws. For so long there had been restrictions on Sunday business activity, and in some places restrictions continued with some modifications. Large crowds showed up when the Cumberland County Board of Commissioners approved an amended blue law in October 1981. Passage of the new law came only after some heated debate. It allowed a variety of businesses to remain open all day Sunday and grocery stores to open in the afternoon. The stores could sell anything they had in stock except alcoholic beverages. This law applied only to the unincorporated areas of the county, since each municipality had its own blue laws. Two years later, in December 1983, both the city of Fayetteville and Cumberland County voted to abolish the blue laws altogether, leaving the whole area wide open for business on Sunday. Perhaps also helping to stimulate business was an increase in the North Carolina minimum wage from $3.10 per hour to $3.35 per hour, thus matching the federal hourly minimum. This change went into effect in January 1983, thus putting more spending money in the pockets of Fayettevillians who were paid the minimum wage.

Although Fayetteville had made some significant economic strides in the twentieth century by bringing a variety of industries to town, the eighties demonstrated that the city and, indeed, the entire Cape Fear area were still dependent upon Fort Bragg to a considerable degree. A 1981 study made by the office of the post comptroller showed that Fort Bragg purchases had a seven-hundred-million-dollar impact annually on business in Fayetteville. That amounted to $17,600 per soldier stationed at the military installation.

It was a simple matter. When soldiers were at Fort Bragg, they spent money in Fayetteville and Cumberland County, and business thrived. When they were gone, business declined. All through the eighties soldiers were on post one day and gone the next, as the United States engaged in a variety of deployments around the world. In March 1982 a thousand Fort Bragg soldiers left for Egypt to become part of a multinational peacekeeping force. After occupying the Sinai Desert for a number of years, Israel returned it to Egypt. Not everyone was satisfied with this arrangement. Hence an outside peacekeeping force was deemed necessary in case objectors caused trouble, and the United States chose to participate in keeping the area safe. Fort Bragg troops moved out again in October 1983, this time to Grenada, one of the Windward Islands down in the southern

Caribbean north of Venezuela. The purpose of the deployed American troops was to topple a presumed Marxist military junta that had seized power there.

Five years passed before Fort Bragg troops were called on again to go to a world hotspot. In March 1988, paratroopers from the 82nd Airborne Division were sent to Honduras when it was reported that Nicaraguan forces were threatening to invade that country. The administration of Ronald Reagan was already on record as supporting so-called "freedom fighters" in Nicaragua, opposition forces that were purportedly trying to oust the communist regime of Daniel Ortega in that tiny Central American nation. Intrigue by government officials to get help to these freedom fighters would bring about the much-publicized Iran-Contra scandal that tarnished the reputation of the Reagan administration.

American intervention overseas continued under Reagan's successor, George Bush. In August 1990 a brigade from the 82nd Airborne Division was sent to Saudi Arabia after Iraq invaded Kuwait with the expressed intention of annexing it. By the end of 1990 Fayetteville was said to be experiencing a "soft economy," and the departure of Fort Bragg troops to the Persian Gulf was partly responsible. Approximately 30,000 troops from Fort Bragg and Pope Air Force Base were in the Middle East ready to do battle with Saddam Hussein over Kuwait, and Fayetteville was feeling the economic pinch. In September the jobless rate had been only 3.8 percent. By October the percentage had jumped to 5.5. Fewer goods and services were being purchased in Fayetteville because the soldiers were far away from Fort Bragg. That spelled economic slowdown along the Cape Fear, and the unemployment rate climbed. No one could argue with the fact that the local economy still depended more than a little on Fort Bragg.

Except for soldiers coming and going and the economy fluctuating accordingly, the 1980s witnessed many worthwhile developments in Fayetteville. Also, the city enjoyed plenty of recognition locally, statewide, and nationally. The struggle for racial and gender equality continued, and the area took some real steps forward toward achieving equality on both fronts. In November 1981 Virginia Thompson was appointed chairperson of the Cumberland County Board of Commissioners, the first woman to hold the post. A few months later, in early 1982, steps were taken to create a predominantly black single-member, state legislative district for Cumberland County. Toward the end of 1983 Lucy Talbot of St. Paul's in-the-Pines Episcopal Church became the first woman rector in the Diocese of East Carolina. In September 1984 Diane Wales became Fort Bragg's first Airborne woman's chaplain.

Progress continued for women and blacks in June 1986 when, for the first time, three black members—Ida Ross, Joseph Pillow, and Thelbert Torrey—took their seats on the Fayetteville City Council. And the miracles continued. Six years after Virginia Thompson became the first woman chairperson of the Cumberland County Commission, Mary McAllister ascended to that post in December 1987 to become the first black woman chairperson. Equality for women and blacks was finally being realized in a part of America where segregation and male chauvinism had a long history.

This did not happen without pressure being applied, especially where blacks were concerned. In May 1982 Dr. Joseph Lowery, president of the Southern Christian Leadership Conference, had been the featured speaker at a public meeting at the Market House, a meeting that had amounted to a demonstration in support of black-voter registration and the extension of the Voting Rights Act of 1965. This demonstration brought back memories of the civil rights demonstrations of yesteryear and made the point that African-Americans intended to secure all of their rights. Without such demonstrations, it is safe to assume that equality would have remained nothing but a dream.

Another plus for Fayetteville was the constantly expanding and updating of the city's medical facilities. Progress, however, did not come without controversy. There were those in town and county who wanted to lease Cape Fear Valley Hospital to a for-profit firm called National Medical Enterprises of Los Angeles. In May 1982 the county commissioners voted to lease the hospital to National Med for ten years. Much opposition to such action had been registered, but the commission vote was four to one in favor. Virginia Thompson, who opposed the move, cast the lone negative vote. Under its new lessee, the hospital continued to expand and improve its facilities. A new $430,000 coronary care unit opened in September. In cooperation with Duke University Hospital, the mushrooming medical center on Owen Drive began "Life Flight," in March 1985. This meant that patients who could not get needed treatment at Cape Fear could be transported by helicopter to the world-class medical center at Duke University.

The expansion of Fayetteville's mushrooming hospital continued in October 1986 when ground was broken for a $4.3 million comprehensive cancer treatment center. By this time the hospital was being referred to as Cape Fear Valley Medical Center. In August 1988 the facility dedicated a new $2.9 million emergency department. Meanwhile, the Highsmith-Rainey Medical Arts Center had been dedicated and opened in September 1986, and that was followed two months later by the dedication of the Cumberland County Mental Health Center in the old Highsmith-Rainey Memorial Hospital building on Haymount Hill. Clearly, Fayetteville and Cumberland County were making every effort to provide area people who became ill with excellent medical care. Two very fine hospitals and several other medical facilities were now available to the public.

While Fayetteville's medical facilities were expanding, so were its boundaries and its school system. Until 1983 Fayetteville had been restricted for twenty-four years in regard to the annexation of surrounding areas. That changed when the North Carolina General Assembly approved in June of that year a bill giving Fayetteville and other Cumberland County municipalities the right to annex by ordinance. The Fayetteville city council was not long in making use of this new power. In July 1984 the council expanded the city by taking in more than six thousand people. There was some opposition, but not much. Taken into the city were College Lakes, the Cambridge Arms apartment complex, areas along the All-American Freeway and MacPherson Church Road, plus the subdivisions of Holiday Park, Borden Heights, and Pleasant Valley. More and more of Cumberland County was being brought into the Fayetteville city limits, and the city's population grew by an impressive 23.6 percent between 1980 and 1990. According to the 1990 federal census, Fayetteville's population had climbed to 73,577.

Some local leaders thought that the closer connection between city and county dictated a merger of the two school systems. This idea had circulated for years, but it had not won general support until September 1982. After a year of studying the matter, a six-member committee representing both school boards unanimously recommended merging the two systems. The following April, Billy Clark, Fayetteville representative in the North Carolina General Assembly, introduced a bill that permitted the two school systems to merge. In September 1984 the State Board of Education approved the merger effective 1 July 1985. The merger took place on schedule and thereby created the third largest school system in North Carolina.

As Fayetteville took steps forward in improving medical facilities and education during the eighties, it also advanced culturally. Progressive citizens in town and county had long advocated the establishment of a first-class central library. In November 1982 area voters had rejected a $4.5 million bond issue to build a central library for the county, but determined officials eventually found funding for the library anyway. Finally, after the project had been stymied for several years, ground was broken in September 1984 for a new $4.56 million central library on Maiden Lane in Fayetteville, across the street from where Central School had once stood and on the site that was long occupied by the Dickinson Buick car dealership. Funding for the facility came from a variety of sources—individual and corporate gifts, a gift from the city of Fayetteville, and a federal grant, among others. The largest amount contributed—2.8 million—came from the county. One of the largest private donations—$250,000—came from the Cumberland Community Foundation, which had been established in October 1981 by Dr. Lucille Hutaff, daughter of Fayetteville's Coca Cola Bottling Company founder Charles D. Hutaff. Dr. Hutaff held the distinction of being the first woman to serve as a full-time professor at Bowman Gray School of Medicine in Winston-Salem, North Carolina. Because of her and a number of other civic-minded people, the new Cumberland County Library rose in the form of an impressive, modern structure that soon housed many fine historical and literary sources. It was and is a cultural facility that does enormous credit to Fayetteville and Cumberland County.

Credit also redounded to Fayetteville's cultural progress when, in November 1985, the Fayetteville Little Theater received state recognition. Founded a few years before, the Little Theater had struggled to survive at times, but at the 1985 North Carolina Theater Conference meeting in Raleigh it became the first recipient of an award for leadership in community theater. In receiving the award, the Fayetteville Little Theater was hailed for its statewide leadership, innovative programming, and high artistic standards. The next year the theater took on the new name of Cape Fear Regional Theater.

In spite of Fayetteville's notorious dens of iniquity and its never-ending violent crimes, it had become one of the most important cities in North Carolina. Besides its progress in a number of significant areas, the city enjoyed considerable political clout in the state and national capitals by the 1980s. In the state house, Fayetteville lawyer Tony Rand became one of the most powerful people in the North Carolina General Assembly following his appointment to the state senate in 1981. He served as senate majority leader and secured funding for a number of state-financed building projects in Cumberland County. Meanwhile, in Congress, Fayetteville's own Charles G. "Charlie" Rose III was a force in the national House of Representatives throughout the eighties, and former Governor Terry Sanford headed for the national capital in December 1986 to be sworn in as a United States senator. Some of Sanford's Fayetteville supporters went to Washington to witness the occasion. Since Sanford was already acclaimed as one of the ten most effective state governors of the twentieth century, he immediately commanded respect as a U.S. senator. Fayetteville was well represented in both houses of Congress.

As in the past, the nation's great and would-be great regularly passed through Fayetteville. Entertainers came to perform—some for money, some for a cause—and the politicians came in search of votes or to make an appearance at some important celebration. In November 1983 Martha Raye, Rosemary Clooney, and Kay Starr were on hand to participate in a benefit show to raise money for the construction of a Special Warfare Museum at Fort Bragg. In May 1987 comedian Bob Hope was at Pope Air Force Base taping a television show. Because Hope's birthday coincided with the event, President Ronald Reagan flew in to wish his longtime friend a happy birthday. In making a few remarks, the president quipped that contrary to rumor Bob Hope had not entertained George Washington's troops at Valley Forge. In December 1988, the popular female rap group Salt-N-Pepa came to town. They performed in the new Agri-Expo Center, which had been named for Congressman Charlie Rose. This was the first concert in the new facility, and it drew more than ten thousand spectators. Almost three thousand more had to be turned away.

A variety of politicians made their way to Fayetteville or Fort Bragg during the eighties, President Reagan being the most prominent, of course. But also showing up was former U.S. Senator Gary Hart of Colorado, who was running for president in 1988. Hart gave a lecture at Fayetteville Technical Community College in January of that year, and in it he called for new taxes to balance the budget and bring down the federal deficit created by Reagan's lavish spending on the military. Hart's campaign quickly fizzled. Two political figures who visited the area in 1989 were Senator Edward Kennedy and his nephew Representative Joseph P.

Kennedy. They were on hand to tour Fort Bragg, and, while there, they laid a wreath at the base of the Special Warfare Memorial.

Enjoying the spotlight with the entertainers and politicians who graced the area in the eighties were two Fayetteville beauty queens. In successive years, 1984 and 1985, two Fayetteville women were crowned Miss North Carolina. Francesca ("Francy") Adler was crowned Miss North Carolina in 1984, making her the first Miss Fayetteville to attain that honor since Vivian White had won it thirty-seven years earlier. The five-foot-nine beauty was a graduate of Pembroke State University. A year later she placed the Miss North Carolina crown on Joni Bennett Parker, another Fayetteville beauty, who, like Adler, stood five feet and nine inches tall. Parker was a graduate of Meredith College. The two beauties, Adler a green-eyed blond and Parker a blue-eyed brunette, were two of the tallest Miss North Carolinas to have worn the crown. Unfortunately, neither of them reached the finals in the Miss America contest, but Fayetteville was genuinely proud of them.

There were beauty queens to talk about in Fayetteville during the eighties and there were sports to talk about. In 1984, it had been twenty-eight years since Fayetteville had had a minor-league baseball team. Baseball came back to Fayetteville that year in the form of the Fayetteville Generals, a minor league affiliate of the Detroit Tigers. The Generals opened the season by beating the Spartanburg Phillies 9 to 6. An enthusiastic crowd was on hand to watch. The return of baseball prompted real estate developer Joseph Palmer ("J.P.") Riddle in January 1987 to donate a fifteen-acre site on Legion Road for the erection of a minor-league baseball stadium. Riddle, one of the dominant developers in Cumberland County, had been a leading spirit in the establishment of Cross Creek Mall, Fayetteville's largest shopping center.

But there was more to talk about than just baseball. One local high school won a state championship. In December 1986 Seventy-First High School defeated West Charlotte 3 to 0 to become the state 4-A football champions. Even more noteworthy on the sports front, Raymond Floyd, in June 1986, won the U.S. Open golf championship and became the oldest man ever to win that prestigious tournament. Floyd, holder of the 1969 and 1982 PGA championships and the 1976 Masters title along with his 1986 Open title, has to rank as the greatest sports figure Fayetteville has ever produced.

The highs and lows continued for Fayetteville until the end of the decade. There were great events in history to celebrate, including the two-hundredth anniversary of the United States Constitution and the two-hundredth anniversary of its being ratified for North Carolina in Fayetteville. In September 1987 Fayetteville joined the rest of the country in observing "Bells Across America." The Market House bell tolled for 200 seconds to mark the two hundredth year since the Constitution had been signed in Philadelphia. Other bells sounded and car horns blew in a celebration that went on for two hours. Dozens of the city's residents read from the Constitution, and red, white, and blue balloons floated into the atmosphere.

Almost two years later, in April 1989, there was yet another celebration. The North Carolina General Assembly held a special ceremonial session in Fayetteville to celebrate ratification of the Constitution by North Carolina at the State House on the site where the Market House was later erected. Perhaps because the Constitution had originally allowed slavery, seventeen black legislators refused to attend the event. A few months later, in November, Fayetteville held its own bicentennial celebration with a "Living History Festival." The city took justifiable pride in the fact that it had hosted the convention that made North Carolina the nation's twelfth state on 21 November 1789.

The celebrations of 1989 to commemorate the nation's founding took place amidst exhilaration, but the joys of 1989 soon gave way to the disappointments of 1990. Some of Fayetteville's old landmarks faded into history. For more than eighty years the Coca Cola Bottling Company had bottled coke products in Fayetteville, but the bottling ceased in 1990, as the bottling and canning operations of the company were moved to another plant located in Morganton, North Carolina. On the site of the Coca Cola plant the Cumberland County Social Services building would soon be erected.

Another esteemed landmark was the Prince Charles Hotel, which had long been one of the city's tallest buildings. The famous hotel had been forced to close its doors with the fading of downtown. Serious but unsuccessful attempts were made throughout the eighties to save the hotel and revitalize downtown. The Prince Charles had closed for a time and then reopened again in 1989 as part of the downtown revitalization program. After less than a year, in December 1990, it went into bankruptcy. In many ways, Fayetteville was a better place than it had ever been, but to citizens who had lived there for many years, by 1990 it no longer looked like the same place, not with the Prince Charles sitting there empty and very few businesses still operating downtown.

To make matters worse, war loomed on the horizon in the Middle East, and Fort Bragg soldiers and Pope Air Force Base airmen were shipping out by the thousands. The economy along the Cape Fear was about to spiral downward. What had been an up-and-down decade was coming to a disappointing end. And to add to the gloom, the many hopes for less crime and violence had been dashed. Once again Fayetteville had been plagued by the "M-word" in the middle and latter years of the eighties. The slaying of three-fifths of the Eastburn family in the spring of 1985 again caused thoughtful Fayettevillians to cringe. Six or seven months earlier, mass murderer Velma Barfield had been executed by lethal injection. Now another killer was loose in the Fayetteville-Fort Bragg area.

On Saturday, 11 May 1985, Air Force Captain Gary Eastburn tried to call his wife Katie from Montgomery, Alabama. No one answered the telephone at his residence on Summerhill Road. Unknown to him, of course, on Thursday night or early Friday morning his thirty-two-year-old wife had perished from having her throat slashed. The same fate had befallen his five-year-old daughter Kara and his three-year-old daughter Erin. His third daughter, eighteen-month-old Jana, had been left alone and would be found crying on Sunday morning by a sheriff's deputy. Captain Eastburn had called the Cumberland County Sheriff's Department on Saturday to ask for help in reaching his wife. Another call to the department was made by a concerned neighbor who had not seen any of the Eastburns since Thursday. When the deputy arrived on Sunday morning 12 May he found the three murder victims. Katie Eastburn, who had been receiving harassing telephone calls, was found nude. She had been raped. Told of the tragic news, Captain Eastburn returned quickly to Fayetteville.

Within a few days of the discovery of the bodies, twenty-seven-year-old Sergeant Timothy B. Hennis, a Fort Bragg parachute rigger with the 600th Quartermaster Company and a resident at 2026 Lombardy Drive in Fayetteville, was arrested and charged with rape and murder. His arrest on 16 May came as the result of witness Patrick Cone's seeing a man answering Hennis's description leaving the Eastburn home at 3:30 a.m. on Friday, 10 May. Cone picked Hennis out of a photographic lineup and identified his car as one he had seen parked near the Eastburn home on the morning in question. Hennis had a definite connection with Mrs. Eastburn, for he had been to her house on 7 May to receive as a gift the Eastburn family dog. The Eastburns were giving their dog Dixie away because Captain Eastburn was being transferred to Great Britain. Sergeant Hennis would claim later that the only contact he had with Katie Eastburn after 7 May was when she telephoned him on the night of 9 May to ask how Dixie was doing at her new home.

Based on information furnished by Cone, the authorities charged Hennis with the murders. The Army sergeant was arraigned before Judge Lacy Hair who ordered a probable-cause hearing. Hennis was represented by attorneys Gerald Beavers and Billy Richardson.

It was not until 27 May 1986 that Hennis was brought to trial. He had been free on $100,000 bail since 16 December. Selection of jurors, starting on 28 May, went on for days, as each side excused potential juror after juror. By 9 June twelve jurors had been selected, but it took two more days to select two alternates. The twelve jurors consisted of seven men and five women. Hennis's trial got underway on Friday, 13 June. In his opening statement, one of the defense attorneys contended that all the physical evidence in the case—fingerprints, sperm, hair, and fiber sample tests pointed to another man. Also, claimed the defense attorney, shoe size pointed away from Hennis. A footprint found outside the house measured size nine-and-a-half or ten; Hennis, who was six feet and four inches tall and weighed over two hundred pounds wore a size twelve-and-a-half. Finger and palm prints found at the scene did not match those of Hennis, according to the State Bureau of Investigation. The SBI also confirmed that hair samples found did not match Hennis's.

The prosecutor in the case was Assistant District Attorney William A. ("Billy") Van Story IV. In his opening remarks Van Story admitted that there was little evidence to link Hennis to the murder scene, but contended that there was "nothing to rule him out." The credibility of the state's chief witness, Patrick Cone, had already been forthrightly challenged. It appeared that the prosecution was fighting an uphill battle in their bid to convict Hennis, especially since Van Story sought the death penalty.

The trial, in the court of Judge E. Lynne Johnson, lasted through the month of June and spilled over into July. In making his case the prosecutor relied heavily on the testimony of Patrick Cone, but he presented other evidence, too. He demonstrated that Hennis had been seen around the Eastburn home by several witnesses. Of course, it was true, for Hennis had been there to take the Eastburn dog off Katie Eastburn's hands.

Pointing to the guilt of Hennis was the testimony of Eddie L. Hollingsworth, a Cumberland County sheriff's deputy. Hollingsworth lived a block from the Eastburn home, and he had seen a car like Hennis's—a white Chevette—parked on the street near the Eastburns' at around 11:40 p.m. on 9 May 1985, the night of the murders. Moreover, Franklin Donald Jacks, a neighbor of Hennis's, had seen the accused burning something in a fifty-five-gallon drum on 11 May, possibly bloodstained clothes. Another witness, Lucille Cook, testified that she saw someone who looked like Hennis at a bank ATM (automatic teller machine) where the Eastburns' bank card had been used after the murders.

Of course, the most damning testimony against Hennis was that of Patrick Cone, who positively identified Hennis as the man he saw leaving the Eastburn residence in the wee hours of the morning on 10 May 1985. Yet, at one point in the investigation, Cone had expressed doubts. Those doubts were short-lived, however, and at trial he said with certainty that Hennis was the man. Cone claimed that his first thought upon seeing Hennis was that he was a burglar.

Defense attorneys Gerald Beavers and Billy Richardson painted a quite-different picture. Over and over again, throughout the trial, Beavers attacked Cone's credibility. Defense witnesses took the stand to say that they had seen a smaller man than Hennis hanging around the Eastburn home in the weeks before the murders. A pubic hair from a Caucasian was found in the house, and it matched neither Hennis nor Mrs. Eastburn. It was clear, the defense argued, that all of the physical evidence pointed away from their client. On 30 June the defense rested, and on 2 July both sides gave final arguments.

The courtroom had been filled each day of the trial. When the jury finished deliberating and delivered its verdict on 8 July, there were about sixty spectators on hand. Hennis was found guilty on three counts of first-degree murder and given a death sentence. When asked if he had anything to say, he stated forthrightly that he was not guilty. His execution date was set for 12 September 1986, but it was stayed pending appeal to the North Carolina Supreme Court.

The appeals process took months as the defense attorneys claimed that Judge Johnson had grievously erred in the exclusion of some evidence and the admission of some other. The state's Supreme Court ruled in favor of a retrial, because the prosecution "had used too many inflammatory photographs of the crime scene." The retrial was conducted in Wilmington for seven-and-a-half weeks in early 1989—27 February to 19 April—and was presided over by Judge B. Craig Ellis of Laurinburg. The outcome was altogether different this time, for on 19 April 1989 Hennis was acquitted. He himself had taken the stand in his own defense, while once again the state's case had hinged mainly on the testimony of Patrick Cone. Obviously the New Hanover County jury believed Sergeant Hennis and not Cone and decided accordingly. Defense attorney Billy Richardson cried when the verdict was announced, saying that he felt like ten thousand pounds had been lifted from his shoulders. On the other hand, Captain Eastburn remained convinced of Hennis's guilt and said, "I'll go to my grave thinking that."

After his acquittal, Hennis returned to the Army for a time. By 1995 he was living in Detroit with his wife Angela and working for the Equal Opportunity Commission. While Hennis got nowhere near the attention that Jeffrey MacDonald did, his story did give birth to a book and a television miniseries. Scott Whisnant, a reporter for the *Wilmington Morning Star*, covered the trial and from his notes and interviews produced a book entitled *Innocent Victims*, which was published in 1993. In December 1995 ABC-TV revisited the Eastburn murders in a miniseries also called *Innocent Victims*. Whisnant served as a consultant for the television movie.

Whisnant's book casts serious doubt on the investigation of the Eastburn killings and on the case made at trial by the prosecution. He alleges that Cone's testimony was always open to doubt because of his "questionable record" and his "contradictory stories." Whisnant also wonders why the police did not take a harder look at Julie Czerniak, the Eastmans' fifteen-year-old babysitter. The teenager seemed to be obsessed with Jeffrey MacDonald, and she had "drug-world connections" as well. The author had trouble understanding why Julie's "bizarre associations" did not come out in court. According to one theory that emerged, drug dealers went to deal with Julie Czerniak and found Katie Eastburn at home instead. They then raped and murdered her and killed the two oldest daughters who might have been able to identify them. This, of course, was just a theory, but there was still other evidence that Whisnant believes was not given careful enough consideration by the authorities.

Whisnant concludes that the only way the Eastburn killings can be solved now is through a confession by the killer or killers. Even then it would be difficult to prosecute anybody, because the Cumberland County district attorney and the North Carolina attorney general's office have gone on record as still believing Hennis is the killer. The Eastburn murders are like the MacDonald murders in that a mother and two daughters were brutally slain in both cases, but unlike the MacDonald murders nobody is being punished today for the Eastburn killings. If Hennis is truly innocent—and a jury of his peers declared him to be—then the killer or killers of Katie Eastburn and her two daughters got away with murder, at least until now, many years after the commission of the horrible crime.

As had often been true in the past, the name of a Fort Bragg soldier was tied to the hideous crime of murder. In the Eastburn case, however, the soldier was acquitted. This was not the case regarding two young soldiers who were accused of first-degree murder in the deaths of Paul Kutz, Sr. and Janie Lee Meares Kutz, a couple in their sixties who resided at 1011 Beechridge Road in Eastover, just across the Cape Fear from Fayetteville. During a robbery at the Kutz home on 1 December 1986, twenty-year-old Specialist 4th Class Jeffrey Karl Meyer and seventeen-year-old Private Mark Edward Thompson stabbed the couple to death. The suspects were soon apprehended at Fort Bragg by MP Robert D. Provalenko, who was awarded the Army Commendation Medal for arresting Meyer and Thompson. When taken into custody, the two young soldiers were dressed "ninja" style and had in their possession credit cards and guns belonging to the Kutzes. There were allegations that Meyer and Thompson had been influenced by the role-playing game called "Dungeons and Dragons." In fact, Meyer would later tell a cellmate that he committed the murders and that what he did reminded him of playing that game.

When Meyer went on trial in the spring of 1987, he pled guilty to two counts of armed robbery and one of first-degree burglary. That was on 12 May. Four days later, on the 16th, he pled guilty to two counts of first-degree murder. The next day he was sentenced to eighty years for robbery and burglary. His sentencing hearing on the murder counts began on 3 June. While awaiting the results of that hearing, on 12 June he broke out of the Cumberland County Jail, along with five other inmates. While he was at-large, a mistrial on his sentencing hearing was declared on 14 June. After breaking into Cliffdale Elementary School, Meyer was captured on 19 June. He remained in jail, awaiting a second sentencing hearing that did not begin until 25 September 1988.

To make sure Meyer received a fair hearing, his case was moved to Wilmington. Superior Court judge Giles Clark heard the case, which resulted in a recommendation by a New Hanover County jury that Meyer receive *two* death sentences, and Judge Clark obliged. On 16 November

1988 he sentenced Meyer to die the following January in the gas chamber at Central Prison, unless the young soldier chose lethal injection instead. The judge stayed the sentence, pending appeals to the North Carolina Supreme Court.

During the hearing, Meyer's attorney claimed that the soldier was mentally ill and had retreated into a world of violent fantasies, in which he thought himself a hero. The defense asked the jury to recognize mitigating circumstances, but the jury decided that aggravating circumstances outweighed all mitigating circumstances and unanimously decided to recommend the two death sentences for Meyer. The case took a unique twist in 1990 when the North Carolina Supreme Court overturned the death sentences. The court's ruling was based on a recent U.S. Supreme Court decision asserting that juries in North Carolina were being given improper instructions in how to consider death sentences. In 1995, at the next sentencing hearing another jury imposed death sentences on Meyer. Again the North Carolina Supreme Court overturned the decision, this time on a technicality. When still another jury handed down the death sentences in February 1999, the sentences were allowed to stand, as the state Supreme Court at last upheld them in December 2000. At this writing in 2003 Meyer remains on Death Row in Raleigh, which, ironically, is his hometown.

Mark Edward Thompson, Jeffrey Meyer's accomplice in the brutal murders of the Kutz couple, did not face trial until October 1989. Once again, the case was moved to Wilmington to assure Thompson of a fair trial. Judge D. B. Herring presided over the trial. Assistant District Attorney John Dickson of Fayetteville sought the death penalty. Fred Thompson, father of the accused, testified that his son had no criminal record except for traffic tickets, and Dr. Brad Fisher, who testified for the defense, claimed that Mark Thompson was mentally ill, being in the early stages of schizophrenia and cut off from reality. The New Hanover jury of five men and seven women refused to buy the defense's contention of insanity and found young Thompson guilty of murder on 23 October. Two days later Judge Herring sentenced the young man to life in prison. Actually Thompson ultimately received three life sentences plus forty years for robbery. One of his attorneys, Billy Richardson, said that Thompson didn't really understand that he would never be free again.

Ronald Adrian Gray was not in the news for as long as the "ninja" killers, but he was at least as vicious as they were. Like them, Gray was a young soldier, holding the rank of Specialist 4th Class. In 1987 he went on a Norris-Taylor-like crime spree that saw him convicted on five counts of first-degree rape, five counts of first-degree sexual offense, four counts of second-degree kidnapping, two counts of armed robbery, two counts of first-degree burglary, and two counts of second-degree murder. Two young women, Linda Jean Coats, 22, and Tammy Wilson, 18, were his two murder victims. In November 1987 Gray pled guilty to the many charges against him and was given eight life sentences by Judge Donald Stephens in the Cumberland County Superior Court. The good news about Gray is that once he was apprehended, justice was meted out swiftly.

The same was true in the case of the man who murdered Margaret Best Jensen. Margaret died because she took a day off from her work in the Cumberland County Land Records Office to clean up some damage done to her apartment at 508 Townhouse Lane by a recent rainstorm. This young woman lived at that address with her husband Kristian Hale Jensen, a Special Forces medic. At 7:15 on Friday night 10 April 1988 Kristian came home and found his wife dead on the kitchen floor. He called the police, and Fayetteville detectives began an investigation. When they learned that the Jensen apartment was out of the city limits, they turned the case over to the Cumberland County Sheriff's Department. Margaret's body was sent to Chapel Hill for an autopsy. The autopsy revealed that she had died from blows to her head. She had also been choked, but it was a severe head injury that caused her death.

The investigation led the sheriff's detectives to William Edgar Weller, who had been discharged from the 108th MP Company at Fort Bragg six months earlier. Weller, a native of Houston, Texas, lived with his wife at 105 Hunter Street. After leaving the Army he had found work as a groundskeeper at the apartment complex where the Jensen couple lived. Grass clippings left in the Jensen apartment led the sheriff's detectives to Weller. When questioned, he said he knew nothing about the homicide. His words gave him away, for the detectives had said nothing about Margaret's death being a homicide. They pressured Weller, and he confessed to the killing. He said that Margaret had complained to him repeatedly about his work as he was preparing to cut the grass, and he "lost it." Apparently, Weller went into a rage and killed her, for he claimed that the next thing he knew, she was dead.

Indicted on a charge of first-degree murder, Weller made a plea bargain on a lesser charge. He was sentenced to forty years for killing a young woman in the prime of her life. I knew Margaret when she was a child, but

I don't recall ever seeing her as an adolescent or an adult. She seemed so shy as a young girl that it is hard for me to imagine her ever being assertive enough to provoke someone into killing her. Her death was a double tragedy. First, a young woman's life was taken for no sensible reason, and second, as noted earlier, her mother, Pearl Best, never got over the shock of having her youngest child taken away from her in such a violent way. At Margaret's funeral, her brother Louis, who was the second of the Best's children, delivered a beautiful eulogy in praise of his younger sister. My mother, who was in attendance, told me time and again how deeply she was touched by Louis's eloquent tribute to Margaret.

The eighties brought to Fayetteville rejoicing and sorrow. The economy was up and then down, but the trend was upward. After all, the population was impressively on the rise as Fayetteville grew by almost twenty-four percent during the decade and Cumberland County by nine percent. In 1990 the county's population had reached 270,140, while the city's had climbed to 73,577. It should be noted that because of the city's new powers to annex, many of Fayetteville's new residents had previously been county residents. There was much talk of revitalizing downtown Fayetteville year after year. Some buildings that had served as dens of iniquity were torn down, and some impressive new buildings like Highsmith-Rainey Memorial Hospital had risen on sites where the old Fayetteville High School and Alexander Graham Junior High School had once stood. There were other new buildings, too, but some joints like Rick's Lounge continued to offer the seamy entertainment of days gone by.

And, amidst celebrations honoring Fayetteville beauty queens and commemorating Fayetteville's role in North Carolina's ratification of the U.S. Constitution, murder and other violent crimes were reported all-too-frequently, just as they had been in past decades. In spite of the city's numerous and strong efforts to dispel the "Fayettenam" image during the eighties, many residents must have wondered if the war looming on the horizon in the Middle East might bring back the wild times of the Vietnam era and another long line of notorious joints up and down Hay Street.

Chapter 10

More Revitalization, More Deployments, and Hate Crimes: The 1990s

In spite of all that well-meaning mayors like Bill Hurley in the 1980s and J. L. Dawkins in the 1980s and 1990s could do to clean up Fayetteville's image and slow the pace of crime, the forces of evil simply would not go away. To be sure, more of the unsavory joints were removed from Hay Street and buildings with a useful, wholesome purpose replaced them, but the sin and crime persisted. In the century's early decades people had often fallen into crime because of swilling alcoholic beverages, while in the sixties and seventies illicit drugs provided the catalyst for wrongdoing. Then came the eighties when plain old lust, meanness, and playing out fantasy roles led to murder. Seemingly the nineties were different in that deep-seated animosity toward gays, hatred of African-Americans, and total disrespect for the law produced a crime wave that included several brutal murders.

In 1993, Kenneth Junior French, an Army sergeant disturbed over President Clinton's policy on gays in the military, entered Luigi's Restaurant on MacPherson Church Road with guns blazing, all the while muttering about gays in the military. When the smoke had cleared four people were dead and eight others were injured. On the night of 6/7 December 1995 two young soldiers, members of the 82nd Airborne, went in search of some "niggers" to kill as part of a "Skinhead" ritual. One of the men, Jim Burmeister, who was from Pennsylvania, proudly gunned down a black couple on Hall Street in order to earn his spider-web tattoo and authenticate himself as a full-fledged Skinhead. In 1997, when the Golphin brothers, two black youths from Virginia who were passing through in a stolen car, were stopped on Interstate 95, they proceeded to shoot and kill two officers of the law. All of these killers went on trial for their lives, and Fayetteville remained in the spotlight during the nineties as one of the murder capitals of the nation.

Thus, attempts to improve the city's image enjoyed only partial success, but, in spite of it all, Fayetteville continued to progress, even though it crawled along at what resembled a snail's pace in the last decade of the twentieth century. We will return to the sensational murders of the nineties presently, but first, as in previous chapters, let us consider what else was happening along the Cape Fear during the century's last decade.

As the decade began, thousands of Fort Bragg troops were in the Persian Gulf area ready to participate in Operation Desert Storm, the attack against Saddam Hussein that would eventually be called the Persian Gulf War. In January 1991 Air Force jets attacked Baghdad, Iraq's capital city. Fayettevillians, like other Americans, watched television hour after hour during the relentless air assault. Then, in February, the ground war got underway. Right away there was bad news. Six Fort Bragg soldiers who were in the 20th Engineer Brigade were killed in action. Nine other soldiers from Bragg had already died. Fortunately, the Gulf War ended quickly, and in April Lt. General Gary Luck, who had commanded 100,000 troops in the war, arrived back at Fort Bragg with about 4,300 soldiers. Several thousand people turned out to cheer the general and his men.

There had been numerous deployments of Fort Bragg soldiers in the eighties, and the nineties would be no different. Sometimes small contingents were sent, sometimes large ones, but there would be no full-scale war again after 1991.

One of the war-torn areas of Europe that produced much agonizing by world leaders was the Balkans. In July 1992, twenty airmen from Pope Air Force Base and two C-130s went to Sarajevo, the capital of Bosnia, to take relief supplies. Then, in December 1995, Fort Bragg soldiers were sent to Bosnia as a peacekeeping force. Peace was hard to keep in that ethnically divided region, and the fighting continued. In 1999 thirty people from Pope Air Force Base participated in the air war over Kosovo, and that was followed by Fort Bragg MPs being sent to the area as part of another peacekeeping force.

Another hotspot of the nineties was the Caribbean. In September 1994, it appeared that the United States would launch an invasion of Haiti, a nation being torn apart by civil war. Sixty-one transport cargo planes, with 2,900 82nd Airborne Division paratroopers were on their way to that country, when they were called back in midflight. A last-minute settlement was reached with Haitian strongman Raoul Cedras and other political figures, and the crisis seemed to be over. However, in mid-October, 7,000 soldiers, mainly MPs, were sent to the Caribbean to keep the peace in a place where peace was seemingly elusive.

As was emphasized in the last chapter, the absence of troops from Fort Bragg and air personnel from Pope Air Force Base always sent the area's economy into the doldrums. Christmas 1990 had turned out to be a real downer, because 25,000 to 30,000 less people were in the area to spend their money on Christmas presents. Because their men were gone, many Army wives and their children left the area to return to their hometowns. For a number of months in late 1990 and early 1991 retail sales declined, people lost their jobs, home sales sagged, many apartments and rental houses had no tenants, car sales plummeted, and the number of bankruptcies multiplied. By late 1990 Cumberland County's unemployment rate had shot up to six percent. In February 1991 Senator Terry Sanford introduced a bill in Congress to provide emergency relief aid up to twenty million dollars to communities like Fayetteville, which had seen large numbers of troops sent to the Persian Gulf.

The picture brightened by April when about two-thirds of the troops returned home. During the Gulf War deployment many of the soldiers had stashed away their hazardous duty pay, and Fayetteville merchants waited expectantly for them to spend it in the spring of 1991. They were not disappointed. Soon after the soldiers returned, car sales climbed by an estimated fifty percent. From all sectors of the economy the reports were favorable, demonstrating once again that Fayetteville remained somewhat dependent upon Fort Bragg and Pope Air Force Base for its economic and financial health. Even so, Fort Bragg spending did not bring universal recovery. In November 1991, Holt-Williamson Manufacturing, a company that made yarn, closed its doors, costing the area 250 jobs. A broader recovery would have to wait for the Clinton presidency that began in January 1993.

The bad times were offset to some extent by the fact that, according to one study, Fayetteville residents enjoyed a lower average cost of living than people living in 302 other metropolitan areas. It cost 2.4 percent less to live in Fayetteville than in those other cities. The contrast between living in Fayetteville and in New York City was very dramatic, for, the study contended, a Fayettevillian making $22,500 per year could live as well as a New Yorker making $50,000. That still did not change the fact that Fayetteville had to watch its economy suffer every time Fort Bragg soldiers were deployed abroad in large numbers. In spite of all the manufacturing plants that had come to the area since World War II, it still needed more, if there was ever going to be economic security without Fort Bragg. Recognizing this, economic developers began a new county industrial park, and a group of former military men established a firm that serviced the internet industry and promised to make Fayetteville a serious competitor in the new high-tech world. Plans for still another industrial park in Cumberland County were laid in the spring of 1999 when the county bought 485 acres off Evans Dairy Road for the development of a park there.

To attract tourists to Fayetteville, plans were made to build a world-class Airborne and Special Operations Museum on Hay Street, a building whose projected cost was twelve million dollars. A project that had been launched in 1985, the museum would not be finished until the year 2000, when it finally opened its doors with great fanfare. A million-dollar gift by Ross Perot, the Texas billionaire and former presidential candidate, was part of the money used to finish the building, which ultimately cost $22.6 million and not the $12 million originally projected. Considered an important part of revitalizing the downtown area, the museum, it was hoped, would provide an economic stimulant for the entire Cape Fear area. Promising to live up to expectations, the building opened on 16 August 2000 and drew about 10,000 visitors during its opening days. The museum, along with a new city hall and a new police headquarters—all located on or near where infamous dens of iniquity had stood—purportedly would breathe new life into downtown. And to add more sparkle to Hay Street's new look, the Prince Charles Hotel had reopened in February 1992 as the Radisson Prince Charles.

An impressive museum, public buildings like the one that housed the Public Works Commission, and the grand old refurbished Prince Charles certainly made Hay Street look respectable again, even though it offered only a few thriving stores. The area in and around the Radisson Prince Charles was named the J. L. Dawkins City Plaza, in honor of the distinguished man who served so long as city councilman and mayor. Unfortunately, Mayor Dawkins was destined to die in office on 30 May 2000, making the last year of the nineties a very sad decade for Fayetteville residents.

I must inject a personal note here. I went to high school with J. L. Dawkins. He was two years ahead of me. I never met a more congenial person. I also remember his mother and father quite well. I saw them many times at the baseball games, when I was batboy for the Fayetteville Athletics. Johnny Dawkins, J. L.'s father, was an enthusiastic supporter of Fayetteville's baseball teams and of the Fayetteville High School Bulldogs.

He always had a smile on his face and seemed to be the most happy-go-lucky man I ever saw. J. L. was like that, too. He loved Fayetteville, and the people of Fayetteville loved him, more so, I think, than any other mayor in the twentieth century and perhaps the town's whole history. As a city councilman and as mayor he strove to make Fayetteville a better place, and I believe he was successful—certainly as far as the town's appearance was concerned.

As the nineties chugged along, more revitalization took place. In February 1996 Joseph W. Baggett announced a $2.5 million renovation of the old Huske Hardware House building and Huske Building in the 400 block of Hay Street. The remodeled buildings were to house a pub, microbrewery, grill, retail shops, offices, and apartments. Robert Marvin, a consultant hired to make suggestions for the continuing revitalization effort, offered a grandiose plan in April 1996 that included a downtown park, a lake, new housing, an arts district, museums, and new shops, all of which was to cost an estimated $28.7 million. The Market House, Fayetteville's most visible landmark, figured into the revitalization, too. Eight years and $800,000 were spent to spruce up the venerable Market House between 1988 and 1996.

There were many encouraging signs that pointed to a city that was moving forward. In August 1991, Maidenform, Inc. had broken ground for the erection of an eight-million-dollar distribution center in the Cumberland County Industrial Park. The new plant was expected to hire 300 workers. That was early in the decade. A more exciting development near its end, August 1999, was the establishment of Advanced Internet Technologies, a Fayetteville based web-host company. The new business purchased twenty-four acres of land along the Cape Fear near downtown Fayetteville and announced plans to develop a high-tech business park. Simultaneously, Home Federal Savings & Loan, which had operated in Fayetteville for eighty-three years, announced that it would become a full-service bank with the new name of Green Street Bank.

Unfortunately, the effort to revitalize downtown suffered something of a setback in June 1999, when Fayetteville Partnership, a nonprofit organization formed to help carry out revitalization, dissolved because of some financial irregularities, among which was the personal use of the organization's credit card by the executive director. Another blow to downtown revitalization came in January 1997 when Wachovia Bank announced plans to close its Green Street branch, thus leaving the city's tallest building with a vacant ground floor.

By this time the revitalization of downtown had already been overshadowed by the building of the new Cumberland County Crown Coliseum, an enormous structure located behind the Charlie Rose Agri-Expo Center on U.S. Highway 301. The huge entertainment facility south of town was projected to cost $55 million. Work on the coliseum, which critics sneeringly called the "Bubba Dome," began in June 1995, but only after some controversy. In July 1993 the Cumberland County Board of Commissioners had been authorized by the North Carolina General Assembly to impose a one-percent sales tax on restaurant meals to help finance the construction of the coliseum. A year later the commissioners agreed to pay $2.5 million for a fifteen- to twenty-acre tract of land on U.S. Highway 301 upon which to put the facility. Not all area residents approved, but construction began in the summer of 1995, and the Crown opened in the spring of 1997.

It was thought that the coliseum would draw businesses like a magnet to the area around its location. That did not materialize, but the Fayetteville Force, a minor league hockey team owned by Bill Coffey, played its home games there, and the games were attended by a goodly number of fans. At the grand opening in October 1997 just over 4,000 people turned out to see the Fayetteville Force play the Nashville Ice Flyers. The Crown seats 13,500 people, and its parking lot has spaces for 4,300 cars. Musical concerts—Christian, country, and rap—and professional wrestling seemed to attract the greatest number of spectators. In October 1998 a World Wrestling Federation match attracted 11,100 spectators for a record attendance up to that time. The major complaints about the Crown Coliseum were the high cost of tickets and the increased property taxes county residents had to pay to help keep up the facility.

Although it probably didn't help downtown revitalization much, the city in general no doubt benefited from the completion of the Central Business District Loop, a portion of which was named for famed civil rights leader Martin Luther King, Jr. The Loop, called by some "the road to nowhere," took many years to complete. The segment between Robeson and Hay Streets opened in 1991, but it was not until April 1997 that the Loop, after thirty-five years and $60 million, was finally finished. Coming into Fayetteville on Highway 87 from the south, the Loop goes through Fayetteville crossing under Hay Street just to the west of the old

Highsmith-Rainey Memorial Hospital and proceeds on under Bragg Boulevard to Ramsey Street near where the Coca Cola Bottling Company's plant once stood. Although it is not a true loop in the sense that it goes all the way around town, it is enormously helpful in getting through town without the annoying interruption normally caused by traffic lights. Not to be overlooked, too, is the fact that building the Loop—even if it seemingly took forever to do it—had pumped some money into the local economy.

As Fayetteville experienced all this development, it lost perhaps the greatest developer in the city's history, when J. P. Riddle died at age 73 in May 1995. Riddle knew what poverty meant growing up in Fayetteville during the Depression, but he overcame his upbringing as a poor boy to become the dominant real-estate developer in Cumberland County. Only Dr. Raymond Pittman came close to matching Riddle's entrepreneurial energy and achievements, at least in my lifetime. Riddle was a generous man, too, contributing significantly to education and charity. His energy and genius were important in Fayetteville's post-World War II expansion, and he would long be remembered as one of the city's most important citizens in the twentieth century.

Continuing to help Fayetteville progress—as had been the case since 1918—was what was happening at Fort Bragg. In other parts of the nation the Army was cutting back on its spending, but not at Bragg. Lt. General Hugh Shelton, commander of the post, announced in February 1994 that Fort Bragg would spend $540 million on construction over the next ten years, and that certainly was wonderful economic news to people along the Cape Fear. Throughout the decade Fort Bragg was at work on a "replacement hospital" for Womack Army Medical Center, not finishing the project until 9 March 2000. This one-million-square-foot complex was double the size of the old medical center, which had been dedicated way back in 1958. The facility offered medical services to roughly 160,000 members of the military, retirees from the military, and families of military who were stationed at Fort Bragg or Pope Air Force Base or who lived within forty miles of Bragg and Pope.

Even with such an enormous building project going on, the news coming from the two military posts was not always reassuring. For instance, a scare was thrown into the people of the area in November 1995 when Fort Bragg sent home 2,334 civilian workers because the federal government shut down over a budget dispute between Democrats and Republicans in Congress. Fortunately, the shutdown was short-lived. Six days after it began, members of the two parties managed to negotiate a seven-year balanced budget, and the Fayetteville area breathed a sigh of relief.

Like Fort Bragg, churches and religious groups played a part in pumping money into the area's economy during the nineties. In 1995 alone, Cumberland County churches spent $14 million in new buildings and additions. New churches were constantly springing up as the area's population moved steadily upward.

All in all it was a decade of ups and downs, but the trend for Fayetteville was definitely up. The city had acquired power to annex by ordinance during the eighties, and city officials had taken advantage. More annexations followed in the nineties. In July 1996, outlying neighborhoods and subdivisions containing twenty thousand people were annexed, boosting Fayetteville's population to an unprecedented 110,700. Another 9,300 were brought into the city limits in January 1998. Still another annexation in June 1999 pushed Fayetteville's population past the 125,000 mark. The Fayetteville and Cumberland County school systems had merged in the eighties, and many residents must have begun to wonder if all of Cumberland County was going to be annexed by Fayetteville, especially after the 1999 annexation, which was the third in three years. As the population in the area climbed, the number of students in the school system also rose, reaching more than 50,000 students by 1995.

As Fayetteville boomed during the 1990s it suffered some serious assaults by Mother Nature. Almost every sort of natural disaster except a major earthquake had befallen the city at some time or other during the century. There had been numerous floods, plenty of snow and ice storms, tornadoes, and especially hurricanes. Only a hundred or so miles up the Cape Fear from the Atlantic Ocean, Fayetteville—indeed the entire Cape Fear region down to Southport—seemed to be a prime target for hurricanes. Hurricane Hazel that blew wildly through the area in 1954 had left unforgettable pictures in my mind, but the nineties would see Fayetteville battered by an unprecedented number of hurricanes, some even more destructive than Hazel. In 1995 some nineteen named tropical storms slid by the North Carolina coast without coming ashore, but such was not the case in 1996.

In July 1996, Bertha pounded eastern North Carolina after coming ashore at Wilmington. Fayetteville was largely spared by Bertha, merely experiencing gusty winds. Two months later, in September, Fran struck the state a hard blow. Passing just east of Fayetteville, it dumped eight inches of rain on the city and buffeted it with eighty-mile-per-hour winds. The storm left nearly 40,000 area residents in the dark and caused about $1.5 million in damage. Fran was the strongest hurricane to hit the area since Hazel, and it left trees and power lines down all over. Some people were without electricity for as long as a week. In August 1998 came Hurricane Bonnie, which tended to follow Bertha's path while inflicting a similar amount of damage—sufficient damage for Cumberland County to be declared a federal disaster area. A rash of hurricanes followed in 1999— Dennis, Floyd, and finally Irene.

Dennis soaked eastern North Carolina in August with twenty inches of rain after lingering for days off the Outer Banks. The following month, on 16 September, Floyd came ashore at Oak Island south of Wilmington and moved north up Interstate 95, bringing more flooding than eastern North Carolina had ever experienced. Much of the rain from Dennis a few weeks before had neither evaporated nor soaked into the ground, and Floyd's rain fell on top of it. The rivers of eastern North Carolina rose to unprecedented levels in many places, and some towns along the Cape Fear were simply washed away. Relatively speaking, Floyd spared Fayetteville the kind of destruction it caused in other places. Fran had caused $5 billion in damage to North Carolina; Floyd exceeded that. Fran had killed 24 people in the state; Floyd was responsible for the deaths of 51. In contrast, the powerful storm Hazel had killed only 19 in 1954. Floyd caused more death and destruction than any other storm in North Carolina history, and still the destruction was not over. In mid-October, just as the floodwaters of Floyd began to recede, Hurricane Irene blasted the Outer Banks, propelling tropical force winds into Fayetteville and Cumberland County, an area still reeling from the heavy rain, strong winds, power outages, and crop damages imposed upon it by Floyd. Never had the area been hit so hard by so many hurricanes in such a short time.

Tropical winds were not all that Mother Nature had in store for Fayetteville in the nineties, for, in the last year of the decade, the Cape Fear region experienced some of the worst snow storms of the century. It was noted in the *Fayetteville Observer* that for a few days in January 2000 North Carolina looked a lot like North Dakota. Fayetteville got two to three inches of snow on 18 January and another two inches over the weekend of 22 and 23 January. On 25 January, Raleigh was blanketed by twenty inches, and up to eighteen inches covered many areas along the Cape Fear. Although the most severe problems appeared in Moore County, just to the west, Cumberland County had to close down its schools for five days. One Fayetteville resident was quoted as saying, "I'm 68 years old, and I've never seen snow like this in my life." The city and county would long remember the hurricanes and snow storms of the twentieth century's final decade.

There were storms of a different kind building in Fayetteville during the 1990s. On the one hand, it seemed the city had made admirable strides on racial and gender issues since the Civil Rights movement, but some were convinced that additional steps were necessary—especially on the racial front. Regarding matters of gender, the women pilots and pilots-to-be at Pope Air Force Base were delighted to learn in January 1993 that the new Secretary of Defense, Les Aspen, was issuing orders that would permit women to fly combat missions. And there was a hopeful sign in politics as well. For a number of years local women had sought and won public office, but most of them had been Democrats. In November 1996 new ground was broken when Mia Morris became the first Republican in the twentieth century to win a Cumberland County seat in the state legislature.

Even on the racial front the situation appeared promising when, in January 1993, John R. Griffin became the first black to be named superintendent of the Cumberland County school system. Racial tension surfaced, however, in December 1996 when the NAACP called for an investigation of a "racially hostile work environment" in the Fayetteville Police Department. The organization claimed that black police officers had been fired or reprimanded after complaining about discrimination. Three officers insisted that racist policies existed in the department. This led to a controversy that produced serious political consequences and persisted during all of 1997.

In a closed session in February 1997 the city council voted 5 to 4 to fire City Manager John Smith and appoint Deputy City Manager Roger Stancil as interim city manager. Smith had supported the police chief, Ron Hansen, when the department had been accused of racism. The following month, the council—again in a 5 to 4 vote—hired Cincinnati attorney Cheryl Grant to investigate the charges made by the three black officers. In September the council hired a new city manager, Ron Rabun of Florida, and Roger Stancil returned to his former position. Rabun lasted about two months before a new city council fired him and again made Stancil city manager. Four of the councillors—Ida Ross, Chris Dempster, Jim Smith, and Thelbert Torrey—who had supported the decision to fire John Smith and hire Cheryl

Grant to investigate the department had been turned out of office in the November election. It was obvious that racial tranquility was not a given in Fayetteville, in spite of the substantial progress that had been made.

Despite its problems, Fayetteville continued to move forward in a number of areas. Medical care continued to be ample for city and county residents, as Cape Fear Valley Medical Center continued to expand its services. In January 1992 the center received permission from the state to begin an open-heart surgery program. Almost seven years later, in December 1998, Cumberland County made a decision to provide the only hospital care in the county for civilians. At that time the board of commissioners voted to purchase all of the Fayetteville assets of Columbia/HCA Corporation, which owned Highsmith-Rainey Memorial Hospital, for $37 million. The hospital was then merged with Cape Fear Valley Medical Center. Thus, the only hospitals serving Fayetteville and area residents became publicly owned facilities.

Education in Cumberland County also moved forward in the nineties. Taking steps in 1992 to keep pace with technological advances, the board of education, with almost half the money coming from the state, spent more than $2.5 million improving the school system's computer network. In 1997 Cumberland County voters approved a $98-million bond issue for construction of public schools. The next year the school board took a new direction when it created the Massey Hill Classical High School as an academy for college-bound students. This must have surprised longtime residents, for Massey Hill had never been considered the cultural center of the area. In fact, I remember when, as a schoolboy, I, and many others, turned our noses up at boys and girls from Massey Hill schools. Massey Hill was where millworkers lived, and somehow we came to believe that their children were inferior to those of us who attended school in the Fayetteville city limits. Now, ironically, as the century was about to end, the school board decided to establish an elite school in the same building where those children of millworkers had once gone to begin their education. This was the second of the county's classical schools, since the Seventy-First Classical Middle School had been established earlier. It had gotten a great deal of attention in October 1996 when it became the first public school in Cumberland County to require students to wear uniforms.

Along with the public schools in the area, colleges that called Fayetteville their home were making strides, too. Beginning in 1992 Fayetteville State University was allowed to offer master's degrees in sociology and political science. In September 1999 the institution reported the largest enrollment in its history with 4,916 students. The freshman class jumped from 527 in 1998 to 806 in 1999. Meanwhile, Fayetteville Technical Community College boasted of improved academic standards, and Methodist College, under President Elton Hendricks, launched successful fund-raising efforts to finance the expansion of its physical plant.

Not only were area schools expanding and improving academically, they were also continuing to gain recognition for accomplishments in sports. In December 1991 the South View High School Tigers became state 4-A football champions by defeating West Charlotte High School 10-7. Less than a year-and-a-half later, in March 1993, South View captured the state 4-A basketball title when its team defeated South Mecklenburg High School 53-52 in a squeaker that went down to the final buzzer.

Individual athletes from Fayetteville schools also received some accolades. Brad Edwards, a former student athlete from Douglas Byrd High School, made it to the National Football League. Playing safety for the Washington Redskins, Edwards, in January 1992, became the first football player from Fayetteville ever to play in a Super Bowl game. In May 1996 *USA Today* named Terry Sanford High School basketball star Shea Ralph the national girls' player of the year.

Not all of the recognition for sporting achievements in Fayetteville went to high schools and their athletes. In the early nineties the Methodist College men's golf team won three straight national titles, losing their attempt at a fourth in 1993 to California-San Diego. Revenge was sweet for the Methodist men's team in May 1994 when they took the title back from the California school, defeating their rival by twenty-four strokes. Thus they won national titles in four of five years—quite an achievement!

News concerning sports in Fayetteville did not always come from school campuses. By the end of the decade there was hockey to watch and wrestling, and it was big news when the U.S. Open golf championship was held at Pinehurst in June 1999. Long a golfer's paradise, Pinehurst is less than fifty miles from Fayetteville, and the event benefited the Fayetteville area economically to the tune of an estimated $1.7 million. Fayetteville hotels and motels were nearly full during the event. The flamboyant Payne Stewart won the title in Pinehurst only to meet his death in an airplane crash not long afterwards.

Sports put Fayetteville frequently in the news, but so did continuing visits by various celebrities, and there were local residents who received recognition for achievements outside of sports. In May 1991 Muhammad Ali returned to Fayetteville for a dedication ceremony of the Mosque Omar Ibn Sayyid on Southern Avenue. While in town he entertained students who packed the gym at Westover High School. Coming to town a few months later—for quite a different reason—was Oliver North, one of the key figures in the Iran-Contra scandal. A retired Marine lieutenant colonel, North was in Fayetteville to sell and autograph copies of his book called *Under Fire*. Many of the embattled Marine's supporters showed up for this event in February 1992. A year later, in February 1993, Tony Franciosa and Loretta Swit arrived in Fayetteville to star in the play *Love Letters*, a production of the Cape Fear Regional Theater. Swit was well known for her many years on the television comedy hit show "M*A*S*H," one of the longest-running shows in television history, and Franciosa, too, had long been a recognized television personality. In 1994 another Hollywood celebrity returned to the area to stay forever. Actress and comedian Martha Raye had been a longtime supporter of the Green Berets. When she died in Los Angeles on 19 October 1994 at age 78, her body was flown to Fort Bragg where Special Forces soldiers gave her a military funeral before her remains were lowered into a grave in the Fort Bragg Cemetery.

Noticeably absent among the visitors to the area in the nineties were politicians, perhaps because President Bill Clinton would not have been warmly received due to his position on gays in the military. Other political figures that identified with the president would probably have been given the cold shoulder as well. No doubt they were aware that, generally speaking, Fayetteville, and especially Fort Bragg, were hostile to Clintonians.

Although they were neither sports figures nor celebrities, two Fayetteville women were recognized at the local and state levels during the nineties. Twice in the eighties Fayetteville women had been crowned Miss North Carolina. It happened again in May 1992 when Heidi Sue Williams won the crown and went off to represent the state and city in the Miss America contest. Another woman who won recognition in the spring of 1996 was a close friend of mine named Mary McDuffie. Mary was principal of Seventy-First High School, which my father had attended during the 1920s. A dynamic educator, Mary was named state principal of the year. She went on to serve in the upper echelons of educational administration in several North Carolina counties before taking a very important job with the state. I first met Mary in the early 1980s when we, along with numerous other history teachers, read Advanced Placement tests in U.S. History for Educational Testing Service of Princeton, New Jersey. From my observations of her, I am convinced that Mary McDuffie richly deserved being named state principal of the year. Cumberland County was fortunate to have her in its school system for a number of years.

There were several stories regarding Fayetteville during the nineties that deserve mention here. Two important anniversaries were observed, one in 1993 and the other in 1994. The Fayetteville Independent Light Infantry (FILI) celebrated its two-hundredth anniversary in August 1993, making it the oldest militia in continuous existence in the South and the second oldest in the country. Less than a year later, in June 1994, putt-putt golf celebrated its fortieth anniversary. Fayetteville football hero Don Clayton had opened the first putt-putt golf course on Bragg Boulevard on 21 June 1954. By its fortieth anniversary putt-putt golf was being played on several continents and the island nation of New Zealand. Clayton estimated that two billion people had played putt-putt golf during its first forty years of existence.

A milestone in Fayetteville's political history was reached in January 1996 when twelve-term congressman Charlie Rose announced his retirement by declining to seek reelection to another term. No other member of Congress from Fayetteville ever served as long as Rose did. Nor had any other member of Congress from the city represented his constituents more effectively. Many people throughout North Carolina's Seventh District—not just residents of Fayetteville—were saddened by Rose's decision.

Another story that captured the interest of Fayetteville citizens had more to do with Fort Bragg than the city. When the Army, in 1996, asked for money and permission to purchase Overhills, the Rockefeller estate that bordered Fort Bragg, Congress obliged. In March 1997 the great-grandson of Percy Rockefeller handed to the Army an antique set of keys to the eleven-thousand-acre estate in a symbolic transfer. The Rockefellers received $30 million dollars for Overhills, which now became part of the enormous Fort Bragg military reservation.

One of the most heart-warming stories of the time came at the end of the decade. In December 1999, Jane Smith, a teacher at R. Max Abbott Middle School, offered to donate one of her kidneys to Michael Carter, a student in her eighth-grade class. The student was born with a kidney disease that would take his life, unless he had a transplant. Smith was white; Carter was black. That made no difference to the compassionate

Jane Smith. The transplant surgery was scheduled for 17 December, but Michael developed an infection, causing the surgery to be postponed. Not until 14 April 2000 was the transplant surgery finally performed. It was successful, and Smith called it the highlight of her teaching career. Her generous act brought her widespread acclaim on television and in newspapers and magazines. Moreover, Smith received the National Kidney Foundation's "Gift of Life" medal in June of 2000 and was named Cumberland County's Teacher of the Year that October. Deborah Evans, Michael Carter's mother, called Jane Smith "our guardian angel." Ms. Smith's magnanimous act was perhaps the most positive publicity that the Cape Fear region received during the 1990s.

On the negative side, there was the matter of Fayetteville's perpetual crime problem. Actually, the 1990s produced many surprises with regard to criminal activity. It appeared that Fayetteville was taking effective steps to root out a great deal of such activity. After all, where once there had been rows of topless bars, the much-ballyhooed Airborne & Special Operations Museum was being erected throughout the decade and would officially open in the last year of it. Another positive sign was that the overall crime rate declined for several years during the nineties. It was announced in January 1999 that the number of reported crimes in Cumberland County was down for the fourth year in a row and there was a decline of eight percent from the 1998 report.

In spite of this good news, there was also some bad. The drug problem was certainly better than it had been in the sixties and seventies, but it seemingly would not go away. In January 1992 the Cumberland County board of commissioners authorized the hiring of twenty-one new deputy sheriffs to work in drug-plagued neighborhoods. Moreover, some of the most horrific murders on record took place along the Cape Fear during the decade, and the year 2000 saw the crime rate go up again. As previously indicated, some of the murders were rooted in outright hatred, especially hatred of African-Americans and hatred of gays. There were also pro-life advocates who hated pro-choice advocates and tried to burn down their clinics and/or blow them up.

The volatile issue of abortion affected Fayetteville in the same way it affected other parts of the nation. In August 1991, firefighters had to be called to the Carolina Women's Clinic on Gillespie Street, because anti-abortionists had set fire to it. There were hate speeches and threats aimed at pro-choice people throughout the decade, and once more, in September

1998, two abortion clinics were set afire. A few weeks later bombs were found in the same clinics. Antiabortionists, in Fayetteville as elsewhere, hated what they regarded as the murder of unborn babies, and so they were willing to murder those they considered murderers. Fortunately, the attempts to kill pro-choice people were unsuccessful in Fayetteville.

Hatred of straight people toward gay people ran every bit as deep as did the hatred that pro-life people harbored against pro-choice people. President Bill Clinton took office in January 1993, and right away announced that he wanted to end the military policy of banning gays from the service or kicking them out, if they were already in the service. Clinton's announcement provoked a bitter controversy all over the nation, but especially in areas where there were military installations. Fort Bragg soldiers and Pope Air Force Base airmen were overwhelmingly opposed to the Clinton policy that called for a swift end to the military's prohibition against gays. For whatever reason, the president's intentions drove Sergeant Kenneth Junior French over the edge.

About 10:00 p.m. on Friday night, 6 August 1993, the twenty-two-year-old French entered the popular Luigi's Restaurant at 528 McPherson Church Road. He was drunk, and he carried two shotguns and a rifle. In a loud voice he said, "Clinton's letting faggots in the military," as he opened fire. People screamed and ducked under tables, while some tried to flee the building. French told everybody to be still and quiet, but the owners of the restaurant, Pete and Ethel Parrous, were yelling at him and making noise. He shot them down, muttering "I'll show you Clinton. You think I am not going to do this. I'll show you about gays in the military."

Before the shooting stopped, four people were dead and eight were injured, some from gunshot wounds and some from flying glass. Besides the seventy-three-year-old restaurant owner and his sixty-three-year-old wife, French killed twenty-six-year-old Wesley Scott Cover of Fayetteville and James F. Kidd, a forty-six-year-old man from Wheaton, Illinois. Cover was shot to death while trying to shield Rona Woods, his pregnant fiancée.

According to Dawn Gabriel, a waitress at Luigi's, she missed being killed because she was able to hide under a table. She reported that at one point French sprawled out on the table she was hiding under and stuck the muzzle of one of the guns in his mouth as if he were going to kill himself. Instead of doing that, he reloaded and started shooting again. The slaughter was brought to an end when Richard Pryor, an off-duty police officer who was working at the Kroger grocery store across the street, heard the shots, ran across the street, and shot French through a window. The gunman went down but got back up. By this time the police had arrived on the scene. Lt. Bill Simons crawled through a rear door on his stomach and shot French again. Others officers then stormed the building. Pryor's shot got French in the leg, and Simons's hit the drunken killer in the jaw.

Alerted to what had happened at Luigi's, Mayor J. L. Dawkins went to the restaurant and found many of the people who had been inside during the shooting now outside in the parking lot trying to comfort each other. The mayor said that the Parrouses, who were leaders in the Greek community, were good friends of his and that he was in shock. Indeed, the entire city was in shock. I remember how upset my mother was for many weeks after the horrible shooting took place.

French, who was from Zephyrhills, Florida, served in the 39th Artillery Regiment and lived at Fort Bragg. Not until the spring of 1994 did he go on trial for his life. Naturally, because of inflamed public opinion in Fayetteville, the trial was moved to Wilmington. The state sought the death penalty at the trial presided over by Judge Coy Brewer. Henderson Hill and James Parish defended French. According to them, young French cracked on 6 August 1993 from the pressure of an abusive childhood and a serious drinking problem. Sandy French, the soldier's mother, stated that it was her husband's spirit that did the shooting, because Kenneth had been abused by his father in years past. Many witnesses testified that Junior French, Kenneth's father, had abused his children, including sexually abusing them.

No matter what demon drove French to open fire on a restaurant filled with people, he was guilty of murder. And, on 1 April 1994, a jury composed of seven men and five women found him guilty on all counts, after deliberating for eleven hours and forty-five minutes. French wept silently as each New Hanover county juror stood up and declared him guilty.

During the sentencing hearing, French wrote a two-page speech pleading for his life. Judge Brewer offered the jury a list of aggravating circumstances and mitigating circumstances. The jury split on the proper sentence for French, and it was not clear until 15 April that the jurors could not agree. This meant that Judge Brewer could not impose the death penalty. He gave French the harshest sentence he could under North Carolina law—four life terms. Many were disappointed that French was not sentenced to death, including one juror named Charles Wooten. "Death is what he deserved. It's just the wrong ending," Wooten was quoted as saying.

At the appeals trial before the North Carolina Supreme Court, defense attorney James Parish argued unsuccessfully that Kenneth Junior French deserved a new trial because a graphic videotape and emotional testimony at his trial served no purpose but to inflame the jury. French had also been sentenced to thirty-five additional years for wounding eight people. All of this meant that French would have to serve at least eighty years on his murder convictions before beginning his other sentences. Barring his living to an unprecedented age or getting an executive pardon, French would never live in the world outside of prison walls again.

Apparently, French's troubled mind had sent him on a shooting spree because he hated gays. Two other Fort Bragg soldiers also hated gays, but it was primarily hatred of African-Americans that drove James Norman ("Jim") Burmeister II and Malcolm Wright, two young paratroopers, to go "nigger huntin' " on 6 December 1995 and shoot down Michael James, thirty-six, and Jackie Burden, twenty-seven, a black couple, at about 12:10 a.m. on 7 December on Hall Street in Fayetteville. Burmeister, nineteen, and Wright, twenty, were driven to Hall Street, a dirt road off Campbell Avenue, by Randy Meadows, who, like his two companions, was a member of the heralded 82nd Airborne Division. Upon spotting James and Burden walking down the dirt road, Burmeister and Wright stepped out of the car. The former joked about earning his spider-web tattoo, a sign in Skinhead circles that the wearer had killed a black person. Wright already had such a tattoo, presumably indicating that he had previously committed murder. Within minutes of getting out of the car, Burmeister shot the black couple to death. Before doing so, he tossed the gun to Wright to give him the first shot, but Wright tossed it back, leaving Burmeister to shoot both James and Burden. After hearing the shots, Meadows returned to the scene of the shooting and was picked up by the Fayetteville police. Burmeister and Wright were soon arrested and charged with first-degree murder, while Meadows agreed to plead guilty to conspiracy and accessory charges in the murders.

It was January 1997 before Jim Burmeister went to trial charged with two counts of first-degree murder and one count of conspiracy to commit murder. During the trial some interesting facts came to light about this young paratrooper who hated black people. He grew up in Thompson, Pennsylvania, a small town of several hundred residents. Few blacks lived there. Burmeister's father ran an auto body shop and garage. The elder Burmeister was an opinionated man who did not hesitate to state his position on all matters. Racial epithets were common in his discourse with others, but, according to his wife, Kathy Burmeister, her husband did not teach his son to hate.

Young Burmeister started drinking beer in his mid-teens and eventually became an alcoholic. Jim took great pride in being in the 82nd Airborne, but he suffered an ear injury and was no longer allowed to jump. He complained of the menial jobs that he was assigned to do, and his drinking accelerated. Just after New Year's in 1993, he lost his cherished sister, Lisa, to leukemia. Kathy Burmeister testified at the sentencing hearing that her son took Lisa's death very hard. "It was devastating to him. It was devastating to us all," she said.

But defense attorneys Carl Ivarsson and Larry McGlothlin were not very successful in making a sympathetic figure out of Burmeister, and the young, former paratrooper's conviction was almost a foregone conclusion following the testimony of Randy Lee Meadows. District Attorney Ed Grannis painted Burmeister as a neo-Nazi Skinhead who hated Jews and blacks and hunted down his victims, Jackie Burden and Michael James, and shot them because of the color of their skin. Grannis asked for the death penalty, as did the families of the two victims. Randy Meadows, who had pled guilty to conspiracy and accessory, gave the key testimony that sealed Burmeister's fate.

Taking the stand on 14 February 1997 Meadows testified that Burmeister admitted to him that "he had shot and killed two niggers." He noted that on another occasion, after the three men had been arrested, that he and Burmeister were watching television. A commercial came on about having criminals do community service. When Meadows asked Burmeister, jokingly, if he was going to do community service, the former said, "I have done my community service and they put me in jail for it." On cross-examination, Carl Ivarsson tried to undermine Meadows's credibility by insinuating that the twenty-two-year-old former paratrooper had been promised a probationary or suspended sentence if he would turn state's evidence. Meadows insisted that all he intended to do was "tell the truth and get out of this thing the best way I can." Meadows also claimed that he was not racially prejudiced, in spite of the fact that he drank beer with Skinheads, listened to their music with its racial slurs, watched the Skinheads give Nazi salutes, and laughed at their jokes about minorities and homosexuals. After testifying, Meadows was returned to jail. He would not learn his own fate until after the trials of Burmeister and Wright.

On 27 February the jury voted to convict Burmeister. It took the jurors nine hours spread over three days to reach their decision. Burmeister showed no emotion when the verdict was announced. Defense attorney Larry McGlothlin said that he, his colleague, and the Burmeisters were disappointed, "but we'll be back tomorrow." On 28 February the same jury returned to court to consider whether to recommend the death penalty or life without parole. At the sentencing hearing, Burmeister's lawyers attempted to portray their client as the product of forces beyond his control, forces that shaped him during his childhood and adolescence. Kathy Burmeister tearfully apologized to the victims' families, saying, "I am so sorry that anything like this happened. . . . I apologize. This has torn our family apart." The families of Burden and James were not moved to accept the apology or to forgive. Karon Knox, a sister of Michael James, said, "She shouldn't have waited until she got before the jury to tell us she was sorry."

Perhaps because of his age—a mere twenty-one years—or possibly because the jury thought there were mitigating circumstances, Burmeister was sentenced to two consecutive life terms with no possibility of parole. Defiant in defeat, the young, former paratrooper said he would not quit, he would not accept defeat, and he vowed that it was not over. Given the evidence against him, it would seem that he would have been satisfied by not receiving the death penalty. Anything can happen, but it is highly unlikely that Burmeister will ever be free again.

The same is true of Malcolm Wright from Louisville, Kentucky. He was a year older than Burmeister, and he already had his spider-web tattoo before the murders of that dark hour on 7 December 1995. Oh, yes, Wright was already a bona fide Skinhead, and he urged his younger buddy to become one, too, by killing a black person. However, Jonathan Broun, one of Wright's lawyers, contended during opening arguments that Wright only agreed to harass prostitutes and drug dealers and never intended to kill anybody. This was an argument that the jury would ultimately reject.

Wright's trial was held in Wilmington with Judge Coy Brewer presiding. Fayetteville District Attorney Ed Grannis led the prosecution, which relied on circumstantial evidence to prove that Wright egged Burmeister on and acted in concert with him. Karon Knox, speaking on behalf of the families of the victims, said, "We feel very strongly that he [Wright] masterminded and brainwashed Jim Burmeister to kill." There was considerable evidence that Wright was a racist and a neo-Nazi. Once again, Randy Meadows pointed an accusing finger at the defendant and offered damning testimony against him. Wright's conviction was just as certain as Burmeister's had been.

A predominantly white jury deliberated six hours before convicting Wright on 2 May 1997 of two counts of first-degree murder and one count of conspiracy to commit murder. As the verdict was announced, the former paratrooper glanced quickly at jurors and then stared straight ahead. His ultimate fate lay in the hands of the same jury that convicted him. Again the prosecution and the families of the victims wanted the death penalty, but again they were disappointed. The jury recommended life without parole, and Judge Brewer handed down the same sentence that had been imposed on Burmeister—two consecutive life sentences with no possibility of parole. Like Burmeister, Wright, because of his irrational hatred of black people, will spend the remainder of his life behind bars.

Randy Meadows got off easy, compared to his two friends. In Wilmington on 13 May 1997 Judge Brewer sentenced Meadows to thirteen to sixteen months in prison, but gave him credit for the 515 days he had already spent in jail. In effect, this meant that Meadows had already served his time. Although the victims' families were not pleased with the light sentence, Ed Grannis was. He told Judge Brewer that if Meadows had not walked back to the crime scene and been placed under arrest, no one would have been brought to justice for the murders of Jackie Burden and Michael James. The district attorney said that Meadows's cooperation was crucial in convicting the two other defendants and that Meadows would probably be murdered himself, if he went to prison. He asked Judge Brewer to go easy on Meadows, and the judge obliged by setting the young man free for time served. However, he tacked on a suspended sentence of fifty to seventy-eight months. Brewer told Meadows to return to his hometown of Mulkeytown, Illinois and to stay straight. The judge warned the young man not to break the law, or he would be returned to North Carolina and put behind bars for up to six and a half years. During his sentencing Meadows did something that neither Burmeister nor Wright had done—he apologized to the families of the victims. Although he had been a misguided young man, it was obvious that Meadows had a conscience and was not a cold-blooded killer like Burmeister and Wright.

Not all of the vicious murders of the nineties were committed by soldiers. Kenneth Junior French hated gays, and his hatred drove him to kill four people. Jim Burmeister and Malcolm Wright hated gays, too, but they also, being committed Skinheads, hated black people and Jews. Their hatred led to the shooting deaths of Jackie Burden and Michael James so that Burmeister could earn his spider-web tattoo. Racial hatred was a two-way street, however. Tilmon Charles Golphin, Jr., 19, and Kevin Salvador Golphin, 17, both of Richmond, Virginia were two black brothers who had contempt for society and no respect for the law. Their hatred led to the shooting deaths of two white police officers on Interstate 95 just east of Fayetteville on 23 September 1997, just a few months after Jim Burmeister and Malcolm Wright were sentenced to life without parole for killing two black people.

The Golphin brothers, who according to neighbors in Richmond were constantly in trouble with the law, stole a Toyota Camry in Kingstree, South Carolina. On 23 September they were driving the stolen car to Richmond, when they were stopped on Interstate 95 just north of the North Carolina 24 overpass. Lloyd E. ("Ed") Lowry, a state trooper with twenty-nine years of service, pulled them over and called in the license plate. When he was told that the car was stolen, he requested assistance. David W. Hathcock, a Cumberland County sheriff's deputy for nineteen years, was nearby and responded to Lowry's call for help. After he arrived on the scene, he and Lowry were gunned down by the brothers, who pulled out an AK47 and started shooting. When passing motorists stopped to see what was happening, they found that both officers were dead. The Golphins sped northward on I-95.

Seeing what had happened, Ron Waters of Lexington, South Carolina followed the Golphins in his Jeep Cherokee. The brothers pulled off the Interstate onto Murphy Road. Waters followed and saw them trying to remove the car's license plate. When the Golphin boys spotted his vehicle, they opened fire on it, hitting it three times. Waters used his car phone to call the Harnett County sheriff's office. Harnett deputies responded and caught up with the two brothers near the Harnett/Cumberland line and chased them to the Long Branch Road exit. The stolen Camry ran off the road, hit an embankment, flipped over, and landed right side up. The Golphins ran from the wreck as numerous police cars arrived on the scene. Terry Hyatt, a truck driver, who observed it all, said, "All hell broke lose. I ain't seen that many guns in my life."

Two women police officers caught one brother, while the other was finally tracked down and seized by a "herd" of male officers. The AK47 used to kill officers Hathcock and Lowry was found near the wrecked Camry.

Amazingly, when Tilmon and Kevin Golphin went to trial in March 1998, they pled not guilty. Judge Coy Brewer presided over the trial, and District Attorney Ed Grannis prosecuted the Golphins. Concerns that an impartial jury could not be found in Cumberland County led to jurors being bussed in from Smithfield in Johnston County. For five-and-a-half weeks the jurors were bussed back and forth everyday of the trial from Smithfield to Fayetteville. The evidence against the Golphins was overwhelming, and they were found guilty at the end of April. On 13 May 1998 the two brothers were sentenced to death, plus nineteen to twenty-six years in prison on other charges. The Golphins joined 180 others who already waited on North Carolina's Death Row.

Kevin Golphin, the younger of the brothers, criticized the jury for sentencing a black man to death. He singled out Genet Watson, a black woman juror, and said, "All eyes is on you, Ms. Watson." He went on to say that he was sorry for the families of the slain officers until he saw that they wanted him put to death. "North Carolina have no kind of justice at all," the young man was quoted as saying. The mother of the two brothers also spoke up and said that the verdict was racial. One does have to wonder how it was that the Golphins were sent to Death Row and Kenneth Junior French, Jim Burmeister, and Malcolm Wright were not. All were killers who murdered out of hatred, and, it would seem, that all deserved to die for their crimes.

Unfortunately, these three murder cases in the nineties are by no means the only examples that could have been used. They alone would make that decade stand out as one of the most murderous of the twentieth century, but there were other vicious murders.

For instance, in October 1995 Sergeant William J. Kreutzer, an 82nd Airborne infantry squad leader, opened fire on approximately 1,300 paratroopers lined up for a run at Towle Stadium at Fort Bragg. He was arrested and charged with premeditated murder for killing Major Stephen Mark Badger and attempted murder for wounding eighteen other soldiers.

In 1998 during a gang initiation two women were murdered and an attempt was made to murder a third woman. The three people who shot the women went on trial in 2000. They were Francisco "Paco" Tirado, Eric "E" Queen, and Christina "Queen" Walters. All three were found guilty and sentenced to death. The twenty-two-year-old "Queen" Walters was one of only six women on Death Row, and she was the youngest of the six.

Then, of course, there was the murder of Captain Marty Theer in December 2000, just days before the decade of the nineties and the twentieth century ended. The "Fayettenam" era of the sixties and seventies had defined Fayetteville as a sin city and a murder capital, but the decade of the nineties took a back seat to no other time period of the century when it came to murder.

The last decade of the twentieth century was a strange one indeed. An article in the *Fayetteville Observer* looked back on the year 2000 and called it a year of triumph and tragedy. The same thing could have been said about the entire decade. Fayetteville citizens looked on as the population expanded dramatically through annexation, reaching 125,000 by decade's end. Efforts to revitalize downtown were at least partly successful, as the old topless bars and other honkytonks gave way to public buildings, a world-class museum, a refurbished Prince Charles Hotel called the Radisson Prince Charles, and a few new businesses. Of course, Hay Street didn't measure up in commercial activity to what it had been before the suburban malls came along, but there were a few stores that thrived. The new Crown Coliseum on U.S. 301 South added luster to the city and gave area residents the potential to have more entertainment events than ever before. And the city produced another Miss North Carolina and a remarkable teacher named Jane Smith who magnanimously gave one of her kidneys to one of her black students who needed a kidney transplant to survive. Triumph? Yes, all of this spelled triumph.

What of the tragedy? As had been the case so many times in the past, the worst of the tragedy manifested itself in murder, and, as seemed to be the case more and more, the killers were connected in some way with Fort Bragg—Kenneth Junior French, Jim Burmeister, Malcolm Wright, and William Kreutzer. These soldiers were filled with hate, but so were the Golphin brothers and the elusive culprits who set fire to abortion clinics and planted bombs inside them. As far as murder was concerned, the decade of the nineties was among the worst of the century.

One must wonder if Mayor J. L. Dawkins ever thought about giving up on Fayetteville. Undoubtedly not, for he was always positive, always committed to trying to improve the city. His death seven months before the decade and the century ended brought much sadness to the city he loved and had worked to improve for a quarter of a century. I feel sure that J. L.

never gave up, just as my mother never gave up on Fayetteville. Less than two months after the mayor died, I put my mother in a nursing home in the town where she was born and where she wanted to die. For eighty-six years she lived there, always glorying in the city's triumphs and always grieving over its tragedies. Undoubtedly, the "mayor for life," as people often called J. L., did exactly the same, and the townspeople loved him for it. Snyder Memorial Baptist Church was packed for his funeral service, and thousands lined the streets of the city as his funeral procession passed. Y2K had not produced the chaos that many had predicted, but it was a tragic year for Fayetteville, just as the nineties—because of so many horrific murders—was a tragic decade.

Conclusion

On 1 January 1901 Fayetteville was only a small town of around 7,000 people, sitting quietly on the banks of the Cape Fear River about 110 miles north and slightly west of where the river flows into the Atlantic Ocean at Southport. It was a rural community surrounded primarily by cotton farms, and cotton, along with other farm products, was sold at the Market House in the center of the town. Eventually tobacco also became an economic staple in the area, and tobacco warehouses emerged so that the region's farmers could market their bright-leaf tobacco near where it was grown.

By the end of the century, as the twenty-first century dawned, Fayetteville had become a city of more than 125,000 residents. It had become an army town and, to a considerable extent, an industrial town. Fort Bragg, first as Camp Bragg, had been established ten miles to the west of town in 1918, and that changed Fayetteville forever. For more than twenty years after the Great War of 1914–1918 brought the enormous military installation to the area, Fayetteville grew slowly, as the number of soldiers stationed nearby was not significant. Fort Bragg's impact on the Cape Fear region was modest during those first two decades. Then came the greatest war of them all, World War II, and it was quickly followed by the Korean War (or "Conflict"), and then the Vietnam War. Off and on for thirty-five years our nation was at war, and thousands upon thousands of soldiers and airmen passed through Fort Bragg and Pope Air Force Base, which stood just north of Bragg. The town changed dramatically as it grew into a bustling city, one of the important cities in North Carolina and the nation.

After World War II the city's population moved rapidly upward, and a variety of industries chose to locate in and around Fayetteville. There were Black & Decker, Rohm and Haas, DuPont, and Kelly-Springfield Tire Company—the biggest of them all—to name the more significant ones. The cotton farms and the tobacco farms were still out in the country from town, but agriculture played a smaller and smaller part in the area's economy as the years went by, for Fayetteville and the Cape Fear region remained dependent, to a great extent, on the Fort Bragg payroll. The coming of the industrial plants whittled away at that dependence, but the numerous deployments of Fort Bragg soldiers and Pope airmen in the 1980s and 1990s revealed that Fayetteville was still an army town as far as its financial and economic health was concerned. When the troops were gone, as they seemed to be more and more frequently, the local economy suffered. The Persian Gulf War hit local merchants especially hard at Christmas time in 1990, but there were many other times when the people along the Cape Fear felt the economic and financial pinch caused by the absence of troops from Fort Bragg.

In spite of the periodic downturns in the area's economy—some caused by troops being deployed and some by national recessions—Fayetteville grew and made great progress. Unfortunately, along with the impressive growth and development came a noticeable increase in crime, including the horrible crime of murder. Alcoholic beverages had long served as a catalyst in the commission of criminal acts. Somebody killed somebody over a whiskey still, or somebody got drunk and killed somebody in a drunken rage. That was old hat along the Cape Fear. A new catalyst appeared in the 1960s—a variety of illicit drugs. The Vietnam War contributed to the problem, and in Fayetteville and at Fort Bragg things got out of hand. A disturbing number of soldiers and Cumberland County residents, too, became addicts, and Fayetteville, which had been a moderately wild town in the past, seemed to take on the character of Sodom and Gomorrah. Dens of iniquity were ubiquitous along Hay Street where respectable businesses had once operated. Fayetteville came under national scrutiny by the media and got the unflattering nickname of "Fayettenam." After Vietnam, when life in the area began to return to normal, mayors like Bill Hurley and J. L. Dawkins made an earnest effort to clean up the city and dispel the "Fayettenam" image.

The opprobrious image was difficult to shake off, for Fayetteville had also come to be regarded as the murder capital of North Carolina, and it sometimes registered murder rates each year that were as high as big cities in the northern United States. To be sure, murder was committed along the Cape Fear long before World War II and the Vietnam era, but the vicious-ness associated with the murders of the latter part of the century seemed far greater.

Early in the century a drunken black man had shot and killed the chief of police in Fayetteville. The confiscation of Marshall Williams's whiskey still in 1921 had led to the shooting death of a deputy sheriff by a young man who later brought fame and glory to himself and Cumberland County.

Six years later a young mechanic was shot and killed, and those accused of killing him were not convicted. In 1939 a young man from a prominent Fayetteville family shot and killed a police officer that had placed him under arrest. Convicted of the crime, the young man, Lenward Hair, was soon out of prison, and he went on to kill again a few years later. Prominent politician and businessman Wall Ewing beat his wife to death in 1946 and stayed in prison less than seven years for doing it. In 1949, Lenward Hair's younger brother, Raymond, shot and killed a college classmate, Roy Coble, over a gambling debt. Apparently, young Hair was drunk at the time. As his older brother had, he served only a fraction of his sentence for the murder before being released from Central Prison. Five years after Raymond Hair killed Roy Coble, a former taxi driver killed Ricky Monsour, presumably in a domestic dispute involving Ricky's wife.

None of these murders was publicized outside Cumberland County, except that of Raymond Hair. Because Hair was the object of a nationwide manhunt for nearly a month, his case received considerable attention. Marshall Williams's case became the subject of national attention more than thirty years after the commission of the crime, because, in the meantime, Williams had invented the M-1 carbine and had acquired the reputation of being a firearms genius. A movie about his life revealed his crime to the nation, but Hollywood, true to its reputation, distorted the facts. News of Ricky Monsour's murder gradually spread far and wide because Ricky ran a bar frequented by hundreds of soldiers, many of whom Ricky befriended. Fort Bragg soldiers scattered around the world had a "grapevine" over which that news was conveyed.

In spite of the murders mentioned above, Fayetteville would never have become known as a "murder capital" if had not been for the cases of Jeffrey MacDonald and Velma Barfield. Both of them were convicted of killing family members, although MacDonald is still maintaining his innocence thirty-three years after the murders at his Fort Bragg home. MacDonald was found guilty of murdering his wife and two daughters, and he is serving three life sentences for it. Velma Barfield was found guilty of poisoning Stuart Taylor, her fiancé, but she admitted to poisoning three other people, including her own mother. MacDonald and Barfield were both in the news—local, state, national, and world—for years, and all that time the spotlight was on Fayetteville and Fort Bragg.

And, while the world continued to hear about Velma Barfield until her execution in 1984 and Jeffrey MacDonald through the 1990s, other horrible murders were being committed. A goodly number of those were by the hands of Fort Bragg soldiers. The "ninja killers," Jeffrey Meyer and Mark Thompson, brutally stabbed an elderly couple to death in 1986. Both young men were stationed at Fort Bragg, as was Ronald Adrian Gray, who killed two young women in 1987. The next year, William Edgar Weller, only six months out of the service, killed Margaret Best Jensen, the twenty-nine-year-old wife of a soldier.

Fayetteville's reputation as a murder capital continued into the 1990s, when Sgt. Kenneth Junior French shot up Luigi's Restaurant and killed four people, because he didn't like President Clinton's policy on gays in the military. In 1995, a few weeks before Christmas, a paratrooper named Jim Burmeister gunned down a black couple on Hall Street, while fellow paratrooper Malcolm Wright looked on and encouraged his buddy to authenticate himself as a Skinhead by murdering a "nigger."

The list of murderers that killed along the Cape Fear goes on: Sgt. William Kreutzer, Tilmon and Kevin Golphin, Paco Tirado, "E" Queen, and "Queen" Walters. And, just as the century was coming to a close in December 2000, Air Force Captain Marty Theer met his death in a hail of bullets. His wife's lover, Sgt. John Diamond, was charged in the crime and convicted of premeditated murder and conspiracy to commit murder. Diamond claimed later that it was Michelle Theer, the captain's wife, who did the shooting and that he (Diamond) helped her cover it up. Not until the twenty-first century was two years old would Michelle Theer be charged in the death of her husband.

On the one hand, it is perfectly understandable that Fayetteville came to be regarded as a Sodom and Gomorrah and a murder capital in the last half of the twentieth century. Yet, to a native who was born there in the fourth decade of the century, grew up there during the forties and fifties, and observed its growth and development from the time he left in the late fifties until the end of the century, it seems a little unfair. Mention Fayetteville and the name of Jeffrey MacDonald comes to the minds of many. It is regrettable that names like Alexander and Frank Porter Graham, Terry Sanford, Charlie Rose, J. L. Dawkins, Pat Lee, Seavy Carroll, and J. P. Riddle are not thought of first. Ask outsiders to name a woman they associate with Fayetteville, and up comes the name of Velma Barfield, when the names that should come to mind are Jane Smith, Dr. Lucille Hutaff, Katie Lee, or my own mother and grandmother.

In my experience with Fayetteville over many years, I encountered some of the finest people ever to walk the streets of any city. It is a matter of supreme regret that the world at large never knew those people, many of whom are gone and all but forgotten. Yes, in the twentieth century there was murder along the Cape Fear—far too much of it. I can only wish that people everywhere might come to realize that the city known as Fayetteville that sits along the banks of that river also produced hundreds of wonderful people and also registered a goodly number of impressive achievements.

A Note on Sources

In writing this book my primary source for general information was the *Fayetteville Observer*, the oldest newspaper in North Carolina that is still being published. With regard to some of the murders committed early in the twentieth century, the *Observer* was the only source I had.

Some information about Fayetteville's growth and development came from *The Story of Fayetteville*, a book written and compiled by John A Oates, a Fayetteville attorney who had a strong interest in local history. Oates's work is primarily an encyclopedia of facts about Fayetteville up to the 1950s and is a valuable source. So is Weeks Parker's *Fayetteville, North Carolina: A Pictorial History*, which adds information about the town into the 1980s and enhances the story with very informative pictures of many significant events and people that are part of the town's story.

Another valuable source was personal experiences—my own as well as those of other natives who lived through parts of the story and offered eyewitness accounts and/or accounts passed on to them. For example, I had firsthand knowledge of Velma Barfield, when she was Velma Burke, and my cousin, Charles Cox, knew her even better than I did. He shared his observations of her with me and expressed to me why he thought she poisoned her mother and at least three other people. Regarding the death of Thomas Burke, Velma's first husband, Charles has doubts—contrary to the opinion of some Burke family members—that Velma deliberately let Thomas burn up in a house fire. My uncle, Gilbert Herring, offered firsthand observations of "Carbine" Williams and Lenward Hair, two of the high-profile murderers in this story. This is information that I could have gotten nowhere else. Finally, my own observations about Ricky Monsour are, I believe, unique.

For more details on the famous murder cases of Jeffrey MacDonald and Velma Barfield, I found indispensable information in several books, and I relied heavily on what I found in them. The MacDonald case gave rise to two in-depth books. Joe McGinniss's book entitled *Fatal Vision* was published in 1983, and it became the basis for a made-for-television movie by the same name. McGinniss went through the entire trial with MacDonald in 1979 and had access to nearly all of the documents surrounding that event. The book contains countless details about the MacDonald case.

The other book on the MacDonald case appeared in 1995 and was written by Jerry Allen Potter and Fred Bost. It is entitled *Fatal Justice* and is, in effect, a refutation of *Fatal Vision*. Potter and Bost subject McGinnis and his book to heavy scrutiny and cast serious doubts on McGinnis's credibility. They make a plausible argument for their position, offering an abundance of evidence to support it. People interested in the MacDonald case should thoroughly examine both *Fatal Vision* and *Fatal Justice* for the complete story. The detail in both books is impressive.

Regarding the case of Velma Barfield, the very best source is Jerry Bledsoe's *Death Sentence*, published in 1999. Besides his own prodigious research, Bledsoe had the input of Velma's son, Ronnie Burke. Excellently written, the book offers incomparable detail about the case. For my own treatment of the case, I relied on Bledsoe, Velma's own account, newspaper accounts, and my own personal experiences.

Before Bledsoe's book there was another called *Woman on Death Row*, published in 1985—some months after Velma's execution. Although Velma herself is the ostensible author, it is really her story as told to a ghostwriter. It, too, is a valuable source, but it does not have the in-depth perspective presented in *Death Sentence*.

Regarding the other murder cases highlighted in this book, I relied primarily on the accounts in the *Fayetteville Observer*. I did, however, in some instances, compare the accounts in that newspaper with accounts in the Raleigh *News and Observer*. As a historian I am well aware that my colleagues in the profession question the reliability of newspaper accounts, but in some cases such accounts are all the evidence we have. Besides, everybody knows that no source is *absolutely* reliable. Hence, the historian is compelled to take the available evidence he or she has and try to come as close to the truth as possible, realizing that absolute truth will never be within his or her grasp.